VMware vSphere™
FOR
DUMMIES®

by Dan Mitchell
& Thomas Keegan

WILEY

Wiley Publishing, Inc.

VMware vSphere™ For Dummies®

Published by
Wiley Publishing, Inc.
111 River Street
Hoboken, NJ 07030-5774

www.wiley.com

For general information on our other products and services, please contact our Customer Care Department within the U.S. at 877-762-2974, outside the U.S. at 317-572-3993, or fax 317-572-4002.

For technical support, please visit www.wiley.com/techsupport.

Wiley also publishes its books in a variety of electronic formats. Some content that appears in print may not be available in electronic books.

Library of Congress Control Number: 2011920891

ISBN: 978-0-470-76872-3

Manufactured in the United States of America

10 9 8 7 6 5 4 3 2 1

WILEY

About the Authors

Dan Mitchell: Dan Mitchell is an early adopter. At age 11, he was the youngest beta tester for what is now America Online. By age 13, he had become a staff writer for the Boston Computer Society. And at the age of 19, Dan started his first technology consultancy and has been active in cutting-edge technology ever since.

In recent years, Dan served as Technical Director for Dunes Technologies (USA). After Dunes Technologies was acquired by VMware in September 2007, Dan joined VMware's Professional Services Organization. Dan departed from VMware in June 2008 to become Technical Director for DynamicOps, a software spinout from Credit Suisse specializing in Virtualization Management and Cloud Automation.

Dan lives in Ashland, Massachusetts, with his wife and four sons.

Thomas Keegan: Tom Keegan never intended to be a technology whiz. He first started programming at ten years old by following a BASIC program out of *321 Contact Magazine.* After many hours of typing and code modifications, he succeeded at showing a dot orbiting another dot on his Apple IIe and was understandably thrilled.

In college, Tom wanted to hook his Macintosh up to the campus network. After being told by campus computer services "Macs can't access the Internet," he proved them wrong and was immediately offered a job by the college. This put him on the track to solve business problems in creative ways, which he still does today. Virtualization, even in the early years was exciting, and Tom has been working with VMware products for ten years. He is certified as a VMware VCP and a Certified Advanced Professional on vSphere 4-Datacenter Design.

Tom currently is a Technical Director at Fresenius Medical Care and lives with his family in Massachusetts.

Dedication

From Dan: I dedicate this book to my grandparents, whom I love and admire. Thank you all for setting such strong examples of honesty, dedication, work ethic, humility, and selflessness. I will do my best to pass on these noble qualities to my own children and grandchildren.

From Tom: I dedicate this book to my children, Elizabeth and Andy. You continually amaze me with your wonderful perspective on the world!

Acknowledgments

From Dan: First, I'd like to thank Matt Wagner of Fresh Books for bringing me to the *For Dummies* people and giving me the opportunity to write about technology I work with everyday. Thanks for believing in me and recognizing my passion to educate people about VMware and virtualization.

Next, I'd like to thank Katie Feltman, Colleen Totz Diamond, Kelly Ewing, Melba Hopper, and the rest of the team at Wiley for putting your faith in me and the incredible effort put forth to make this book a reality.

Additionally, I must thank my coauthor, Tom Keegan, for jumping in and making a significant contribution to this book. Your understanding of VMware virtualization is phenomenal, only rivaled by your work ethic and ability to get the job done.

So many folks in the technology industry have helped and inspired me over the years. In no particular order, I want to thank Mike Adams, Ed Bugnion, Sonja Pelichet, Leslie Muller, Burke Azbill, Kyle Smith, Rich Krueger, Rich Bourdeau, Brian Emerson, Mike Laverick, Doug Brown, Jason Nash, Dan P, Diane and Mendel, Steve Wozniak (AppleFest Boston 1988), Steve Case (from AppleLink-PE days), and numerous others. Thanks also to all my peers, past and present, from the Boston Computer Society, Dunes, Foedus, VMware, and DynamicOps, for making every day another learning experience.

Most importantly, I give my sincerest appreciation to my family. Special thanks to my wife, Julie, for everything she does, every single day. Thanks to my boys, Tommy, Johnathan, Joshua, and Dylan, for your patience and understanding while I was writing this book. Thanks to my mom and dad for fostering my love of technology from childhood and replacing the motherboard in my Apple IIe when I blew it up (sorry). Thank you for all your love, help, and support. I couldn't ask for a better family.

From Tom: Dan Mitchell, my coauthor, invited me to join him in this endeavor. I've written articles and chapters behind the scenes in the past, but this book is the first time I have been in the spotlight, and I thank him for his confidence in me and his support.

I also want to thank the folks at Wiley for their guidance. Katie Feltman, Colleen Totz Diamond, Kelly Ewing, and Melba Hopper contributed immensely to the book. As an author, you don't realize how much your writing skills can improve until you see the edit marks that these experts provide.

I've worked in various roles in technology books for ten years, and it all started because Tony Northrup asked me to help edit a book he was writing. Thanks, Tony, for helping me to get my start!

I appreciate you, Mom and Dad, for caring enough to provide appropriate computers at home, and letting me modify the computer every year to make it faster. I'd like to thank my kids, Elizabeth and Andy, for months of going to bed at 7 p.m. so that I could get enough time to work on the book. I'm sure the early bedtime would not have worked as well if you knew how to tell time, or if the seasons did not result in earlier darkness each day. I am inspired by you as you grow each day.

Lastly, I am most thankful for my beautiful wife, Heather, for her support and understanding. From muttering as I work on my laptop to asking her to weigh in on technology matters I know she has no interest in, she showed patience and support throughout the project.

Publisher's Acknowledgments

We're proud of this book; please send us your comments at http://dummies.custhelp.com. For other comments, please contact our Customer Care Department within the U.S. at 877-762-2974, outside the U.S. at 317-572-3993, or fax 317-572-4002.

Some of the people who helped bring this book to market include the following:

Acquisitions and Editorial

Project Editor: Kelly Ewing

Acquisitions Editor: Katie Feltman

Copy Editor: Melba Hopper

Technical Editors: Jason Nash, Thomas Keegan

Editorial Manager: Jodi Jensen

Editorial Assistant: Amanda Graham

Sr. Editorial Assistant: Cherie Case

Cartoons: Rich Tennant
(www.the5thwave.com)

Composition Services

Project Coordinator: Sheree Montgomery

Layout and Graphics: Samantha K. Cherolis, Joyce Haughey

Proofreader: Evelyn C. Wellborn

Indexer: Palmer Publishing Services

Special Help
Colleen Totz Diamond

Publishing and Editorial for Technology Dummies

Richard Swadley, Vice President and Executive Group Publisher

Andy Cummings, Vice President and Publisher

Mary Bednarek, Executive Acquisitions Director

Mary C. Corder, Editorial Director

Publishing for Consumer Dummies

Diane Graves Steele, Vice President and Publisher

Composition Services

Debbie Stailey, Director of Composition Services

Contents at a Glance

Table of Contents

Introduction

Every so often, a technology comes along that changes the way we go about our everyday business. This technology is called a *disruptive technology* and has such a significant benefit or improvement that people are willing to change their normal way of doing things to incorporate the new technology. Virtualization is one of those disruptive technologies, and vSphere leads the charge.

From the outside peering in, vSphere is intimidating. It appears to be this massive monster of complexity, able to span thousands of servers, connect to terabytes of storage, and even move around machines without turning them off. You probably feel like you're in over your head before you've even set foot in the pool, right? The reality is, vSphere can be as big or small as you want it to be. And once you get into it, you'll wonder how you ever got by without it. Not so scary after all.

This book is packed with real-world experience, compiled from our day-to-day adventures working with VMware technology. It gives you the know-how to get vSphere up and running, and stay that way. Use this book to get the most out of vSphere and enjoy all the benefits we've enjoyed over the years thanks to VMware virtualization.

About This Book

This book is a comprehensive introduction to VMware vSphere 4. It gives you the information you need to plan, install, and manage a vSphere virtual infrastructure. The book covers the most common elements of vSphere and how to make them work for you. While you're welcome to read this book from cover to cover, each chapter sticks to a specific topic, making the book a reference guide as well. Chapters are further divided into sections, so you can quickly get to the information you need.

This book isn't a vSphere manual. In fact, it's the vSphere anti-manual, meant to give you as much or as little information as you need about vSphere in plain English, without all the mumbo-jumbo and limited use of TLAs (Three Letter Acronyms).

There are no exams or quizzes, so you don't need to memorize the contents of this book. Put what you use from this book into your head, and leave the rest right here between the pages. If you need to look something up, you should have no problem finding this bright yellow book in your desk drawer. The whole point of the *For Dummies* series is to help you find the information you need to figure something out and get you back to your life.

How to Use This Book

This book is an introduction to a complex technology, written in the *For Dummies* conversational manner. Some of the concepts we describe talk about how and why things work the way they do. Other concepts are based on a process or a comparison. To keep it as simple as possible, we break them out like this:

- ✔ In bulleted lists, often you will find the concept name in bold, followed by the definition of the concept.
- ✔ A simple list of information is just regular text.
- ✔ Numbered steps of a process are shown in bold, followed by additional details and descriptions shown in regular text.
- ✔ Commands and Web site URLs are shown in monofont.

What You're Not to Read

This book is geared toward a few different audiences, each with different needs:

- ✔ If you're a *technical manager,* you may want to read the entire book, but you can skip the information and lists with the Technical Stuff icon.
- ✔ If you're a *system administrator,* you may want to read the entire book, plus read Chapter 21 more than once. Feel free to peek at Chapter 24 and put these tips in the back of your mind before you get deep into configuration.
- ✔ If you're an *experienced VMware administrator,* you can jump directly to Chapter 4 to see the differences between VMware Virtual Infrastructure 3.5, vSphere 4, and vSphere 4.1. Then check out the introductions in each chapter to see whether the information is new to you.

You also don't have to read information in the little gray boxes, known as sidebars. While interesting, the information isn't necessary to understand the topic at hand.

Foolish Assumptions

Although this book is written with the virtualization newbie in mind, we've made some assumptions about you, the reader:

- ✔ You've mastered using a desktop or laptop computer for stuff like e-mail and Web browsing.
- ✔ You know what a server is, how to remotely connect to it, and either have experience managing one or more servers or know someone who does.
- ✔ You have a basic understanding of networking and storage area networks (SANs).
- ✔ You have VMware vSphere 4.1 and at least one server on the VMware Hardware Compatibility List (at www.vmware.com).

How This Book Is Organized

This book is divided into seven parts, each of which describes a phase of a vSphere deployment:

Part 1: Deciding on vSphere

This part of the book is an introduction to VMware vSphere and virtualization. vSphere has a lot of features and functionality, and this part touches on all of them. If you're transitioning from the previous version of VMware ESX, you can even find a chapter to tell you the differences between versions.

Part 11: Getting Ready for vSphere

The best way to ensure a successful vSphere deployment is to plan and prepare for the rollout. The chapters in this part show you how to plan for your vSphere deployment, and they offer several points to consider while doing your planning. This part also provides the details you need to prepare your environment for vSphere installation.

Part 111: Installing vSphere

Getting the installation right is key to a properly functioning vSphere environment. This part takes you through each step in detail to install VMware ESX, vCenter Server, and the vSphere Client. The chapters in this part are independent of one another, so you can quickly access the installation steps of the product you're installing.

Part IV: Configuring and Connecting vSphere

This part of the book is all about configuring your new vSphere infrastructure. The chapters in this part help you configure your vCenter Server and get connected to your network. You also attach storage to your ESX hosts and configure them into a cluster.

Part V: Administering and Maintaining vSphere

The chapters in this part of the book discuss the day-to-day operation and ongoing maintenance of your vSphere infrastructure. You can create and clone virtual machines, organize your resources, and monitor the setup after the machines are built. You also get a quick overview of the virtual infrastructure from a high level.

Part VI: Tuning and Troubleshooting vSphere

As your vSphere environment grows, you want to make sure that every virtual machine is getting its fair share of resources. The chapters in this part help you tune the performance of groups of virtual machines and address fault tolerance and uptime considerations. Also, an entire chapter is dedicated to troubleshooting the most common vSphere issues, how to identify them, and where to go for resolution.

Part VII: The Part of Tens

Finally, this book ends with the famed *For Dummies* Part of Tens, where each chapter lists ten items or topics. A chapter in this part includes a list of tools to help manage your vSphere infrastructure and a chapter with some great online resources to further your vSphere know-how. The final chapter includes ten tips from the pros for a successful vSphere deployment.

Icons Used in This Book

Throughout the margins of this book, you see little pictures, known as *icons*, that highlight various types of information:

This icon flags useful, helpful tips or shortcuts.

This icon marks a friendly reminder to do something.

This icon marks a friendly reminder *not* to do something.

This icon alerts you to overly technical information and virtualization geek discussions of the topic at hand. The information is optional reading, though you never know if it will come in handy someday.

Where to Go from Here

If you're new to virtualization, start at the beginning of this book. Get familiar with the terminology. Explain the concept of vSphere and virtualization at your next family gathering. Most importantly, don't get overwhelmed. After all, it's just software.

Take some time to explore the Web sites and resources in "The Part of Tens" section at the end of the book. Those resources exist to make your job easier.

You can also visit Dan's Web page for more information or as a diversion: www.startswithv.com.

Enjoy the book and thanks for reading!

Part I
Deciding on vSphere

The 5th Wave   By Rich Tennant

"Well, I suppose we should plan on getting rid of those coal-burning servers."

In this part . . .

This part introduces you to VMware's vSphere virtualization platform. Chapter 1 covers how to get the
most out of vSphere in your environment. Chapter 2 provides the background of virtualization and a basic primer
on how it works. Chapter 3 explores the key features of
vSphere and why each of them is important. Chapter 4
shows you what changed between VMware Virtual
Infrastructure 3.5, vSphere 4, and vSphere 4.1.

Chapter 1

Getting the Most Out of VMware vSphere

In This Chapter

▶ Defining your virtualization mission

▶ Rolling out vSphere effectively

▶ Taking control of your vSphere environment

*W*elcome to the brave new world of virtualization. Your mission, if you choose to accept it, is to reap the benefits of virtualization and leverage VMware vSphere to the fullest extent possible. The mission will be successful with careful planning, the right mindset, and a few tips from the professionals. Once you've successfully completed your mission, you can immediately begin enjoying the convenience, efficiency, and reliability that is VMware vSphere.

This chapter provides an overview of your virtualization mission. Looking down from a high level, you see how to determine where vSphere can best fit into your environment. The next waypoint shows how you can use the information to develop rollout plans for vSphere. Looking beyond your rollout plan, you discover how to request storage and network resources critical for a successful deployment. A preview of deployment comes next, followed by a peek into the day-to-day operation and maintenance of vSphere.

vSphere and Your Environment

VMware vSphere is comprised of many parts, some of which you may never use and others that you'll use every day. Because it's impractical to cover every combination of vSphere components and features, this book focuses on the most common configurations, but still touches on each of the features offered in the product. How you will deploy vSphere depends on your environment, the scope of your initial rollout, and the version of vSphere being deployed.

VMware vSphere is packed with so many features and options that it's highly unlikely you'll ever have the opportunity to use them all. Instead, you're more likely to hit a limitation of your infrastructure before you reach a limitation of vSphere. For this very reason, you need to think about your vSphere rollout with your feet firmly planted on the ground, your budget in hand, and realistic goals for deployment in mind.

A key topic of this book is figuring out what you need to meet your virtualization goals. Starting with a small deployment or pilot is a great way to feel out the boundaries encountered when introducing vSphere to your environment. It also gives you the opportunity to discover how to foster acceptance and adoption of virtualization, which is just as important as getting vSphere to function properly with existing infrastructure.

VMware vSphere is exciting technology. Although you may have the urge to jump ahead to full-on deployment, heed the saying, "Look before you leap." You must meet several prerequisites before you even install the software; missing just one could earn you countless hours of troubleshooting. Also, the more complex the deployment, the greater the risk of impact to other systems. Connecting to network and shared storage with reckless disregard may inadvertently take down other systems or, worse, cause irreparable data loss. If you're working with VMware ESX for the first time, take your time. Careful attention to detail during the planning phase will pay off in the long run.

Rolling out vSphere

Putting vSphere to work in your environment without proper planning works about as well as feeling your way through a cactus store with your eyes closed. In either situation, you're likely break some stuff, and while you'll eventually get through, you'll do so only after encountering some painful challenges. In order to prevent these encounters from happening, take the time to plan and prepare before you deploy.

Mapping out an unfamiliar terrain

Experienced hikers know the importance of mapping a route before venturing off into the wilderness. They prepare for the expected, pack for the unexpected, and have a plan that gets them to their camping site safely — all before the trip begins. Hikers plan because they know poor preparation is a recipe for catastrophe, and not knowing where to go can only amplify the situation.

Like an experienced hiker, mapping a path to a successful deployment is key to your vSphere rollout. You need to know safe stopping places in your rollout plan in case something unexpected arises and causes delays in your deployment. Working with key stakeholders, you collaboratively define deployment goals and understand their respective deadlines. Having a plan in place, especially one built with the key stakeholders involved, sets the right expectations upfront and provides you with partners so that you don't lose your way.

You'll need one of those

Have you ever started on a project, reached the halfway mark, and become stuck because you didn't have everything you needed? This kind of situation happens all the time in poorly planned vSphere deployments. Either something wasn't configured properly or the resources provided are fewer than requested.

A misconfiguration during deployment results in one of three scenarios: wasted time spent on troubleshooting, a "workaround" being put in place to get past the issue, or reinstalling the software only to end up right back in the same broken state. None of these scenarios are desirable, but all are preventable by confirming and reconfirming that you have everything you need before you start.

A resource deficiency is comparably frustrating, especially since you're able to complete installation and configuration, leading you to believe the problem is a misjudged requirement. Not until later does the real trouble show up — when it starts impacting the virtual environment. At this point, the effort to correct the issue is exponentially greater than it would have been if you had addressed the issue early on. Stick to your numbers when it comes to getting the resources you need, and you'll prevent a giant headache in the future.

Thinking about Networks and Storage

When virtualization-savvy people discuss their VMware vSphere infrastructure, they focus on the server hardware — number of CPUs, how many cores per CPU, how much memory — allowing the server hardware to take precedence over the other two-thirds of the infrastructure. Like tires and brakes to a car, network and storage are critical to every vSphere deployment. Leave out the critical components in either case, and all you have is a high-powered paperweight.

Keep in mind that a machine running VMware ESX is more like a tiny datacenter than a server. The network interfaces become a connection point between the outside world and the virtual switch hidden within the ESX host. The same holds true for storage area network (SAN) connections. The connections to support these capabilities differ from your common server and need to be configured as though they were being connected to additional network switches. Also, due to the nature of shared storage across ESX hosts, the storage capacity you'll be requesting from your SAN administrator will be larger than normally required for a server but optimal for an ESX host.

Administrators unfamiliar with these requirements may give you what they think you need, rather than what your ESX host actually needs. Work closely with your network and storage administrators to get what you need the first time. Not only does this make for a smooth deployment the first time, but it also educates the network and storage administrators on what needs to be provided going forward.

Taking Care of vSphere

Like anything else, a vSphere environment requires regular care and feeding. VMware occasionally releases patches and updates for your VMware ESX hosts and vCenter server. Unless it's a critical security patch, try not to be the first to apply it. Instead, browse around the vSphere discussion forums and see what experiences other administrators are having in their environments after applying each update. Don't wait too long though, or you run the risk of hitting the issue the patch is meant to fix.

The other part of looking after a vSphere environment is literally feeding the environment resources as they grow. It's inevitable — your vSphere environment will eventually run out of storage space, and running virtual machines will max out the capacity on your ESX hosts. Plan ahead to secure the resources needed to keep up with the growth in the environment, or you might have a deprived virtual infrastructure on your hands.

The vCenter of Your Universe

When all is said and done, vCenter Server is undoubtedly the piece that holds the vSphere environment together. vCenter Server is how virtual machines get cloned and customized, how ESX hosts get clustered, and how vSphere is able to do so much with such a small footprint.

vCenter Server is the brains behind ongoing management of a vSphere environment. vCenter is also the integration point for most third-party virtualization management platforms and is the foundation by which a vSphere environment is incorporated into cloud computing, which may sound like a lot, but there's more. vCenter allows for plug-ins for your favorite vSphere-related utilities, such as VMware Converter. vCenter owns licensing responsibility as well, so anything licensed in the vSphere environment leverages at least the license server capability of vCenter Server.

Like any disruptive, yet emerging, technology, *cloud computing* bears a name that represents a concept with more than one meaning. Some people hear the term cloud computing and think of a service where you can rent server resources by the hour. Other people think of cloud computing as a safe place where you can run your applications with compute power limited only by your wallet. Cloud computing experts agree on at least one point: Cloud computing involves using some set of compute resources as a service. vSphere lets you create a pool of compute resources internally, and you can manage those resources as a cloud, dynamically providing compute capacity to virtual machines, instead of passing them on as discrete components. This is why vSphere is touted by VMware as a cloud OS.

vCenter Server boasts support for management of more ESX hosts, virtual machines, and even more vSphere client connections than its predecessors. Another feature now available allows multiple vCenter Servers to be linked together, providing some level of redundancy at the management level. For a successful vCenter Server deployment, pay special attention to vCenter Server installation, configuration, and feature deployment.

Chapter 2

Introducing Virtualization

*V*irtualization is disruptive technology, forever changing the way we think about IT infrastructure. Most people have heard about virtualization, cloud computing, and VMware. It's great that it works so well, but what is virtualization?

This chapter takes you through the concepts of server virtualization. You see some comparisons between virtualization and everyday ideas and discover some of the terminology along the way. You also find out the benefits and pitfalls of virtual machines and how they compare to the physical world.

Thinking Virtual

Virtualization is not new, not magic, and not as complicated as you may think. Half the challenge of understanding virtualization is properly interpreting the terms surrounding it. The other half is accepting virtualization as the simple concept it is, and not trying to make it into something more complex.

People naturally shorten, abbreviate, or create acronyms for the terms they say a lot. You never hear people say "Self-Contained Underwater Breathing Apparatus" unless they're telling you what the acronym "SCUBA" stands for. Information technology is almost always "IT," the World Wide Web has been shortened to Web, and connecting to the Web is called "going online." So then, what does virtualization mean?

For most people, the term *virtual* refers to something artificial, as in "virtual reality." Others think of virtual as something being almost real, as in "I'm virtually done." In server virtualization, the term virtual is best defined as something that has been abstracted but that is still associated with a real resource, such as a virtual CPU or virtual disk. Both run on their real counterparts, but in order to allow virtual machines to run on different server models, a layer is inserted between the virtual and the physical. The abstraction layer that maps virtual resources to physical hardware is called a *hypervisor.*

For all intents and purposes, *virtualization* is usually the shortened version of "x86 server hardware virtualization." In the following list, we break down that terminology:

- ✔ **x86:** Refers to a processor with its instruction set made popular by the Intel 80386 32-bit CPU. Operating systems, such as Windows and Linux, primarily run on x86-based processors. (vSphere requires x64-based processors, which are x86 family processors with an extended 64-bit instruction set.)

- ✔ **Server:** Refers to an instance of an operating system (OS) and a multiuser application, such as a Web server or database server. Server is also used to describe the physical computer hardware the OS and applications run on.

- ✔ **Hardware virtualization:** When multiple operating systems run on the same physical hardware, but isolated, each OS thinks it's the only one running on the machine.

In short, the OS and applications once tied to x86-based physical hardware have been reduced to a bucket of bits, which can be placed next to other buckets of bits, all running on the same physical server, but unaware they're sharing the hardware with the other buckets.

While cloud computing and virtualization are related, they're not one and the same. Cloud computing may incorporate virtualization and virtual machines as the underlying platform, but cloud computing extends beyond the infrastructure. Instead, cloud computing is providing resources (like virtual machines, or a hosted application) as a service.

Virtual machines aren't so different

Virtual machines and physical machines are pretty much the same. Both have CPUs, memory, hard disks, operating systems, network connections, and even a BIOS. You can load applications on them and connect to them remotely, just as you can with a physical machine. Virtual machines are so much like physical machines that the OS doesn't even know it's in a virtual machine. If someone connects to the machine remotely, they probably won't even know they're using a virtual machine unless you tell them (or they spot the VMware Tools icon).

Virtual machines can be made to extend even further into the physical world to support specific cases where real physical resources are required. Certain clustered applications require sharing disk volume at the physical level. VMware vSphere is able to connect a virtual machine to a physical disk volume using Raw Device Mapping (RDM). RDM is one more way vSphere closes the gap between physical and virtual servers.

Real virtual hardware

OS vendors have the monumental task of trying to support as many pieces of hardware as possible. Virtual machines take a different approach by presenting a virtual version of the most common components in the industry, with the most built-in support across operating systems. This approach means that you can easily install popular operating systems without having to load extra drivers. It also allows the virtual machine to be run on servers with different models or brands of components, without any changes required to the virtual machine.

VMware takes virtual hardware one step further by providing optimized drivers for vSphere-specific virtual hardware. One example of this vSphere-specific hardware is a virtual network interface called VMXNET. This virtual network adapter is enabled when you install its custom driver, which is part of the default driver set contained within the VMware Tools toolkit available for most VMware virtual machines.

Arriving at Virtualization — Again

Server technology and fashion trends have something in common. In fashion, old styles never die; they just come back as retro. With server technology, any concept that was "the bee's knees" in its day comes back on smaller, faster, cheaper hardware.

Virtualization is so 1960s

Once upon a time, the mainframe was king of the datacenter. Aside from pure processing power, there was another huge advantage. System operators could schedule different programs with specific tasks (called *jobs*) to run at the same time on the same piece of hardware. Even better, the jobs could be reprioritized, allowing a given job to get more processing time than another job. The biggest obstacle for mainframe was and still is the cost to purchase, operate, and maintain the system.

In 1965, Intel cofounder Gordon Moore made the following prediction: "The number of transistors incorporated in a chip will approximately double every 24 months." This prediction came to be known as *Moore's Law*. As computer processors got smaller and manufacturing them got less expensive, a huge shift began to take place in corporate IT. Companies started buying desktop computers, each capable of running their programs independently without having to be attached to a central system. Success in stand-alone desktop computers kicked off a trend of companies procuring dedicated computer hardware for a single purpose or application. Improvements in networking technology gave the trend momentum, enabling dedicated computer systems to work collaboratively. Moore's Law pressed on, and servers' processor speeds were improving exponentially. Suddenly, the processing power offered by the new systems dwarfed the needs of applications once requiring all the resources of a dedicated server.

The one-application, one-server model did eventually paralyze some companies — with datacenters full of space-consuming, heat-producing, power-using, underutilized server hardware, and no remaining capacity for growth. Some datacenters simply ran out of power to add more servers, while others didn't have the physical space to install more hardware. The answer was there all along: more applications on less hardware. Virtualization of the x86 platform brought it back into style.

Supervisor turns hypervisor

Virtualization originated from the mainframe. Different programs shared the mainframe by taking turns running on the processors. A batch of work being processed by a program, or a job, was assigned to one or more processors. Each job was allowed a percentage of the total processing capacity, or a *slice*. Dividing processing cycles over a period of time is called *time slicing*. A scheduler, or *supervisor,* tells each program when to take its turn, with prioritized jobs being allocated more time slices than other jobs. This time-tested concept is still applied today in hypervisors, but on the x86 architecture. Most business-class computers now include Intel VT-x or AMD-V technology, both of which allow for hardware-assisted virtualization. When a virtual machine needs to process some instructions, it sends those instructions to the vCPU. While most instructions will already be executed on the processor directly, executing some specific instructions can affect other virtual machines on the same host. Those instructions must be translated into code that runs in a way that is isolated and will not affect the other virtual machines. Hardware-assisted virtualization allows those instructions to be translated and executed right on the chip. In contrast, early x86 virtualization technology used full virtualization, requiring the CPU instructions to be emulated in a software hypervisor, adding significant overhead to each request being executed.

Virtualization Simplified

One way to think about server virtualization is to compare it to car pooling. The next time you're driving to work, look around at the number of vehicles with empty seats (see Figure 2-1). Think about how many of those cars might be going to the same office. Then consider how many of the people driving those cars might live near each other, yet drive separately to the same destination every single day. It sounds like a waste of fuel, doesn't it?

Aside from the financial benefit, car pooling also reduces the number of cars on the road at a given point in time, which translates to less traffic. The passengers of the vehicle are consuming a resource — a ride to work. By putting the passengers with a common destination together into fewer cars, as shown in Figure 2-2, consolidation is being achieved.

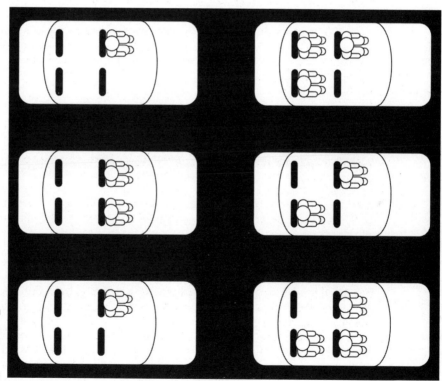

Figure 2-1:
Before car pooling.

In Figures 2-1 and 2-2, the consolidation involves 12 passengers and 6 cars. Translating the diagram to IT, each car represents a physical server, and each passenger represents an application or job that needs to be executed. The goal is to use the least number of cars to support all the passengers. Figure 2-3 shows the result of the passenger consolidation.

According to Figure 2-3, consolidating the passengers into just three cars resulted in a 50 percent reduction of cars, with the cars at 100 percent utilization. While this consolidation ratio may seem a bit far-fetched for car pooling, it's not unreasonable to see significant increases in utilization and a noticeable reduction in physical server hardware demand. There's always some overhead in consolidation. For the car poolers, the car will have at least a slight drop in fuel economy for the simple reason that it takes more fuel to move more weight. In server virtualization, the hypervisor creates some overhead, with hypervisors running directly on the physical server hardware taking up less resources than hypervisors running on top of an OS.

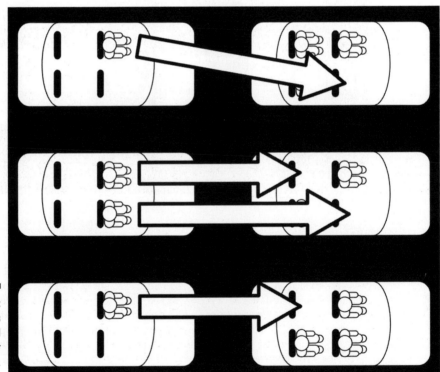

Figure 2-2:
Passengers
consolidated
into fewer
cars.

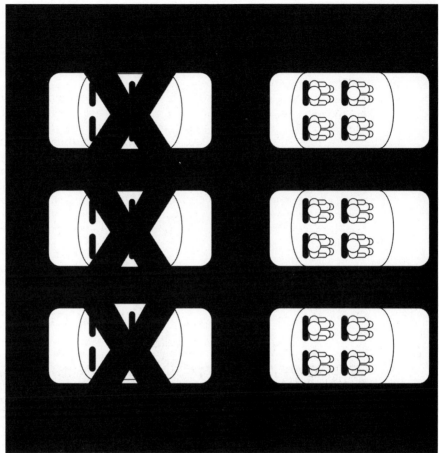

Figure 2-3:
Carpooling —
after con-
solidation.

Picturing virtualization

Ask any VMware administrator how virtualization works, and that person
will most likely draw you a picture. The picture is the Mona Lisa of virtualization diagrams, famously recognizable among VMware users everywhere.
It's a simple diagram that describes how VMware ESX, the foundation of the
vSphere virtualization platform, lets you run virtual machines on physical
machines loaded with the VMware ESX hypervisor. The diagram in Figure 2-4
describes the components of a virtual infrastructure based on VMware ESX.

Why is this simple diagram so popular? First, anyone with a basic knowledge
of computers can understand the diagram. Second, it's the foundation of the
VMware product story, and VMware led the way in bringing virtualization to
the masses.

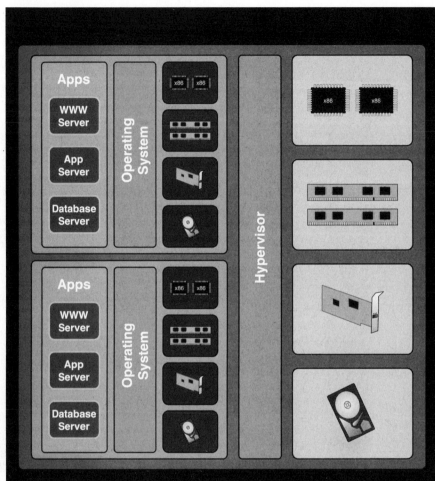

Figure 2-4:
x86
virtualization.

This is your machine

You're probably familiar with the components of a traditional server, like the one represented in Figure 2-5. You go online to order a server from your favorite manufacturer, and while you're shopping, you're asked to provide the desired configuration for the system you've selected. Some choices are required, such as the number of CPUs, the amount of Random Access Memory (RAM), and how much hard disk storage to install at the factory. Other choices are optional, such as a second network interface or a DVD drive. The sum of these choices *defines* the machine. The manufacturer assembles a server with the components you requested and ships it out to you.

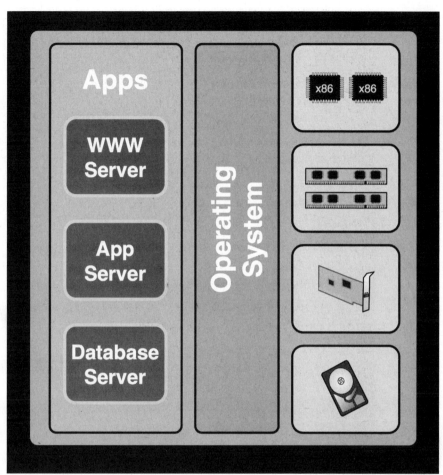

Figure 2-5:
A traditional
server.

The server arrives, and you install an OS, such as Microsoft Windows or Linux. Once the OS is loaded, applications are installed on top of the OS. At a high level, the server matches the diagram in Figure 2-5.

This traditional server configuration dedicates an entire server (CPU, memory, network, and disk) to running a single instance of the OS and a related set of applications. The majority of physical servers dedicated to a single application are grossly underutilized, only using about 5 percent of the server's actual capacity. Simple math tells you that when the OS and the applications consume 5 percent or less of the server's total capacity, the remaining capacity (95 percent) goes unused. Unfortunately, the cost of running a server (power, cooling, rack space) is about the same, whether it's being utilized at five percent or at 95 percent of its capacity.

This is your machine on virtualization

The next question is, "Is there any way I can use the leftover processing on my server?" Here's where the diagram starts to transform and the concept of virtualization begins to take shape. Figure 2-6 grows a bit to show where the virtualization layer comes into the picture.

In Figure 2-6, the traditional server is no longer a stand-alone piece of hardware. A virtualization layer is inserted between the physical server hardware and the server's OS. The physical server is directly loaded with hypervisor software. The hypervisor is the program responsible for scheduling of processor compute time and allocation of memory in the virtualization layer. A hypervisor that doesn't require an underlying OS to run on is known as a *bare-metal* hypervisor, since it runs directly on the "bare metal" of the physical host. VMware vSphere is a bare-metal hypervisor platform, and the physical server running VMware ESX is called the *host*.

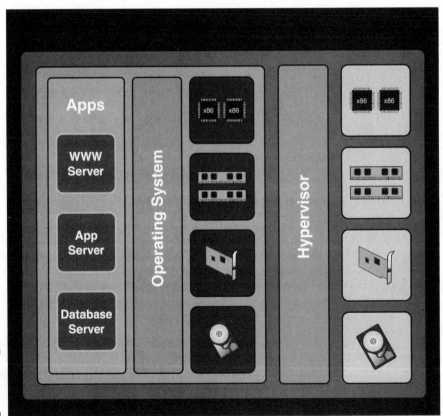

Figure 2-6:
Virtualization
layer.

The traditional server is replaced with the virtual machine, also referred to as the *guest*. A virtual machine is a collection of files with the machine's specifications, settings, and hard drive contents. When a virtual machine is running on the hypervisor, it looks just like a physical server on the inside. The virtualization layer presents virtual hardware components (based on popular physical hardware components) to the virtual machine. Behind the scenes, the virtualization layer maps the virtual components to physical counterparts in the underlying host. This allows the physical components to be shared across multiple virtual machines.

The hypervisor governs requests for processing time and schedules them to be executed on a real processor. Some requests to execute code will affect other virtual machines. Those requests are trapped and translated into code to be run in a way that doesn't affect the other machines. With each new generation of CPU, more of this translation activity is being pushed to the processor level where code translations can be executed faster and with less overhead. The AMD-V and Intel VT-x features are examples of chip-based, hardware-assisted virtualization technologies.

Ups and Downs of Virtualization

Virtualization has had a major impact on the IT industry, particularly in the areas of datacenter efficiency and cost reduction. Most IT professionals agree virtualization's impact has been positive, but with a few caveats. Even with the strides companies like VMware continue to make, at least a few cases will remain where virtualization doesn't make sense, or where it can't be achieved due to current limitations of virtualization.

Positively virtual

A lot of the positive attributes of virtualization came by way of its creation. Virtualization had been in use for many years in the mainframe world before it was reinvented into the x86 virtualization world. Much of the functionality introduced was an answer to a problem or limitation that existed in the physical machine realm. Here is a list of the positives that virtualization enables:

  ✔ **Do more with less.** Virtualization provides a viable alternative to a one-to-one ratio between applications and servers. IT organizations are able to run more applications on less hardware, and in many cases, reduce the datacenter footprint through consolidation of existing machines to a virtualized infrastructure.

✔ **Run a virtual machine on dissimilar hardware.** Another major positive often overlooked in the realm of virtualization is the capability of a virtual machine to run on dissimilar hardware. In vSphere, the OS of a virtual machine is presented with a standard set of virtual components (virtual CPUs, virtual hard drive controllers, virtual memory, and virtual network adapters are examples). Because the virtual machine sees the virtual hardware and not the physical hardware behind the hypervisor, the virtual machine needs to support only the virtual hardware. The virtual machine may then be moved to another vSphere host with different hardware and be powered back on in its new location without the need for any additional hardware drivers in the OS.

✔ **Virtual Machine Disks are files.** A Virtual Machine Disk (VMDK) is a file (or set of files) containing the virtual equivalent of a physical machine's hard drive. The difference is the portability of the file.

✔ A **File system tuned for virtual machine storage was introduced.** VMware introduced Virtual Machine File System (VMFS) in the early days of VMware ESX and was the only option for storage of VMware virtual machines. VMFS was designed to meet the demanding needs of virtual machines reading from and writing to disk, with a strong focus on Input/Output (I/O) transfer capability.

✔ **Bare-metal virtualization has very little overhead.** VMware ESX started out as a bare-metal hypervisor, consuming a small footprint by not requiring an OS between ESX and the hardware. vSphere slims down the ESX hypervisor even more in ESXi by eliminating the service console, a Linux-based command-line interface used for low-level administration and to host the vCenter management agent.

✔ **Cost-efficient disaster recovery.** Disaster recovery (DR) is at the forefront of peoples' minds, and many organizations have disaster recovery plans in place. The traditional model for server DR requires two identical machines — one at the local datacenter and the other in some remote location. The hardware at the remote location can sit unused for years without ever being called into service as part of a disaster recovery scene. By using virtual machines instead of physical machines for disaster recovery, the chance of hardware obsolescence decreases, and the virtual machines require far less work to bring online than their physical counterparts require.

✔ **Improved uptime and availability for applications.** Even the simplest application can enjoy uninterrupted server time when running on vSphere. Even a virtualization beginner can get vSphere running in a High Availability (HA) configuration without much effort.

Some side effects of virtualization

Virtualization is not without its pitfalls. Most users of virtualization agree its benefits far outweigh its negatives. Just the same, it's still important to be aware of the negatives so you can steer clear of them whenever possible. Here is a list of potential issues associated with virtualization:

- ✔ **The "Eggs in One Basket" effect:** Formerly used as an excuse to delay adoption of virtualization at its outset, the "All Your Eggs in One Basket" argument suggests that virtualization introduces risk by putting more applications onto a single piece of physical hardware. The risk is having a far greater number of applications go down in the event the physical hardware fails, whereas there would be far less impact if just one application were running per physical server.

- ✔ **Virtual machine sprawl:** Creating a virtual machine is far easier than deploying a physical machine when much of the process to procure a machine is bypassed or nonexistent. Users see the rapid provisioning times of virtual machine cloning and begin to decouple the cost to have and run the virtual machine from the virtual machine itself. Before long, numerous temporary machines exist in the environment, abandoned, forgotten, or stashed away for use another day "just in case."

- ✔ **Increased hardware requirements:** Getting the biggest return out of vSphere virtualization is best accomplished by exploiting the high-value features of vSphere, such as memory sharing and thin provisioning of virtual machine disks. The more machines running the same OS, the greater the efficiency. In order to fit all those machines onto a single host, the server industry has been so kind as to build bigger, more powerful (and even more expensive) hardware to accommodate more virtual machines per host. Although fewer physical machines are being provisioned overall, the cost of deploying larger hosts can match or exceed the cost of deploying the equivalent capacity in less powerful servers using the one application, one server model.

- ✔ **More complexity throughout the environment.** Besides increased hardware at the server level, virtualization requires additional network and storage networking. The unique requirements placed on both the network and the storage infrastructure may require some upgrades to the computing foundation.

- ✔ **New skill requirements:** Since you're reading this book, you already know that virtualization requires updated IT skills, even between major product releases. Adequate training for vSphere management is a must. An administrator self-taught in vSphere may yield a less efficient virtualization deployment than one trained for the task. In the long run, a sloppy deployment will cost far more than adequate training resources.

When Virtual Is Improbable

Virtualization is an exciting technology, especially once you've realized the far-reaching potential and benefits of its deployment. Like the microwave oven, the Internet, or any other disruptive technology, people tend to get wrapped up in the technology, feeling out the boundaries as they go. Before saddling up to become a virtualization trailblazer, here are some cases where virtualization is not a viable option:

- **Hardware-based multimedia applications:** Installing a multimedia interface card into a vSphere server does not allow you to map the card's capabilities to a virtual machine.

- **Telephony applications:** Internet-based voice communications have seen mainstream adoption over the past few years, but the days of telco-based phone services are long from extinct. Several vendors still offer telco adapter cards for use in call centers, voicemail systems, and other interactive voice-driven applications. These card-based telco adapters don't map to virtual machines and shouldn't be installed in servers running vSphere.

- **Other virtualization products:** Installing another hypervisor in a virtual machine usually doesn't work, and when it does work, the performance is poor at best.

- **Unsupported on virtualized platforms:** Believe it or not, some software vendors out there still will not support their product if it's running in a virtual machine. That doesn't mean it won't work in a VM; the software will just deny you support for an issue if it's running in a VM when the problem occurs.

- **Licensing:** Some software has licensing restrictions specific to virtualization, such as running a desktop OS licensed for use on a physical desktop computer.

When is unsupported really unsupported? Many times, even if virtualization isn't supported, you can get specific case-by-case support from vendors if you work closely with them. Before you rule out an application, try to contact your vendor. Depending on how large a customer your organization is, you may be surprised!

Chapter 3

Exploring the Capabilities of VMware vSphere

. . . .

In This Chapter

▶ Why standard VMware vSphere is so unique

▶ Going to the next level with advanced vSphere options

▶ vSphere virtualization for the enterprise

. . . .

*V*Mware has led the software industry through innovations in virtualization technology since its introduction of VMware ESX several years ago. VMware continues to lead the way with its vSphere platform, incorporating new, enterprise-ready features targeting support for mission-critical applications. Still, the standard features of vSphere have created a standard by which other virtualization platforms are compared.

In this chapter, you find out about the standard features of vSphere and what makes those features unique. We discuss the advanced features as well as the features in the Enterprise edition of vSphere. You also discover some features available only in the Enterprise Plus edition of vSphere.

Exploring the Unique Features of vSphere

VMware differentiates itself through a mix of features available only on vSphere and through continuous innovation. This innovation leads to new Enterprise features that drive adoption of virtualization in mission-critical environments.

The vSphere licensing model breaks out groups of features into three main categories: Standard, Advanced, and Enterprise. The rest of this chapter explains the differences and similarities among the three.

Taking a Peek at Standard vSphere Features

VMware vSphere continues to reign over the enterprise virtualization market, but the standard features at the heart of the product are the reason people choose vSphere over other virtualization platforms. VMware-specific technologies, such as the way memory overcommit is handled, all the way up to the high availability capability at the cluster level, reinforce VMware's position. This section covers the standard features in vSphere.

Memory overcommit

One of the biggest benefits of running vSphere is VMware's mastery of memory management. vSphere has three different ways to handle memory contention by virtual machines (VMs). Each way is best for a specific condition, so it's common for more than one method to be applied at a time.

Sharing common memory across virtual machines

Every vSphere deployment contains multiple virtual machines running identical operating systems, which means the VMs also have some identical data (called *pages*) in memory. Instead of storing redundant pages in the ESX host's physical memory, the host uses Transparent Page Sharing (TPS) to remove redundant pages. TPS works transparently, scanning the memory of all VMs on an ESX host, looking for identical data in the memory of multiple VMs. When TPS finds such data, it consolidates that data to a single copy in the ESX host's physical memory and points the VMs to the common memory. This process happens entirely at the ESX host level and has the least overhead of the three memory overcommit mechanisms.

Consider leveraging the benefits of Transparent Page Sharing (TPS) when planning your vSphere farm. Placing similar VMs on the same host or grouping similar VMs to a particular cluster maximizes the effect.

The mysterious VMware balloon driver

The VMware balloon driver has been around since the introduction of VMware ESX. The balloon driver is part of the VM Tools package installed in every VM. As its name suggests, the balloon driver inflates to take up as much free memory space as is available in a VM. The ESX host grabs that memory to redistribute to other VMs in immediate need of memory.

When a shortage of memory occurs, the balloon driver may squeeze memory out of a lower priority VM (as defined by you) and give it to a higher priority VM. The idea is to cause the guest OS to experience a low-memory condition, triggering a cleanup process to optimize the area in memory already reserved for use.

Memory compression — because it's better than swapping

Transparent Page Sharing (TPS) and the balloon driver are usually sufficient to reduce memory contention on an ESX host. When TPS and ballooning aren't enough, ESX swaps inactive data in a VM's memory to a disk file created for each VM until that data is needed again in active memory. Since it's being written to disk, an inherent latency causes this method to take longer to read from swapped out memory.

VMware realized that compressing data and putting it back into physical memory is much faster than swapping the data to disk and added this method as the last attempt at freeing up memory before data starts getting swapped to disk. The compressed data is stored in a per-VM compression cache and is regularly updated.

Virtual machine cloning

VMware vCenter has made it incredibly simple to make copies of existing virtual machines. Once a VM is built, you can convert it into a template and redeploy it with its own unique identity. The ease of use offered by vCenter Server sets the bar for VM deployment from templates.

The secret to vSphere's ability to rapidly deploy unique VMs through vCenter Server lies in the preparation. vCenter Server uses Customization Specifications, which hold the common data used to configure systems in the infrastructure. Naming conventions, OS license keys, admin usernames and passwords, network address details, and domain membership information reside in the Customization Specification, which you can adjust at the time it's selected to use in cloning a VM.

You create the specification using a wizard through the vSphere Client, and you can edit it at any time. The data in the Customization Specification drives vCenter's VM customization engine that applies the settings to the cloned VM without any other interaction.

VMware vCenter also allows you to take any VM and either convert or clone it into a VM template. The template differs from a standard VM in that it cannot be edited or powered on without being converted back into a standard VM. The VM template is used to deploy new virtual machines by creating a clone with a unique name. Once the copy is complete, the cloned VM is customized by vCenter, using its VM customization engine to apply the identity and settings derived from the customization specification. Cloning can also take advantage of thin provisioning (see next section) to deploy a VM that consumes only the space of the data contained on its virtual disk growing as needed, up to the actual provisioned size.

Thin provisioning

VMware vSphere offers a thin-provisioning feature for virtual disks. The virtual disk file consumes the space equal to the actual data contained on the virtual disk. The virtual disk file grows as needed to accommodate new data, up to the actual provisioned size.

To make the cloning process even faster, you can create VM templates with thin-provisioned virtual disks. Using the thin-provision disk format for templates reduces the template footprint. It also allows for faster provisioning of the template, since vSphere doesn't have to copy empty virtual disk space to the cloned VM's target location.

High availability

VMware High Availability (HA) is one of the early features that made VMware ESX unique. Prior to the introduction of VMware HA, applications couldn't be clustered unless they were specifically designed for clustering, and even then they still required a specialized configuration to work. VMware HA needs just two VMware ESX hosts configured as a cluster with shared storage and network and can bring failover capability to any VM.

The premise behind VMware HA is to improve the availability of any application running in a VM. VMware HA offsets the impact of a clustered host becoming unavailable, whether due to host hardware failure or loss of network connectivity. The ESX hosts must have shared access to the same storage; otherwise, the remaining ESX hosts won't be able to access the virtual disks of the VMs being brought back up from the failed ESX host. The same holds true for common access to networks across ESX hosts, enabling the recovered VMs connectivity to the appropriate networks.

VMware ESX hosts in a cluster configured for HA look out for one another. The hosts are in constant communication, each transmitting a beacon through the network to indicate to peers that the host is still up and running. If a host goes down, the other hosts take notice and are aware of the VMs that were running on the host prior to failure. When an ESX host in a cluster fails to signal its beacon for a second time, its peers spring into action and bring up the VMs from the failed host as configured by the cluster's administrator. Capacity can even be reserved on each ESX host in a cluster, guaranteeing resources to bring up VMs in the event of a failure elsewhere in the cluster.

vMotion live migration of VMs

VMware set the standard for migration of running virtual machines across hosts when it introduced vMotion. VMware vMotion has matured from a neat feature to a must-have for host maintenance and infrastructure optimization.

vMotion allows the movement of a running VM from one ESX host to another without interruption. It's a pretty simple feature to use, with a few prerequisites. A network connection specifically enabled for vMotion traffic is required, as are ESX hosts sharing the same network and storage used by the VM. You select a VM, a different ESX host to receive the VM, and a priority level (high or low). In a matter of seconds, the VM disappears from its original host and reappears on the new host, all without skipping a beat.

Administrators first viewed this feature as a novelty, but later realized its importance. vMotion has two main uses:

 ✔ Evacuating a host of its running VMs so that it can undergo maintenance

 ✔ Migration of VMs from highly loaded ESX hosts to less loaded ESX hosts

Both uses have found their way into standard operating procedures of enterprise organizations over the years, and vMotion has become a needed feature rather than a novelty.

Getting a Look at Advanced vSphere Features

The standard edition of vSphere (see preceding section) is already quite robust, but customers may require just a bit more for their vSphere deployment. The Advanced edition brings true high availability with fault tolerance and hot-add of virtual CPUs and memory, practically removing any reason for your mission-critical VM to experience downtime. The advanced edition also includes the Virtual Serial Port Concentrator (described in Chapter 4), designed with command-line–based enterprise applications in mind.

Distributed Resource Scheduler

Distributed Resource Scheduler (DRS) is a unique feature to vSphere that allows vCenter to optimize the environment by moving VMs around for the best balance of workloads. DRS can leverage vMotion to automatically migrate machines from one ESX host to another without interruption and without operator intervention. Conversely, you can keep DRS in a manual mode, offering migration suggestions to the operator.

DRS constantly evaluates the load of each ESX host in a cluster and how each VM is impacted by the others. Based on this data, DRS calculates the impact of moving certain VMs to other hosts to alleviate the load on other VMs. You can set DRS to act at a minimum performance improvement threshold, with five different levels, represented by *stars*. One star means that moving the VM yields a slight increase in performance. Five stars means a significant increase in VM performance as a result of the move.

When DRS is set to be fully automatic, it moves any VMs that meet the minimum star rating. In semi-automatic and manual modes, it makes suggestions for optimal balance.

DRS also plays another role in balancing VMs across a cluster. Anytime a VM is powered on, DRS suggests the optimal ESX host on which to power up the VM, thus helping to balance the load even before contention begins. In full and semi-automatic mode, DRS chooses the host for you without operator intervention. In manual mode, you're prompted to choose a host to run the VM. This same functionality is at work when a VM is created on a cluster. DRS makes a suggestion as to where the new VM should created based on existing workloads of the ESX hosts.

A newer feature of DRS is the ability to set rules relative to other VMs. This feature addresses situations where two VMs are supposed to be separated on different hosts for redundancy (such as domain controllers or file servers). This feature allows you to specify which VMs should never reside on the same host, or in the case of a multi-VM application, which VMs should be kept together on the same host.

Hot-add of CPU and memory to running virtual machines

The concept of adding CPU and memory resources to a running application was founded in the mainframe world. CPU and memory get reassigned to higher priority jobs and then returned to be shared by the other jobs once the high-priority jobs are completed. VMware took this concept and made it a reality in the x86 virtualization realm by implementing the concept in vSphere.

You can configure virtual machines running operating systems capable of handling the addition of virtual CPUs and memory to allow hot-add of vCPU and memory. As the vSphere administrator, you must configure the VM manually, as the feature is disabled by default to prevent accidental corruption of a running VM not capable of handling dynamic vCPU and memory changes. Once a VM is configured to allow hot-add of virtual CPUs and memory, you can make these changes without powering off the VM, and in most cases, without a reboot of the VM.

Delving into vSphere Enterprise Features

Enterprise and Enterprise Plus editions of vSphere are as good as virtualization can get. Truly meant for enterprise implementations, vSphere Enterprise adds Distributed Switch capability, as well as the option to add a Cisco Nexus 1000V virtual switch. The Host Profiles feature is ideal for managing large numbers of ESX hosts. Lastly, Storage I/O Control and Network I/O Control (described in Chapter 4) allow fine-grained control and prioritization of both network and storage resources.

Storage vMotion live migration

Storage vMotion is a feature that allows you to move virtual disk files of a running VM from one datastore to another datastore without interruption. It leverages the same prerequisites as vMotion, but it's licensed separately from vMotion. Migration of a VM's virtual disks takes longer to complete due to the size difference (memory versus disk).

Storage vMotion resulted from the recurring theme of growth on VMware storage infrastructure. As VMware ESX capabilities advanced, so did the size of VM File System (VMFS) datastores. Organizations needed a way to move live VMs from their existing datastore to a larger one so the original datastore could be reclaimed. Storage vMotion addresses this need, and with the same simplicity as vMotion.

vSphere fault tolerance

VMware made major investments in vSphere to ready it for hosting mission-critical applications not previously considered as virtualization candidates. The result of their investment is vSphere Fault Tolerance (FT), a true continuous availability feature that, before now, was available only with specialized server hardware.

VMware knew it needed something truly spectacular for people to consider vSphere as a viable option for hosting mission-critical applications. VMware FT is how VMware answered the call for a way to ensure continuous availability of virtual machines. When FT is enabled for a given VM, a copy of that VM is created on another ESX host. The copy is actually running and gets updated in real time by way of vLockstep technology. If the original VM fails, the FT copy is already running and up-to-date and gets connected to the network to take the place of the original VM. The failover is completely transparent with zero downtime.

vShield Zones

The first iteration of vShield was more of a concept than a feature. The idea was to integrate security components, such as firewalls, into the virtual infrastructure. VMware vSphere made the vShield concept a reality by introducing real, manageable security components to vSphere.

VMware vShield provides a simple way to introduce network filtering to the vSphere virtual infrastructure. vShield components are deployed as vApps, allowing configuration from outside the virtual appliance contained within each vApp. One vShield VM is required on each ESX host being protected. You can deploy vShield Manager inside or outside the protected environment, but it must be capable of communicating with vCenter Server and the vShield machines in order to manage them. Although vShield lacks the capabilities of more advanced firewalls, the filtering capability at the virtual infrastructure level makes up for that lack.

vNetwork Distributed Switch

Introduced in vSphere, the vNetwork Distributed Switch provides a unique twist to virtual networking. The Distributed Switch leverages real networking to build seamless virtual networks across hosts. This feature is limited to the Enterprise Plus edition of vSphere.

The Distributed Switch concept is built upon the idea behind Virtual LANs (VLANs). By marking data packets with an identifier that can be used to restrict who receives the packet, the illusion of multiple network segments on a single physical network is possible. The simplest implementation of the Distributed Switch creates a common port group on all the member ESX hosts, tied together by a common VLAN. The advantage to using the Distributed Switch over individual port groups is the centralized management capability it brings to VM networking across the member hosts.

More advanced deployments can leverage the vNetwork Distributed Switch feature enabling use of Private VLANs. Private VLAN capability is a prerequisite at the physical network level and must be enabled on the connected switches. Implementing a Private VLANs allows you to further segment common VLAN. This approach effectively creates a "VLAN of VLANs" that can be defined at the Distributed Switch, without having to reconfigure the physical network switching fabric each time a new Private VLAN is needed.

Host Profiles

A longstanding challenge in managing larger virtual infrastructure deployments has been keeping the ESX host configurations consistent. A related matter is the time it takes to deploy an ESX host whose configuration is nearly identical to an existing ESX host. vSphere Host Profiles solves both of those problems.

Responding to customers' increasing needs to ensure that ESX host configurations are kept consistent, whether for compliance or for general manageability, VMware introduced vSphere Host Profiles. You can choose a specific ESX host to act as the role model for its peers. You capture the host's configuration and associate it with the other ESX hosts in the farm. You can quickly see whether an ESX host's configuration differs from the source host's configuration, ignoring unique identifiers such as network address and host name. If the ESX host configuration differs, the host is marked as out of compliance. As the administrator, you can then use Host Profiles to apply the correct configuration to the nonconfirming host to bring it back into compliance.

Another time-saving use for Host Profiles is its ability to completely configure a new ESX host by applying a configuration template derived from a source ESX host to the new member of the farm. You're prompted for unique identifiers, such as network addresses and host name. vSphere then proceeds to configure the network, storage, and everything in between, based on the configuration template and the information you supplied. This feature is a huge timesaver, especially when rolling out a new vSphere host farm.

Chapter 4

Comparing Virtual Infrastructure 3.5 with vSphere 4.x

*V*Mware vSphere 4.0 raised the bar in the virtualization space with new technology, improved performance, and major strides in highly available, fault-tolerant architecture. VMware did it again with vSphere 4.1, boosting performance and capacity to new heights, making it more efficient and manageable than ever before.

This chapter explains the enhancements made to ESX between Virtual Infrastructure 3.5 (VI3) and vSphere 4.0. You discover the new features added in vSphere 4.0 and then explore new features and improvements made between vSphere 4.0 and vSphere 4.1.

Quickly Comparing VI3 with vSphere 4

The introduction of vSphere 4.0 brought with it higher powered virtual machines (VM) and a more flexible architecture. Virtual Infrastructure 3.5 (VI3) moved VMware into the production datacenter, but vSphere 4.0 took it deeper with features and capabilities made for hosting mission-critical applications. In this section, you find out about the improvements in VI3 and the new features in vSphere 4.0 that take it to the next level.

Bigger, better virtual machines

ESX/ESXi 4.0 introduced a long-needed update to VM components with the release of its new default standard, Virtual Machine Hardware Version 7. Here are the changes:

- **Virtual CPUs:** The maximum number of virtual Central Processing Units (vCPUs) per VM went up from 4 vCPUs to 8 vCPUs. Also, a VM can have between 1 and 8 vCPUs in single vCPU increments. VI3 allowed for only 1, 2, or 4 vCPUs.

- **VM memory:** The maximum amount of RAM for a VM is now 255GB. This amount is up from the 64GB maximum in VI3.

- **Virtual network adapter:** VMware's very own virtual network adapter adds some subtle performance improvements as it reaches its third generation (VMXNET3).

- **More virtual hard disk types:** Up through VI3, you had only two virtual hard disk options: LSI SCSI adapter and BusLogic SCSI adapter. Two more options have been added: an LSI SAS adapter, which supports Windows Server 2008 Failover Clustering configurations, and an Integrated Drive Electronics (IDE) adapter, for operating systems without SCSI support.

- **Virtual machine performance counters tied to Windows performance:** This feature enables the VMware Tools agent running in each VM to get its data directly from Windows, removing discrepancies between vCenter Server readings and other Windows performance monitoring tools.

- **More support for guest operating systems:** vSphere 4.0 adds support for the following guest operating systems:

  - Asianux 3.0 Server

  - CentOS 4

  - Debian 4 and 5

  - FreeBSD 6 and 7

  - OS/2 4 and 4.5

  - MS-DOS 6.22

  - Windows 3.1

  - Windows 95 and 98

  - Windows 7 (experimental)

  - Windows Server 2008 R2 (experimental)

  - Windows Preinstallation Environment 2.1

- SCO OpenServer 5
- SCO UnixWare 7
- Solaris 8 and 9 (experimental)

vCenter Server (formerly VirtualCenter)

vCenter Server has a new name and a new look in vSphere 4.0, but that's not all. Major improvements found in vCenter Server 4.0 include

- ✔ **Guest OS customization:** vCenter Server can now customize Windows Server 2008 (32-bit and 64-bit), Ubuntu 8.04, and Debian 4.0.

- ✔ **Centralized licensing:** You no longer require a license server or host license files as required in VI3. All product and feature licensing now consist of 25-character license keys managed from vCenter Server 4.0.

- ✔ **Storage vMotion:** This highly coveted feature can now be managed through vCenter Server and works across a Network File System (NFS), Internet Small Computer Systems Interface (iSCSI), and Fibre Channel (FC) storage. Storage vMotion has been updated to take advantage of new VMkernel code that copies blocks of storage data more efficiently. The feature can also be used to convert virtual disks from thick format to thin format.

- ✔ **Performance chart enhancements:** vCenter now offers a proverbial "single pane of glass" for performance metrics of CPU, memory, disk, and network without a lot of clicking around. Thumbnail views of VMs, hosts, clusters, resource pools, and datastores were added for simpler navigation. Also new are aggregate graphs to show resource consumption.

- ✔ **Monitoring (events and alarms) enhancements:** Low-level hardware and host events are now reported. Time-based controls on alarm triggers have been added to limit false alarms. Notifications can be set for critical errors and events as well.

- ✔ **More database choices:** vCenter Server 4.0 adds support for Microsoft SQL Server 2008 and Oracle 11g.

- ✔ **More server OS choices:** vCenter Server now runs on Microsoft Windows Server 2003 (x64 — in 32-bit compatibility mode), Microsoft Windows Server 2008 (x64 — in 32-bit compatibility mode), and Microsoft Windows Server 2008 (x86).

- ✔ **HA clustering with Windows Server 2000, 2003, and 2008:** Support for Microsoft Cluster Services (MSCS) has been expanded to include more OS options and support for both 32-bit and 64-bit guest operating systems. Boot-from-SAN VMs are now supported, as is some application-level clustering such as that used by Microsoft Exchange 2007.

ESX — a host of improvements

ESX is all grown up, now able to leverage massive amounts of memory, CPU, and disk like never before. The following are some of the key improvements in ESX 4.0:

- **1 terabyte (TB) of host memory:** In case you happen to have a server with 1,024GB of RAM, up to a *terabyte* of memory is supported per host.

- **More CPUs:** 64 logical CPUs per host, up from 32 logical CPUs in VI3. Also, an ESX host can support up to 512 vCPUs per host, up from 192 vCPUs in VI3.

- **64-bit VMKernel:** The core of the ESX hypervisor, VMKernel is now 64-bit, significantly expanding support for more memory and increasing performance overall.

- **64-bit service console:** The Linux-based service console for ESX is now 64-bit, improving management console performance.

- **iSCSI storage:** Updated iSCSI support improves performance and reduces overhead for the software-based iSCSI adapter built into ESX, as well as hardware-based iSCSI adapters.

- **NFS datastores:** 64 NFS datastores can be shared by an ESX cluster. The VI3 default maximum was 8 shared NFS datastores, but could be configured to allow up to 32 shared NFS datastores.

- **Jumbo frames on network-based storage:** Network-based storage connections can go faster thanks to Jumbo Frame support, allowing more data to be pushed over the network at a time. Support is for iSCSI and NFS on 1 Gigabit per second (Gbps) and 10 Gbps network interface cards (NICs).

- **Enhanced vMotion Compatibility (EVC):** EVC automatically configures ESX hosts with Intel FlexMigration and AMD-V Extended Migration technologies to make them compatible with ESX hosts with older CPUs.

- **Distributed Power Management (DPM) with IPMI and iLO:** DPM powers off ESX hosts when not in use to save power. DPM now offers support for powering on ESX hosts via Intelligent Platform Management Interface (IPMI) and HP Integrated Lights-Out (iLO), in addition to using Wake on LAN.

Pushing up the uptime

Downtime is a bad word in corporate datacenters. Some improvements for high availability, or *uptime,* include the following:

✔ **HA maintenance mode:** High availability mode now respects an ESX host in maintenance mode and suspends failover actions (such as moving over VMs from a failed ESX host) targeted for the host while undergoing maintenance.

✔ **HA improved admission control:** Prior to vSphere, budgeting capacity for HA failover was figured manually. HA admission control lets you choose a policy to reserve room for failover in a cluster of ESX hosts.

✔ **VMware data recovery:** This vCenter-integrated backup solution officially supports file-level restore, allowing you to recover individual files from a backup. Enhanced Windows file sharing CIFS is added, and overall performance improved.

Finding Out What's New in vSphere 4

Numerous improvements over VMware Virtual Infrastructure 3.5 make vSphere 4 a mature player in enterprise-level server virtualization, earning vSphere a place in the business-critical corner of the datacenter. vSphere 4 adds features to help you keep virtual machines running, get more out of your underlying physical infrastructure, and boost performance all around. Explore the capabilities of vSphere 4 and see how you can benefit in your own environment.

Additions to availability

Driving vSphere into production server environments is what VMware had in mind with the release of vSphere 4.0. Here are some of the new features supporting that effort:

✔ **vCenter Server — Linked Mode:** Managing large vCenter Server implementations just got easier. Linked Mode allows administrators to interconnect their vCenter Servers to share roles and licenses across them. Administrators can also see an overview of all linked vCenter Servers from a single vSphere client.

✔ **VMware Fault Tolerance (FT):** This new feature protects VMs from downtime and data loss in the event of server hardware failure. FT is enabled on a per-VM basis and allows a second copy of the VM on another ESX host to run in lockstep with the original VM. Because everything about the two VMs is identical, the second VM can pick up at exactly the point where the original VM failed. The second VM even keeps its memory synchronized with the original VM, so switching over is transparent.

✔ **Hot-add of memory and vCPU:** Using the updated VM hardware (version 7) and a hot-add-friendly operating system, memory and vCPUs can be added to a running VM.

✔ **Hot-plug (add/remove) of virtual devices:** VMs enabled for hot-add of vCPU and memory also gain the ability to add and remove virtual devices while the VM is still running. Some of these devices include virtual network adapters, virtual SCSI disk adapters (and virtual disks), virtual CD-ROM drives, and virtual sound cards.

✔ **Hot-extend for virtual disks:** Virtual disks can be made larger while the VM is still running.

Some operating systems, such as Windows Server 2003 and Windows Server 2008, can take advantage of the hot-extend for virtual disks feature without a reboot.

Net new networking

Networking grows up in vSphere 4.0, introducing new technologies and adapting to current ones. Here are some of the new networking capabilities:

✔ **IPv6 support:** vSphere 4.0 adds IPv6 networking support for the ESX kernel, the service console, and vCenter Server. This allows vCenter Server to manage ESX hosts in a mixed network environment with IPv4 and IPv6. Network storage with IPv6 is still experimental (functional but unsupported).

✔ **vNetwork Distributed Switch (vDS):** VMware introduces a new concept in virtual network management with the addition of the vNetwork Distributed Switch (vDS). A vDS is centrally managed from vCenter Server, but spans several ESX hosts. It also introduces Private Virtual Local Area Network (VLAN) support and Network vMotion.

• **Private VLAN support:** Private VLANs allow greater segmentation of traditional network VLANs. Private VLANs are ideal for setting up restricted communication among certain VMs sharing the same network segment. This feature requires a physical network switch with Private VLAN support.

• **Network vMotion:** The vDS enables monitoring of a VM's network connection(s) while the VM is being moved (using vMotion) around the virtual infrastructure.

• **Third-party distributed virtual switches:** vDS includes support for third-party distributed virtual switches from vendors such as Cisco.

Storage starters

vSphere 4.0 brings several new capabilities in the area of storage:

- **Thin-disk provisioning:** vSphere 4.0 brings game-changing technology to the virtual storage space with native thin disk provisioning. This feature allows VMs to consume disk space only on an as-needed basis, allowing for over-allocation of storage. vCenter alerting, alarms, and reports let you closely track usage and allocation, providing a safe way to optimize available storage space.

- **Fibre Channel over Ethernet (FCoE):** New support for FCoE on Converged Network Adapters (network adapters that support both LAN and SAN traffic) provides another option for ESX to connect with SAN storage.

- **Managing SAN-based VMFS snapshots:** Create an identical snapshot of a VMware-formatted Logical Unit Number (LUN) on your SAN; then connect it to an ESX host or cluster. ESX automatically gives the LUN snapshot a new identity and allows its use in addition to the original LUN.

- **VMDirectPath for virtual machines:** This feature reduces CPU load on the ESX host caused by VMs with excessive amounts of network and disk traffic. VMDirectPath allows a VM to directly access certain physical hardware devices, such as 10-gigabit network adapters. Some Fibre Channel and Serial Attached SCSI (SAS) storage adapters are also available as experimental (working but unsupported) capability.

- **Native support for SATA disks:** ESX now supports internal SATA disks for use as VMFS datastores.

- **Paravirtualized SCSI (PVSCSI) adapters:** A new virtual SCSI adapter option that provides better throughput with less CPU usage — intended for use in VMs that are very disk-intensive. The PVSCSI adapter is used in addition to the primary SCSI adapter and is connected to the I/O-intensive disk, while the primary SCSI adapter stays connected to the virtual disk containing the operating system and applications.

Security sentiments

VMware introduced a few security-specific features for vSphere 4.0:

- **vShield Zones:** This add-on provides firewalling and network traffic inspection capabilities at the virtual network switch level. vShield Zones are managed by vShield Manager, which is provided as a virtual appliance and configured using a Web-based user interface.

✔ **VMware VMsafe:** A new technology rather than a feature, VMsafe is designed to give security vendors the ability to develop VMware-aware security products.

✔ **Granular permissions for networks and datastores:** Administrators can set specific user/group access permissions at the network and datastore level.

Virtual management medley

VMware vSphere 4.0 introduces some ways to simplify administration of your virtual infrastructure. You can use vApps and Host Profiles to introduce standard configurations. Power management and Storage Awareness put you in touch with your infrastructure, while the Host Update Utility assists in upgrading to vSphere 4.0 from previous versions of VMware ESX. VMware vCenter Orchestrator brings the power of automation for repetitive, time-consuming tasks.

✔ **vApps:** A way to deploy, manage, and monitor a group of related VMs, including their configurations and interdependencies, as a single entity. Powering on or off a vApp is just a single step, as vSphere hides the complex contingencies like requiring the vApp's VMs to start up and shut down in a specific order. Additionally, vCenter Server can import and export vApps in the Open Virtualization Format (OVF) 1.0 standard.

✔ **Host profiles:** Designed to drive configuration consistency across ESX hosts. A host profile captures the configuration of your ideal ESX host setup, including networking, storage, and security settings and then lets you apply that configuration to other ESX hosts. Host profiles then allow you to monitor for compliance on the ESX hosts, comparing the applied host profile with the actual host configuration and reporting on the differences.

✔ **Power management:** ESX 4.0 supports processor-based power management technologies from Intel and AMD, allowing ESX to save power by turning down the processing power when not running at maximum capacity.

✔ **vSphere Host Update Utility:** Meant to ease the pain of migrating from ESX 3.x to vSphere 4.0, this GUI-based tool allows remote upgrade of ESX 3.x hosts to ESX 4.0. It even includes a rollback feature.

✔ **vSphere Storage Awareness:** Storage Awareness provides visibility into storage utilization per VM and per datastore. It also generates friendly storage-to-host-to-virtual machine topology maps for exploring their relationships.

✔ **vCenter Orchestrator:** Formerly a separate product, vCenter Orchestrator is a workflow engine that allows you to build workflows using existing code snippets and then execute the workflow from a Web UI.

Discovering the Differences in vSphere 4.1

VMware describes vSphere 4.1 as "what vSphere 4.0 should have been." This version is all about performance and scalability, and the drastic increases in the capacity limits between versions speak for themselves.

vCenter Server

The major focus points in this release of vCenter Server are performance and scalability. Here are some of the key points in this release of vCenter Server:

✔ **64-bit transition:** Starting with vSphere 4.1, vCenter Server is offered only in a 64-bit version and requires a 64-bit operating system to run on. Moving to 64-bit eliminates the memory limits associated with 32-bit operating systems and inherently improves performance.

✔ **Improved Host Profiles:** Adding to the capabilities introduced in vSphere 4.0, Host Profiles now include

• **Administrator password configuration:** Administrators can centrally change the administrator password on their ESX hosts.

• **Privilege settings:** All permissions configurable from the vSphere Client can be configured through Host Profiles.

• **Physical NICs specified by ID:** Physical network adapters can be specified by their device ID in the server and assigned for specific network connections. This feature ensures that the NIC meant for IP-based storage is configured to carry storage traffic or that the NIC on the vMotion network is configured to carry vMotion traffic.

• **Active Directory configuration:** Now that ESX 4.1 hosts can authenticate logins directly using Active Directory, Host Profiles can provide the domain name and user credentials required to connect an ESX host to a domain. This feature can also be used to manage complete Active Directory configuration on an ESX host.

✔ **Higher limits for vCenter Server Managed infrastructure:** Improvements across the board allow vCenter Server to manage more systems with response times and performance as shown in Table 4-1.

Table 4-1	vSphere Configuration Limits		
Limits	*vSphere 4*	*vSphere 4.1*	*Improvement*
Hosts per vCenter Server	300	1000	3x
Registered VMs per vCenter Server	4500	15000	>3x
Powered-on VMs per vCenter Server	3000	10000	3x
Concurrent vSphere clients	30	120	4x
Hosts per datacenter	100	500	5x
VMs per datacenter	2500	5000	2x
Linked Mode	10000	30000	3x
vCenter Server concurrent operations	100	500	5x
Port Groups per vCenter Server	512	1016	≈2x
Distributed Switches per vCenter Server	16	32	2x

ESX 4.1

ESX 4.1 introduced some new technology to vSphere and incorporated numerous performance improvements overall.

- ✔ **Active Directory integration:** ESX 4.1 hosts are now capable of authenticating user logins via Active Directory. Prior versions of ESX used a traditional Linux-based authentication model with local accounts and no centralized account configuration.

- ✔ **Virtual Serial Port concentrator:** Many administrators rely on serial port console connections to manage physical servers, which is connected back into a central remote access point, or *concentrator*. vSphere 4.1 adds the Virtual Serial Port as yet another virtual peripheral for VMs. This option can be configured to redirect the VM's serial port over a network link using telnet or Secure Shell (SSH) for remote access by the VM's administrator.

- ✔ **Memory compression:** This feature brings vSphere's existing memory over-commit technology to a new level. Traditionally, an operating system will move lower-priority memory data from high-speed RAM to a file on disk (called *memory swapping*) to free up space in the RAM for higher priority data. Accessing data on a disk is significantly slower than accessing data in RAM, affecting performance during peak memory usage. Memory compression sits between RAM and the memory-to-disk mechanism and attempts to compress the data and then store it in the VM's compression cache. Most of the VM performance is recovered because accessing compressed memory is faster than accessing memory swapped to disk.

✔ **Storage I/O Control (SIOC):** New in vSphere 4.1, SIOC ensures that your most important VMs get priority access to storage I/O, especially during times of congestion. Similar to the "shares" model used to give VMs preference to CPU and memory resources, SIOC enables administrators to assign shares of storage I/O to VMs. When SIOC detects latency (slow response times) while communicating with a datastore, SIOC considers the datastore congested. SIOC responds by throttling the storage I/O of other VMs on the same datastore, while respecting all of the VM's storage I/O shares. The net effect is freeing up storage I/O resources for prioritized VMs.

✔ **Network I/O Control (NetIOC):** A new network traffic management feature of the vNetwork Distributed Switch (vDS), NetIOC adds the capability to isolate and prioritize certain types of network traffic. This feature is useful when different network traffic types (such as VM, management, iSCSI storage, NFS storage, Fault Tolerance logging, and vMotion traffic) contend for bandwidth on an ESX host's physical network uplinks. Traffic priorities are set at the vDS, with bandwidth being allocated by percentage shares, bandwidth limits, or both.

✔ **Load-Based Network Teaming (LBT):** Another new feature of the vNetwork Distributed Switch (vDS), LBT dynamically adjusts the mappings of virtual ports to teamed physical network adapters, optimally distributing the inbound and outbound network traffic of each ESX host across the team. When LBT detects utilization of 75 percent or more for at least 30 seconds on a physical network adapter in the team, LBT will attempt to move one or more virtual ports to a less utilized network adapter within the team, rebalancing the traffic load.

✔ **Higher limits for ESX hosts and clusters:** While VM density per host and host density per cluster stayed the same, there were some other massive increases in capacity for ESX clusters and vNetwork Distributed Switches, as shown in Table 4-2.

Table 4-2	Improvements in vSphere 4.1		
Limits	*vSphere 4*	*vSphere 4.1*	*Improvement*
VMs per host	320	320	None
Hosts per cluster	32	32	None
Virtual machines per cluster	1280	3000	3x
Hosts per Distributed Switch	64	350	>5x

VMware continues to raise the bar for performance, availability, and ease of management. Drastic improvements such as scalability and disk-related performance shine through in vSphere 4.1. Availability meets performance with new features such as Storage and Network I/O Controls. Improvements in management capabilities appear in the form of management capacity increases. These improvements, combined with the already robust vSphere platform, enable VMware to retain its position as the gold standard for production virtualization.

Part II
Getting Ready for vSphere

The 5th Wave   By Rich Tennant

"I assume everyone on your team is on board with the proposed changes to the system architecture."

In this part . . .

This part helps you plan and prepare for your vSphere rollout. Chapter 5 discusses important considerations and how to plan for a successful vSphere rollout. Chapter 6 shows you how to prepare with the right network and storage resources.

Chapter 5

Planning for a vSphere Rollout

Rolling out a vSphere infrastructure without a plan is like building a house without any blueprints — you end up with something resembling what you wanted, but it's generally unstable and costs a lot of money to redo properly. In the event more space (capacity) is needed, you can't tell whether adding on will improve the situation or just make it worse.

This chapter gives you the key factors to consider in planning your vSphere rollout. You find out how to size an initial vSphere deployment to meet the needs of your organization while keeping the design scalable. This chapter also walks you through VMware's vSphere licensing model so that you can choose what licensing you'll really need.

Right-Sizing the Environment

Figuring out how much virtual infrastructure your organization requires seems like obvious math, but infrastructure planning is more than just adding up all the CPUs, memory, and disk space for each machine. Virtualization, and vSphere in particular, brings capabilities that don't exist in the physical server world. Much of this functionality helps to put more virtual machines (VMs) on less physical hardware and optimizes shared resource usage while maintaining performance. The features you'll come to know and love are the same ones that can bite you if not given the necessary care and feeding they require.

Enough is not always enough

Running out of capacity is probably the last thing you'd expect to happen in your vSphere environment, but it can happen under even the most normal of circumstances. While running out of capacity may seem like more of an inconvenience than a catastrophe, depleting one particular resource can cause one or more VMs to fail.

The resources provided to a VM are

- ✔ **CPU:** An ESX host can't run out of CPU resources for VMs, but it can spread the CPU cycles so thinly across its VMs that they slow to a crawl.

- ✔ **Memory:** An ESX host's memory can be consumed in its entirety, at which point the host turns to swapping chunks of memory to disk, bringing its VMs to a standstill.

- ✔ **Network:** A completely saturated network connection can impact other VMs on the same network, but won't cause them to actually fail. Network saturation can impact the availability of applications on the VM.

- ✔ **Disk:** A full datastore means that any running VM residing on it could fail. A VM will fail when it needs to write critical data to a completely filled datastore (such as swap data or growth of a thin-provisioned virtual disk).

Using certain vSphere features will impact the amount of disk space a VM requires to operate:

- ✔ **Snapshots:** A VM snapshot can vary in size based on the power state of the VM, the quantity of snapshots being created, the duration for which each snapshot is kept, and the activity level of the VM.

  - • **Power state:** Creating a snapshot of a running VM can add to the snapshot's disk-space needs by up to the total amount of random-access memory (RAM) assigned to the VM. A snapshot of a VM in the powered-off state does not use any RAM.

  - • **Quantity:** Creating a snapshot of a VM means no longer writing any new data or changes to the current virtual disk, so all changes from that point forward are written into a new file. The sum of the original disk and its subsequent snapshots make up the live virtual disk seen by the VM. Since modified data is written to the snapshot file instead of the original virtual disk, multiple copies of that data (the original and modified) exist. Each snapshot can consume up to the size of the original disk (if every bit of data was modified), but rarely does. To calculate the maximum space required, multiply the size of the original disk by the number of snapshots that might be created.

- **Duration:** The longer a snapshot is active, the more space it takes up. Only intermediate snapshots (those between the original disk and the current snapshot) stay the same size. The maximum size each snapshot can grow to is equal to the size of the original virtual disk.

- **Activity level:** Because a snapshot is really just a collection of changes made to a virtual disk, the activity level of a machine directly impacts how quickly a snapshot grows. Snapshots of VMs with high volatility in data (database server) or lots of transactions (e-mail server) tend to grow much faster than snapshots of less active VMs (domain controller).

✔ **Thin provisioning:** A thin-provisioned VM is just like any other VM, except that its virtual disk takes up datastore space only at the time it's needed, up to the allocated size of the virtual disk. Conversely, a thick-provisioned VM's virtual disk grabs all its datastore space up front, guaranteeing the disk space will be available to the VM. Allocating more disk space than is physically available is known as *storage oversubscription.* There is always the risk that several thin-provisioned VMs suddenly need to consume all of their allocated disk space, causing space contention. It's the job of the administrator to keep track of oversubscription and manage the environment accordingly to prevent contention, or to limit use of thin provisioning to nonproduction machines or to VMs with very little growth over time. (See the section "Selling the same disk space twice (or more)," later in this chapter, for more details.)

Measure twice, deploy once

Giving a VM the right amount of resources means knowing what will be running on the VM. Knowing the application that will be running on the VM means understanding how the application and the operating system (OS) underneath it will use the resources provided. Moving from a physical server to a VM (commonly referred to as *physical-to-virtual,* or P2V) at least gives you the opportunity to observe the application in its natural habitat. Fortunately, physical-to-virtual migration is a mature process. VMware Converter and several third-party products are available to help. Sizing a new VM is partly science, but it's mostly knowing what makes VMs different than their physical siblings.

Here are some points to consider when sizing a VM:

✔ **Operating system:** Does the OS version being used have any configuration limits, such as maximum number of Central Processing Units (CPUs) or amount of memory? Can the OS make use of multiple CPUs or additional memory? Certain OS versions are limited to using a single CPU or 4GB of RAM, and additional resources will yield no benefit.

✔ **Application performance:** Is the application designed to take advantage of a multi-CPU machine? If so, how many CPUs can it use? Many administrators have a common misconception that more is better, but a single Virtual CPU (vCPU) in a VM can actually outperform a VM with multiple vCPUs because of the capabilities of the VMware processor scheduling algorithm. In the case of virtual CPUs, the ability to configure a VM with more than one vCPU exists to support applications and operating systems designed to run optimally (and sometimes exclusively) in a multi-CPU environment.

✔ **Disk space (operating system):** How much disk space does the OS consume? Is additional space needed for OS patches and updates? OS vendors *really* want you to use their automatic update feature, which consists of downloading an update from the vendor's Web site and applying it automatically. This is convenient for administrators, especially those not running their own update servers, but consumes space at an unpredictable rate.

✔ **Disk space (application):** How much space does the application consume once installed? Will the application's log files grow indefinitely, or is there a limit to their size? Log files are notorious for eating up all available disk space on a system volume and eventually crashing the machine. Pay special attention to log rotation settings and the logging "level" that dictates how much detail is output to the log files. Unmanageable logging should go onto a separate volume to prevent crashing the machine, or some other process should be put in place to move or delete the logs as they become obsolete.

✔ **Disk space (database):** Does the application use a local database? How big will the database grow? Does this size include transaction logs? Is the backup of the database stored locally, and how much space does it consume? Whenever possible, local databases should be stored on a second volume to protect against consuming all the disk space on the boot (system) volume. Adding a second virtual disk to the VM is recommended, as most operating systems allow growing a nonboot (data) volume while keeping the volume online.

✔ **Network interfaces:** Does the machine need to be on more than one network simultaneously? Is it within security policy to connect a machine to the proposed combination of specific networks? Occasionally, a user will request a VM to be attached to two networks that, in the physical world, would be strictly prohibited. Because VMs bypass the step of placing a request for a physical switch connection, the administrator can be exposed to the risk of breaking network security policy.

✔ **Redundancy:** Does the application's server requirements call for multiple disks and/or a particular redundant configuration of those disks (referred to as a Redundant Array of Inexpensive Disks, or RAID)? Are the requirements intended for a physical machine? Not all software vendors have come to accept virtualization as a production environment and still give their minimum system requirements in terms of physical servers. A vendor may request multiple hard drives in a RAID-5 configuration or two network cards for redundancy. vSphere abstracts the hardware component of the configuration, so you may need only a single virtual disk and one virtual network interface to satisfy the requirement.

✔ **Backups:** Has installation of a backup agent been requested? vSphere provides the capability to back up VMs and then restore them in their entirety or file-by-file. Your network administrator may not be aware of this capability as an alternative to the pay-per-system model commonly associated with traditional physical machine backup solutions.

Department of redundancy department

Having a Plan B is the foundation of risk mitigation. This simple concept drives the way we protect the things most important to us. The same applies to the important applications on which organizations rely — and as such, the computer infrastructure hosting those important applications. VMware has done a great job of embracing that concept by continually enhancing its ability to keep servers running.

The best way to put Plan B into your design is to always look at the "what if." Take networking, for example. Say that you have a vSphere host with a 4-port network card. You could connect all four ports to a network switch so that, in the event one of the ports fails, you're still up and running. Now ask yourself, "What if the network switch fails?". The answer is obvious — you're out of luck and without a network connection. Instead, you're better off connecting two network ports to one switch and the other two to a second switch. Problem solved, right? Wrong. All four ports are on a single network card, and if the network card fails, so does your connection. If you're in a position to get two 2-port network cards, great; but if not, you still need a plan B.

At this point, Plan B looks like it won't be solved at the hardware level. This point is where vSphere's high availability capabilities kick in to offset the risk at the underlying physical hardware level. Depending upon the criticality of the VM, you can even go so far as to implement vSphere Fault Tolerance (FT), where two copies of the same VM run in lockstep on different hosts.

When thinking about Plan B, always remember that the purpose of vSphere's high availability feature set is to pick up where the hardware leaves off and ultimately provide you with the Plan B you require.

Selling the same disk space twice (or more)

Realizing that most VMs use only a portion of the disk space allocated, VMware wanted to give customers the ability to make better use of their storage. With the release of vSphere, VMware introduced a new feature called *thin provisioning*. Prior to thin provisioning, VMware ESX created a virtual disk file on a datastore that consumed the full amount of space allocated to the VM, including empty space. Thin provisioning allows a VM to have a virtual disk of a predetermined size, but instead vSphere stores only the actual data residing in the virtual disk, ignoring the empty space. As the virtual disk fills, the virtual disk file on the vSphere datastore expands, up to the predetermined size.

Using thin provisioning is incredibly efficient, but a risk is associated with its use. In the case where a datastore is *oversubscribed* (more space allocated than exists), you have the risk of thin-provisioned VMs growing more rapidly than anticipated and not having a place for them to store their data. This risk can be mostly mitigated by monitoring VM growth and maintaining a reasonable oversubscription ratio.

VMware vSphere fault tolerance requires the use of a thick-provisioned virtual disk. If the virtual disk is thin provisioned, it will be automatically converted when fault tolerance is enabled.

Keeping Scalability in Mind

Being conservative can be just as bad as being aggressive when rolling out a vSphere implementation. It's human nature to try to keep some extra resources aside, "just in case." Following this instinct will almost definitely backfire when (not if, but when) vSphere adoption catches on within your organization, and usage suddenly accelerates, growing beyond even your loftiest expectations. The best way to prepare is to determine exactly what to do with your "just in case" resources when the time comes to put them into use.

Storage considerations

Going back to the introduction of VMware ESX, experts have debated over the best way to divvy up the raw storage being presented to the ESX hosts. Even with the introduction of thin provisioning in vSphere, the answer is always the same: It depends.

vSphere supports several different types of storage:

- ✔ Fibre channel
- ✔ iSCSI
- ✔ Network Attached (NFS)

Of those types of storage, several vendors offer varying degrees of functionality. Combining vSphere-native capabilities (such as thin provisioning) with array-based capabilities can amplify your storage efficiency. Storage array-based de-duplication is one of those capabilities.

Storage array-based de-duplication identifies identical blocks of data on a disk and replaces the duplicated data with pointers to a single instance of the data. Storage array-based de-duplication technology can yield huge savings, especially when you have dozens of VMs running the same operating system. De-duplication reduces space consumed by the OS by pairing it down to a single set of common data. The result is virtual disk data made up of block-level pointers to the common copy of the OS data blocks and combined with the unique data for each VM. Combining vSphere thin provisioning with storage array-based de-duplication slims down a VM's footprint even more.

Adding hosts versus adding clusters

Building out vSphere infrastructure in clusters is the best way to roll out a highly available, fault-tolerant virtual infrastructure. However, not everyone needs a high level of fault tolerance, but instead may want to take advantage of the other benefits associated with using vSphere. This need is fulfilled by adding ESX hosts individually to vCenter Server, where they can still share storage and clone VMs from each other's templates, but without all the overhead of clustering.

Thinking about the differences between vSphere editions, ask yourself how important these features are to your environment:

- ✔ **High Availability (HA):** vSphere HA relocates and restarts a VM on a different host in the event the VM's original host fails. If an ESX host fails, you have to bring the VMs back up manually after the host is repaired. If the VMs happen to reside on storage shared between the failed ESX host and another ESX host, you can register the machines on the other ESX host to bring them back online, but, in that case, you need to manually unregister each VM from the new host, then bring back up the failed host, and reregister each VM there. Are your VMs so important that they can't wait for their ESX host to be fixed? Are you willing to go through the process of relocating your VMs if they can't be down while their ESX host is being fixed? (Remember, your time costs money, too!)

✔ **Uptime during maintenance:** vSphere offers two unique features — vMotion to move running VMs across hosts, and vStorage vMotion to move the virtual disks of running VMs across datastores. Can you afford to have your VMs powered off during maintenance? If you need to move a VM across datastores, can you afford to have that VM down during the move (which can sometimes take hours)?

Comparing vSphere Small Business Editions

VMware created two editions of vSphere for small businesses. These editions are called Essentials for Retail and Essentials Plus for Retail. Offering these editions allows VMware to let small businesses get started in enterprise-grade virtualization.

Essentials for Retail

vSphere Essentials for Retail is designed as an entry point to vSphere virtualization for small businesses. Using this edition provides

✔ **Supported host specifications:** Provides up to six cores per processor and 256GB of memory.

✔ **Thin provisioning:** Allows administrators to optimize utilization of existing storage resources using over-allocation of datastore space.

✔ **Update Manager:** Using this feature saves time and effort by allowing vSphere to retrieve and deploy patches and updates to vSphere hosts and other virtual systems. Update Manager is managed using the vSphere Client.

✔ **vCenter server management:** A vCenter Server Agent license is included to allow this version to be managed by all editions of vCenter Server.

Essentials Plus for Retail

vSphere Essentials Plus for Retail is designed as an entry point to vSphere virtualization for small businesses, but this version also includes high availability and backup features. Using this edition provides every feature included in the Essentials for Retail version, plus the following:

✔ **High Availability (HA):** Enabling this feature provides basic fault toler-ance when two or more vSphere hosts are deployed together in a cluster configuration. In the event a vSphere host fails, HA will move one or more of the VMs that were running before the failure over to a func-tioning vSphere host. HA then starts the VMs on the functioning host according to a policy previously defined by the administrator.

✔ **Data recovery:** Deploying this feature is a simple way to back up VMs and recover them quickly if the need arises. This feature copies your VMs to secondary storage as defined by your backup policy. In the event of a failure, the administrator may recover either the entire VM or individual files from the backed-up copy. Data recovery even uses de-duplication technology to optimally utilize backup storage and the backup window.

Looking at Mid-Size and Enterprise Business vSphere Versions

VMware offers four editions of vSphere designed to support mid-size and enterprise businesses. These editions are called Standard, Advanced, Enterprise, and Enterprise Plus. Offering these versions allows VMware to let businesses of all sizes get started in enterprise-grade virtualization.

Standard Edition

vSphere Standard is designed as an entry point to vSphere virtualization for mid-size and enterprise businesses. Using this edition provides

✔ **Supported host specifications:** Provides up to six cores per processor and 256GB of memory.

✔ **Thin provisioning:** Allows administrators to optimize utilization of exist-ing storage resources using over-allocation of datastore space.

✔ **Update Manager:** Using this feature saves time and effort by allow-ing vSphere to retrieve and deploy patches and updates to vSphere hosts and other virtual systems. Update Manager is managed using the vSphere Client.

✔ **vCenter Server management:** A vCenter Server Agent license is included to allow this version to be managed by only the Foundation and Standard editions of vCenter Server.

✔ **High Availability (HA):** Enabling this feature provides basic fault tolerance when two or more vSphere hosts are deployed together in a cluster configuration. In the event a vSphere host fails, HA moves one or more of the VMs that were running before the failure over to a functioning vSphere host. HA then starts the VMs on the functioning host according to a policy previously defined by the administrator.

✔ **vMotion:** VMware vMotion is a VMware-proprietary feature that allows the migration of running virtual machines from one host to another without interruption.

Advanced Edition

vSphere Advanced is designed to support production implementations in mid-size and enterprise businesses, but lacks some features desirable for large-scale production vSphere deployments. Using this edition provides every feature included in the Standard Edition, plus the following:

✔ **Supported host specifications:** Provides up to 12 cores per processor and 256GB of memory (twice as many cores as the Standard Edition).

✔ **Data recovery:** Deploying this feature is a simple way to backup VMs and recover them quickly if the need arises. This feature copies your VMs to secondary storage as defined by your backup policy. In the event of a failure, the administrator may recover either the entire VM or individual files from the backed up copy. Data recovery even uses de-duplication technology to optimally utilize backup storage and the backup window.

✔ **Hot-add of VM components:** Adding resources to a VM used to mean shutting down the machine, adding the resources, and starting the VM. Using this feature allows an administrator to add resources, such as CPU and memory, to a running VM.

✔ **Fault tolerance:** Applying fault tolerance to a VM should be done sparingly. Fault Tolerance (FT) places a VM in lockstep with an identical copy of the VM. The VMs remain synchronized, and in the event of a failure, the alternate VM continues exactly where the protected VM stopped. Fault tolerance should be reserved for mission-critical workloads in the virtualized environment.

✔ **vShield Zones:** This feature allows for VM isolation and secures the virtual network from security threats.

✔ **Virtual Serial Port Concentrator:** This feature enables aggregation of Virtual Serial Ports to a central location. Users can then connect to the Concentrator, providing the equivalent of connecting to the serial console port of a physical server.

Data recovery is available as a separately licensed option in the Standard Edition.

Enterprise Edition

vSphere Enterprise is designed to support production implementations in mid-size and enterprise businesses, but lacks some features desirable for large-scale production vSphere deployments. Using this edition provides every feature included in the Advanced Edition, plus the following:

- ✔ **Supported host specifications:** Provides up to six cores per processor and 256GB of memory (six less cores per processor than Advanced Edition).

- ✔ **Storage vMotion:** Similar to standard vMotion, this feature allows migration of a VM's storage from one datastore to another without interruption to the running VM.

- ✔ **Distributed Resource Scheduler (DRS):** This feature allows the movement of running VMs among their interconnected hosts with a goal to optimize the loads of running ESX hosts.

- ✔ **Distributed Power Management (DPM):** Enabling DPM reduces electrical consumption by migrating machines to other hosts and then powering down the unused vSphere host.

Enterprise Plus Edition

vSphere Enterprise Plus is the top-of-the-line product to support higher-end production implementations in enterprise businesses. Using this edition provides every feature included in the Enterprise Edition, plus the following:

- ✔ **Supported host specifications:** This feature provides up to 12 cores per processor and an unlimited amount of memory.

- ✔ **vNetwork Distributed Virtual Switches (dvSwitch):** Configuring a Distributed Virtual Network Switch allows the VM connected to the switch to communicate across vSphere hosts privately. Administrators manage the dvSwitch centrally through vCenter Server.

- ✔ **Network I/O Control (NetIOC):** This feature allows granular management and allocation of network bandwidth resources to VMs.

- ✔ **Storage I/O Control (SIOC):** SIOC enables prioritization of storage I/O resource allocation to VMs.

- ✔ **Host Profiles:** This feature allows for rapid deployment of vSphere hosts by applying a predefined configuration to a new vSphere host. Using Host Profiles drives consistency in host configurations and simplifies the addition of new hosts to the vSphere environment.

Exploring Support and Subscription (SnS) Requirements

VMware requires purchase of Support and Subscription (SnS) on all commercial (nonfree) vSphere editions and all vCenter Server editions. VMware SnS is comprised of two parts: Support and Subscription. Subscription simply provides access to incremental updates, patches, and revisions. Support is available in two levels:

- **Basic support:** This level of support is provided during normal business hours and is best suited for nonproduction environments.

- **Production support:** This level of support is provided on a 24-hours-per-day, 7-days-per week, 365-days-per-year basis (24x7x365), with priority support for customers experiencing downtime in their production environments.

Chapter 6

Preparing Network and Storage for vSphere

*V*Mware vSphere networking and storage are critical components of the virtual infrastructure. However, when you go to set up the infrastructure, you'll need a unique shopping list. Servers are often set up specifically for virtualization, with greater memory and Input/Output capacity.

vSphere, the Network Switch

Connecting an ESX host to your network is different than connecting a typical Microsoft Windows or Linux server. The connections between a network switch and the network interface cards (NICs) of a physical server running Windows or Linux is really just adding one more server to the network. Take the same physical server with the same network connections, but running VMware ESX, and the story changes drastically. Physical network interfaces on a vSphere host are associated with a virtual network switch running as part of the host. This effectively creates a switch-to-switch topology, introducing functionality such as Virtual Local Area Networks (VLANs) and NIC teaming, while keeping the day-to-day virtual network configuration with the vSphere administrator.

Connecting ESX hosts to your network is easier when you're familiar with the concepts that make up virtual networking. These concepts are covered in the next section.

Understanding virtual and physical network switches

Virtual network switches are quite similar to physical network switches. Both are used to connect machines together so that they can communicate with each other. They can also be connected to other switches to create a larger network.

To better describe physical and virtual network switches, here is a list of related terms and their definitions:

- **Physical network:** A bunch of physical machines connected together by a network so that they can communicate with each other. VMware ESX hosts are physical machines.

- **Virtual network:** A bunch of virtual machines connected together logically so that they can communicate with each other. Virtual machines run on physical machines.

- **Network Interface Card:** A built-in or subsequently added network port on a physical machine. The NIC is connected to a physical network switch to enable communication with other physical machines and network devices.

- **MAC address:** A unique address assigned to a network interface by its manufacturer, similar to a serial number or fingerprint; generally it can't be altered. ESX automatically generates randomized Media Access Control (MAC) addresses for virtual machines' NICs. These addresses are unique because they key off an identifier in the vCenter server.

- **Physical network switch:** A physical piece of hardware with several Ethernet ports that passes information between the physical machines connected to the network switch's ports. The network switch learns which physical machine (as identified by its MAC address) is connected to each switch port, allowing it to pass data packets from one connected machine to another without having to ask for directions each time. Physical network switches can be connected together to form bigger networks.

- **Virtual network switch (vSwitch):** A vSwitch is a lot like a physical network switch, with some exceptions. A vSwitch passes information between its connected virtual machines, just like the physical switch does for physical machines. A vSwitch can be connected to a physical network switch by associating the ESX host's physical network interfaces with a vSwitch and then connecting those network interfaces to a physical network switch. When no physical network interfaces are associated with a vSwitch, the vSwitch passes data only between the virtual machines on the ESX host connected to the vSwitch.

- **Port group:** A port group makes the connection between a virtual machine and a vSwitch and also defines options like Virtual Local Area Network (VLAN) policies.

✔ **NIC teaming:** When two or more physical NICs are associated with a vSwitch, they're considered a team. NIC teaming lets members of the team share the network traffic load, effectively increasing the data throughput. NIC teaming can also be used as a passive failover, giving the network traffic an alternate path in the event the primary network connection fails.

✔ **VLANs:** Using the Institute of Electrical and Electronics Engineers Standards Association (IEEE) 802.1Q standard, VLANs allow a single physical network to be logically divided so that groups of ports attached to a VLAN are isolated as though they were on their own physical network.

Here are some advanced VMware-specific network terms:

✔ **vNetwork Distributed Switch:** Acts as a single vSwitch across a set of ESX hosts in a vCenter Server Datacenter, allowing all the hosts in the cluster to share common switches. This lets VM administrators manage the switch from one place and also provides several capabilities that standard vSwitches do not have.

✔ **dvPort:** A port on a vNetwork Distributed Switch that connects to an ESX host's Service Console, VMkernel port, or a virtual machine's network adapter.

✔ **VMkernel Port:** A networking stack that allows ESX to connect to iSCSI and NFS storage and also provides Fault Tolerance (FT) and vMotion communication with other ESX hosts.

✔ **Service Console Port:** Created by default during ESX installation and is used for management communication with network and remote services such as vSphere Client. Certain services, such as iSCSI storage, may require adding another service console port.

✔ **vMotion:** A VMware vSphere-specific technology allowing virtual machines to be relocated to a different ESX host, different shared storage, or both. Enabling vMotion capability requires appropriate vSphere licensing.

Comparing the capabilities of a physical network switch and a virtual network switch reveals that they have many capabilities in common, but still have a lot of gaps left to be filled. The introduction of the Cisco Nexus 1000V Virtual Switch for vSphere closed most of those gaps by virtualizing the familiar Cisco switch interface and feature set, bringing easier management for network administrators with existing Cisco experience.

Asking for the right connections

Different models of physical servers offer a variety of networking configurations:

✔ **Rack-mounted** and **most standalone servers** normally have the option to request more network interfaces be added when the machine is ordered.

✔ **Blade servers** typically don't offer additional network interfaces due to their compact form factor and technical limitations. Every blade server chassis has a backplane blade that servers plug into, supplying each blade server with power and network connectivity. In the case of blade servers with two or three network interfaces each, the ESX host must be configured to address these limitations, including use of VLANs and teamed NICs, to make the most of the situation.

Teaming Network Interface Cards

A Network Interface Card can be a single point of failure for a server. In vSphere, a single point of failure is a bigger concern because a single NIC may service dozens of virtual machines. To address this issue, you should configure NICs to be redundant teams. Redundant teams for NICs can provide additional bandwidth as well as fault tolerance.

In most cases, you want to create NIC teams to your vSphere host. Though we cover NIC teams in Chapter 11, as you design the environment, you need to be aware of the hardware design. For example, many servers today have two 1GB Ethernet connections. So, you can easily team them, right?

You can team them, but you might not be getting all the protection you expect. A team using only the onboard NICs can protect against cable failure, but may not protect against other hardware issues. Many mainboard integrated NICs share a common controller, so if that fails, the team is useless.

When building an ESX host, it's wise to take into consideration the hardware requirements and hardware design of the host. Many servers have multiple Peripheral Component Interconnect (PCI) busses, and placing cards in the appropriate slots will let you maximize the performance and fault tolerance of the server.

VLANs and Other Switching Concepts

Network switching is rather complicated, but understanding a couple of key concepts can go far when you have to work with the networking folks. Speaking their language can be helpful when setting up the vSphere environment.

✔ **VLAN tagged ports versus access ports:** On a physical network switch, you typically configure a switch port to be an access port. With a vSphere host, you'll typically configure a switch port to service multiple VLANS. These VLAN tagged ports, also called *trunks,* allow multiple VLANs to flow over the single network connection. Most vSphere hosts require access to multiple VLANs, and without tags, you'd need a separate NIC for each VLAN. vSphere hosts usually have many NICs, but not that many!

✔ **Mapping out VLANs to virtual networks:** Within vSphere, you can have multiple VLANs run on a single vSwitch, thanks to port groups, which are collections of network ports with common properties, such as VLAN numbers. These VLAN numbers should map exactly to VLAN numbers on the physical network.

✔ **Duplex decisions:** Network connections operate at a specific speed and are connected at half-duplex or full-duplex. A half-duplex connection at 1 gigabit per second (Gbps) shares that 1 Gbps connection for sending and receiving traffic, but a full-duplex connection operates at 1 Gbps for sending traffic and 1 Gbps for receiving traffic.

It's important to set up a vSphere host's connections at full-duplex if your physical network supports it. In any situation, it's even more important to ensure that all the connections that make up a team are set up consistently.

We're always shocked that in 2011, network auto negotiation is still extremely unreliable. In many cases, you may need to explicitly set the network speed and duplex, which you often have to do on both the server and the physical network switch.

✔ **Naming virtual networks:** Port groups and vSwitches need consistent names across all the hosts in your environment. If you have a port group on one host that is VLAN 88 named vlan-88, you need to ensure that all the other hosts with VLAN 88 follow suit. In a cluster, you must have consistent names, but even if you don't connect them all in a cluster, consistent names help when you're administering or troubleshooting.

vSphere, the Keeper of Storage

Storage is the foundation of most servers, and vSphere environments are no exception. vSphere storage is a bit different, however. It's common to use storage not located in the server so that multiple servers can access it.

Storage can be local or remote. Local storage is the disk contained within the server and is useful for the installation of an ESX server, but it's often not used for VMs. In some cases, local storage may be used when a host is for testing or for really small installations. Remote storage is storage from a Storage Area Network (SAN) or a Network File System (NFS) location. Remote storage is provided by a different array or server that presents the disk to the vSphere host.

Getting the skinny on thin provisioning

Thin provisioning in vSphere is simply allocation on demand. A disk is created for a VM, and is initially very small. As data is written to the VM disk, the disk expands up to the size you have set, which is done by vSphere behind the scenes and independent of the operating system or application. Some applications and operating systems write a lot of zeros to format file systems or data files, and in this case, a disk file can grow faster than you expect.

Thin-provisioned disks don't automatically shrink. You can shrink them by running commands within the operating system and vSphere.

Painting yourself into a corner through overallocation

Consider a 1TB volume on which you need to create five VM disk files. You could create five 250GB thin-provisioned disks on it, and they would all work fine initially. Over time, however, they will grow, and you could end up promising more disk than you can deliver. This situation can make the VMs fail, so it's important to watch the allocation carefully.

On the other hand, application experts often overestimate the disk space that they need. In some cases, application specifications may claim to require ten times the amount of disk space than they really do require, resulting in wasted disk space and wasted money. Thin provisioning lets you make your application expert *and* finance person happy by giving them the disk capacity they require while at the same time allowing them to purchase only what is used.

Sharing storage is more than just sharing space

Disks aren't commonly shared. In physical servers, a disk is exclusively owned by one server, unless it is a cluster. Clusters also often provide exclusive access to disks in such a way that the disk might be presented to more than one server, but each disk is accessed by one node of the cluster at a time.

In vSphere, shared disks are common. Large volumes on a SAN are often created and presented to multiple servers, which may be new to storage folks. vSphere contains a file system designed for hosting VMs, and it allows safe access to a presented disk from multiple hosts.

Access Control and Datastores

Because vSphere is so often used with shared storage, it's important to only share what you mean to share. Misconfigurations in the storage environment can result in loss of access, or loss of data, or both.

When you connect a vSphere host to the SAN, you may be giving it the ability to see SAN volumes you don't mean to present to the host. Hiding these unrelated SAN storage volumes from vSphere is a good idea so that you don't corrupt or impact those volumes.

In most SAN environments, the array ensures that only the hosts that you have granted access to can see specific volumes. This security is called *Logical Unit Number (LUN) masking* and is independent of the vSphere installation.

Generally, masking at the array is the way to go. It's easy, secure, and the most common way to provide LUN masking. If you need to, you can also mask at the vSphere host, which you do from the command line by modifying claim rule settings. If you plan to do mask at the vSphere host, it's best to work closely with VMware support.

A SAN should not operate on the same network as regular traffic for reasons of availability, performance, and security. SAN traffic has minimal security around it, and although building a dedicated SAN can be complex to piece together, it is often worth it in the long run. It's best to make sure that you physically isolate all your storage traffic using discrete switches or logically using VLANs.

Advanced Storage Configurations

You need to be aware of a couple of advanced storage configurations. These configurations aren't used that often, but they are really important in special circumstances.

Raw Device Mapping (RDM) is a file that points to a physical device. RDM contains information on how to access a physical storage device and is helpful when you are converting a physical server to a virtual machine or in cases where a VM disk file doesn't make sense.

Many times, if a VM needs access to an exceptionally large disk, an RDM might be used to simplify access. RDMs are also used in circumstances where multiple physical or virtual machines need to access the same disk.

vSphere has several options for choosing a connection path to the storage. These path selection plugins (PSPs) determine how vSphere sends and retrieves data. Most arrays that are on the Hardware Compatibility Guide have a default PSP assigned, and the PSP is often optimal for that array. We cover PSPs in depth in Chapter 12.

Part III
Installing vSphere

The 5th Wave   By Rich Tennant

"Great goulash, Stan. That reminds me, are you still in charge of our system architecture?"

In this part . . .

This part navigates the complete installation of vSphere 4. Chapter 7 guides you through installing VMware ESX server for the first time. Chapter 8 covers the installation of vCenter Server and vSphere licensing. Chapter 9 shows you how to install the vSphere Client for managing the environment.

Chapter 7

Installing VMware ESX 4 for the First Time

*V*Mware ESX 4 is the core of the vSphere virtualization platform, and this chapter guides you through the preparation for your ESX 4 Server installation. You kick off the installation by booting to ESX 4 installation media. This chapter shows you how to configure the network interface, partition the local storage, and set up the initial administrator account for ESX 4. You also confirm the installation using a Web browser and validate the configuration using the vSphere Client.

Gearing Up for Install

Collecting the materials and configuration information for the new ESX 4 host is key to a smooth installation. Keep in mind that an ESX 4 host has integrated infrastructure components normally found external to a physical server, such as network switching and SAN connectivity to multiple storage arrays. Installing ESX 4 on a physical server is easy; it's getting the configuration right that presents the challenge.

Preparing the install media

VMware enables customers to download installation media from VMware's Web site. The version referenced in this chapter is the full VMware ESX 4 installation in the ISO file format. Once the ISO file is downloaded, it can be burned to a recordable DVD for installation on a local physical machine. For a server located remotely (such as in a datacenter or colocation facility), the

ISO file may be copied to a file share local to the server, and attached as virtual media using the server's remote management interface or remote console.

VMware provides the Message-Digest 5 (MD5) checksum value next to the download link for each installer posted. An *MD5 checksum* is a unique value created by analyzing a file's contents. If two files have identical MD5 checksums, then the files are identical. Take a few minutes to validate the MD5 checksum of your completed download against the VMware-provided checksum on the download page. Ensuring that the file downloaded without corruption or error can prevent headaches later on.

Confirming the connections

Deploying VMware ESX 4 into an environment new to virtualization involves introducing unfamiliar configurations to network and storage administrators alike. Servers running traditional operating systems rarely require network link aggregation or VLAN tagging, nor do they require storage volumes to be presented from multiple storage arrays to a single host.

Handing off your requirements to a fellow administrator without explanation can lead to confusion, causing that administrator to think the requirements are a mistake. The friendly administrator subsequently implements a "corrected" configuration, and you're left troubleshooting a perfectly good installation of the software. Providing a basic crash course in ESX 4 to those responsible for supporting its infrastructure goes a long way in getting the configuration right the first time. Familiarizing fellow administrators also helps prevent misidentifying normal ESX 4 operation that could otherwise trigger them to react and potentially take the server offline as a preventative measure. This orientation also gives you the opportunity to introduce your peers to vSphere and show them all the cool new stuff you know.

If your ESX 4 host is connected to Fibre Channel (FC) SAN storage, that's a great place to start. Brands, models, speeds, and menus may vary, but all FC SAN storage connections are fundamentally the same. A server contains one or more Host Bus Adapters (HBAs), which are connected via an FC cable to a FC switch, which ultimately connects to an interface on the SAN called a Storage Processor (SP). Most servers have two FC connections, called *paths*. These paths are configured in active/active (both links are used simultaneously) or active/passive (one link is used, but the server switches to the second link if the first link fails or becomes unavailable). Each time a server containing an HBA is powered on, a configuration option for each HBA scrolls by, telling the administrator to press a specific key combination to enter setup for the HBA. Once inside the HBA setup menu, you're able to see the storage being presented to the server. Confirm that all the expected FC storage is being presented and can be seen by the HBA. When you're done, exit from the setup menu.

Checking the network connections for the server must be done from the network switch side. This check involves validating that VLAN access matches the expected settings defined during the planning phase of your vSphere rollout.

IP addresses, routes, and VLANs, oh my!

Putting your new ESX 4 server on the network requires that the server's network interfaces and their respective network switch connections are in agreement on how they will communicate. Most network switch ports are configured as access ports by default, meaning all data packets sent and received through the port are associated with a single VLAN. Using VLAN trunking lets you funnel the data from multiple network segments through a single network connection, while keeping the data packets isolated by tagging each data packet with a VLAN ID. Most network switches allow you to configure a combination of the two, by setting a default VLAN for untagged traffic, while the rest is passed through as tagged VLAN traffic. During the ESX 4 installation, you're asked whether VLAN trunking is required for the host's management connection and, if so, which VLAN to use. If you're unsure of this information, check with your network administrator.

The network address and the settings around it are also critical to the installation. The ESX 4 host's IP address is important, but the subnet mask and gateway associated with the IP address are critical attributes. The subnet mask is used in routing to decide whether a data packet should be routed on the local network or sent to an external network. The wrong setting either keeps externally bound packets inside or causes packets meant for the local network to be routed outside. The gateway is the network address that data packets are sent to for proper routing. An improper gateway setting causes packets to be returned as undeliverable, or worse, sent into a black hole with no response at all.

Booting Up ESX 4 Installation Media

You begin installing VMware ESX 4 by booting the ESX 4 installation media. Make sure that you have a working copy before you begin the installation process. If the media doesn't boot, check the boot order of the server. The CD or DVD drive must be first in the boot order list, or the server won't boot using the installation media.

Follow these steps to install VMware ESX 4:

1. **Boot the physical server with the VMware ESX 4 installation media.**

   For local machines, insert the DVD media into the drive and boot the machine. The ESX 4 installation boot menu appears, as shown in Figure 7-1.

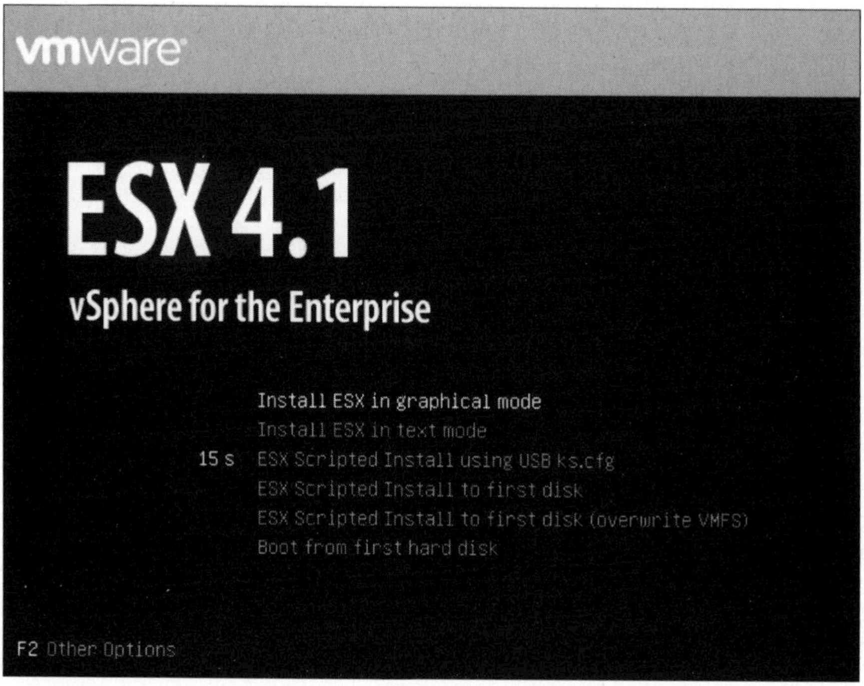

Figure 7-1:
ESX 4
installation
boot menu.

2. **Choose Install ESX in Graphical Mode and press Enter.**

   The VMware ESX 4 Installer loads. The ESX 4 Installer Welcome page appears.

3. **Click Next.**

   The VMware Master End User License Agreement appears.

4. **Select the checkbox to accept the terms of the license agreement and then click Next.**

   The Select Keyboard page appears.

5. **Select the appropriate keyboard type and click Next.**

   The Custom Drivers page appears, as shown in Figure 7-2.

6. **Select the No radio button and then click Next.**

   The Load Drivers page appears, as shown in Figure 7-3.

7. **Select Yes.**

   The Loading Drivers progress box appears.

8. **Click Next.**

   The License page appears, as shown in Figure 7-4.

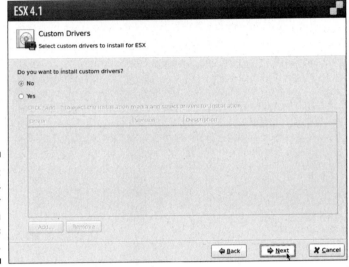

Figure 7-2:
ESX 4
Installer
Custom
Drivers
page.

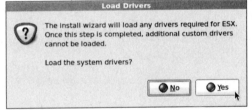

Figure 7-3:
ESX 4
Installer
Load Drivers
page.

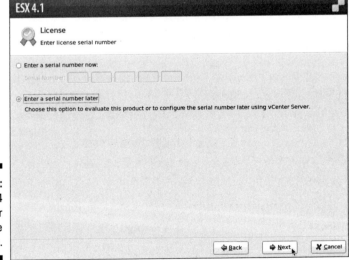

Figure 7-4:
ESX 4
Installer
License
page.

9. **Choose Enter a Serial Number Later and click Next.**

The Network Configuration Adapter Selection page appears, as shown in Figure 7-5.

Using vCenter Server to apply a license to an ESX 4 host is easier than manually entering a serial number when prompted during ESX 4 installation. The process is wizard-driven, GUI-based, and provides a list of available license resources to choose from. Choosing Enter a serial number later during ESX 4 installation will cause the vCenter Server to automatically prompt you to select a license at the time the ESX 4 host is added to the vCenter Server.

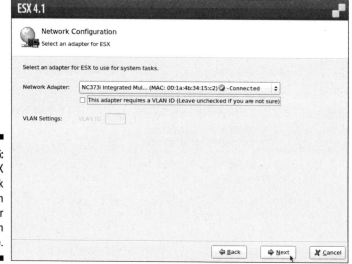

Figure 7-5:
ESX
Network
Configuration
Adapter
Selection
page.

If the wrong VLAN settings are selected at the time of installation, you won't be able to connect to the ESX 4 host over the network. However, you can correct these settings by logging in directly to the ESX 4 host's console. See the VMware ESX 4 documentation for details.

10. **Use the default selection from the Network Adapter drop-down list, and make sure the VLAN checkbox is unchecked (unless you specifically know a VLAN is required for the ESX 4 host's management interface); click Next.**

The Network Configuration Adapter Settings page appears, as shown in Figure 7-6.

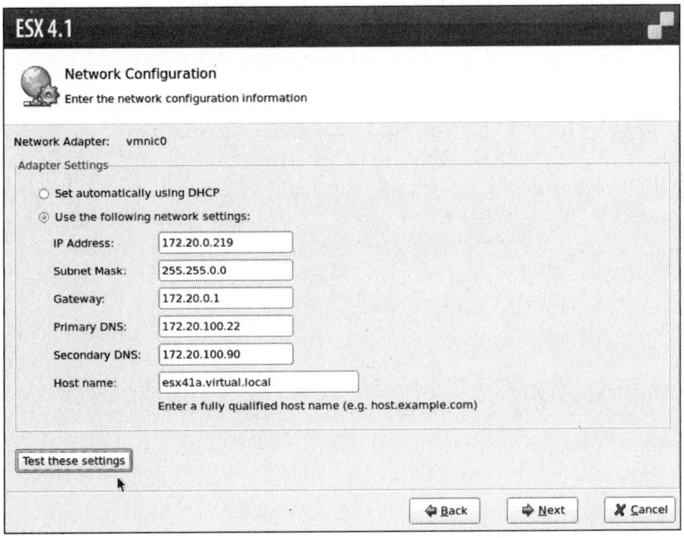

ESX 4.1

Network Configuration
Enter the network configuration information

Network Adapter: vmnic0

Adapter Settings

○ Set automatically using DHCP
⊙ Use the following network settings:

IP Address: | 172.20.0.219 |
Subnet Mask: | 255.255.0.0 |
Gateway: | 172.20.0.1 |
Primary DNS: | 172.20.100.22 |
Secondary DNS: | 172.20.100.90 |
Host name: | esx41a.virtual.local |

Enter a fully qualified host name (e.g. host.example.com)

[Test these settings]

[⇦ Back] [⇨ Next] [✗ Cancel]

Figure 7-6:
ESX
Network
Configuration
Adapter
Settings
page.

11. **Select the Use the Following Network Settings radio buttons and make the following changes:**

 • *Enter the IP address of the ESX 4 host into the IP Address field.* This IP address is used to access the ESX 4 host management interface.

 • *Enter the subnet mask for the IP address of the ESX 4 host into the Subnet Mask field.* This value will be provided with the IP address.

 • *Enter the network gateway IP address in the Gateway field.* This is usually the IP address of the network's router.

 • *Enter the IP address of the primary Domain Name Server (DNS) into the Primary DNS field.* This IP address is used by the ESX 4 host to look up the IP addresses of other hosts.

 • *Enter the IP address of the secondary Domain Name Server (DNS) into the Secondary DNS field.* This IP address is used by the ESX 4 host to look up the IP addresses of other hosts when the Primary DNS server is unreachable.

 • *Enter the fully qualified host name of the new ESX 4 host into the Host name field.* This is the name by which the new ESX 4 host will be addressed. The fully qualified host name is required, which is the host name followed by the domain name (such as `virtual.local`).

 If you're not sure about any of these settings, check with your network administrator.

12. Click the Test These Settings button.

The Network Test page appears, as shown in Figure 7-7. If the results are successful, proceed to the next step. Otherwise, check your network settings and try again.

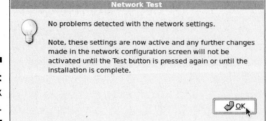

Figure 7-7:
Network
Test page.

13. Click OK.

The Setup Type page appears, as shown in Figure 7-8.

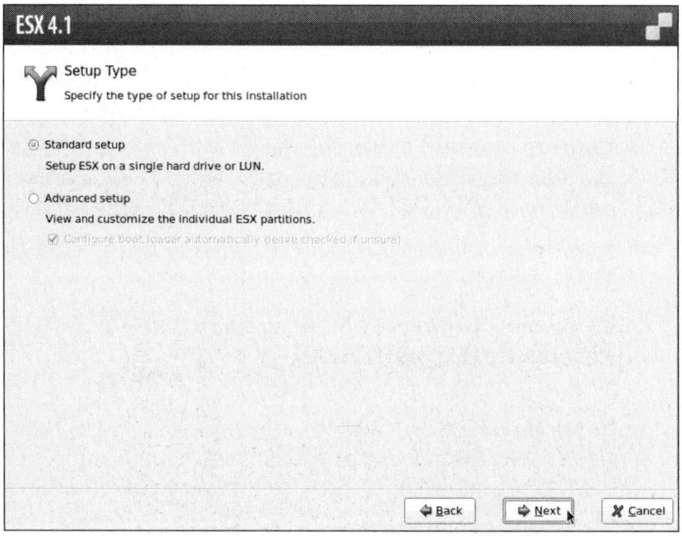

Figure 7-8:
Setup Type
page.

14. Choose Standard Setup and then click Next.

The ESX Storage Device page appears, as shown in Figure 7-9.

15. Choose the appropriate Local Storage Device and click Next.

Make sure that the Storage Device selected approximately matches the size of the drive on which you intend to install ESX 4. If presented, Uncheck the Preserve the Existing Datastore checkbox and click OK to proceed.

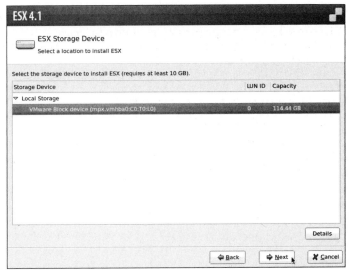

Figure 7-9:
ESX Storage
Device
page.

The Time Zone Settings page appears, as shown in Figure 7-10.

If the host was previously used as a VMware ESX host, a warning may appear offering to preserve the existing VMFS datastore. Double-check that you do not have any data on a VMFS and then uncheck the Preserve the Existing Datastore checkbox. Click OK to proceed.

Figure 7-10:
Time Zone
Settings
page.

16. Choose the ESX host's time zone and then click Next.

The Date and Time page appears, as shown in Figure 7-11.

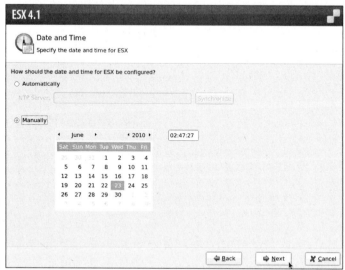

Figure 7-11:
Date and
Time page.

17. Choose the Manually radio button, set the Date and Time (if not already correct), and click Next.

The Set Administrator Password page appears, as shown in Figure 7-12.

18. Provide the password information and click Add.

You enter a password for the root administrator account in the Password field. This password provides full access to the ESX 4 host. Be sure to remember this password.

You then re-enter the password for the root administrator account in the Confirm Password field. This value and the password provided in the previous field must match.

When you click Add, the Add Account page appears, as shown in Figure 7-13.

19. Enter an account name and password and click OK.

The account name is the user name of an additional administrator account. The account can be used instead of the root administrator account to manage ESX 4.

The page closes, returning to the Set Administrator Password page.

20. Click Next.

The Summary of Installation Settings page appears, as shown in Figure 7-14.

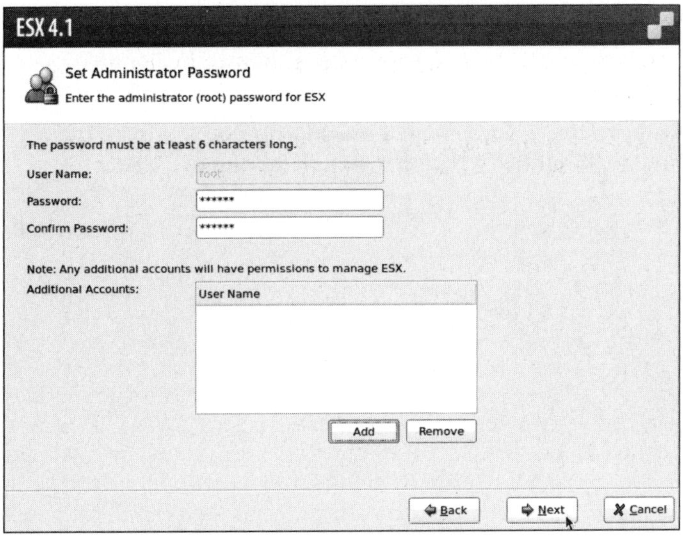

Figure 7-12:
Set
Administrator
Password
page.

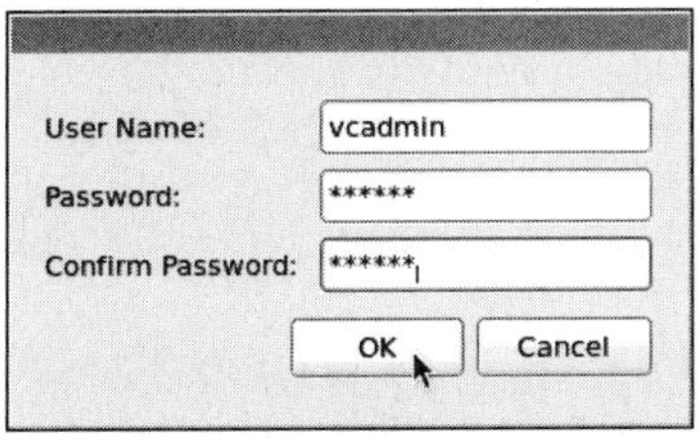

Figure 7-13:
Add
Account
page.

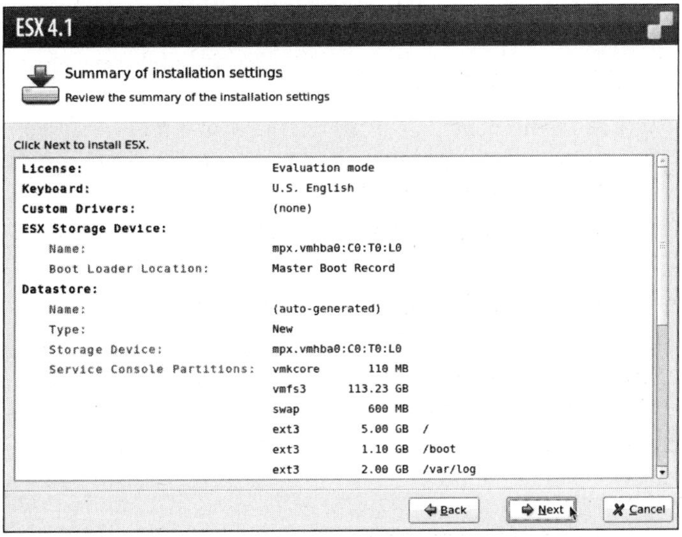

Figure 7-14:
Summary of
Installation
Settings
page.

21. **Click Next.**

    The Installing ESX progress page appears. The installation must complete before proceeding to the next step.

22. **Remove the VMware ESX 4 Installation Media from the server and then click Finish when this step is complete.**

    Your VMware ESX 4 installation is complete.

Confirming ESX Installation

Connecting to a new ESX host lets you confirm that it's configured correctly and ready for use. A successful connection using a Web browser confirms that the network address has been set correctly, and the host is running. If the Web browser connection is successful, follow up by connecting to the host using the vSphere Client. Connecting through the vSphere Client gives a greater level of detail, such as validating the password and ensuring the network and storage connections are correct.

Taking the extra steps now to confirm a successful ESX installation can save time and frustration later because it's difficult to correct configuration errors after the ESX host is added to vCenter Server.

Connecting via a Web browser

The quickest and easiest way to confirm a new ESX 4 host is to connect to the ESX 4 host's management interface using a Web browser:

1. **Launch a Web browser (such as Microsoft Internet Explorer or Mozilla Firefox).**

    The Web browser must be on a computer with access to the same network on which the ESX 4 host resides.

2. **Enter the URL of the ESX host's management interface into the Web browser's address bar.**

    The ESX host's management interface uses a Secure Socket Layer (SSL) connection, so the URL begins with `https://`, followed by the fully qualified host name of the ESX host (which includes the domain).

3. **Navigate to the ESX host's management interface.**

    The VMware ESX 4 Welcome window appears in the Web browser, as shown in Figure 7-15. If an SSL warning appears, click Continue to proceed.

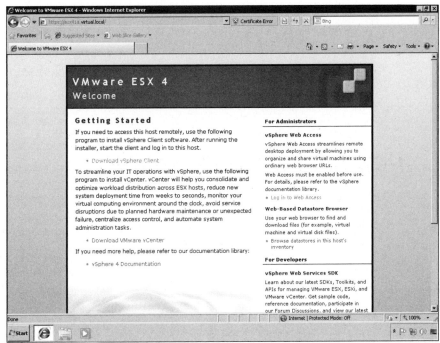

Figure 7-15:
VMware
ESX 4
Welcome
window.

The default SSL certificate used by ESX 4 is a self-signed certificate, and it may display a warning when you first connect. This behavior is normal until a trusted SSL certificate is installed.

Connecting with vSphere Client

Follow these steps to connect to the ESX 4 host using the vSphere Client to check the system specifications:

1. **Launch the vSphere Client.**

   The vSphere Client login page appears, as shown in Figure 7-16.

2. **Enter the host name of the ESX 4 host in the IP Address/Name field.**

   Use the fully qualified host name (including domain) of the ESX 4 host.

3. **Enter root in the User Name field.**

   This represents the root administrator account.

4. **Enter the password of the root administrator account in the Password field.**

   This password was set when ESX 4 was installed.

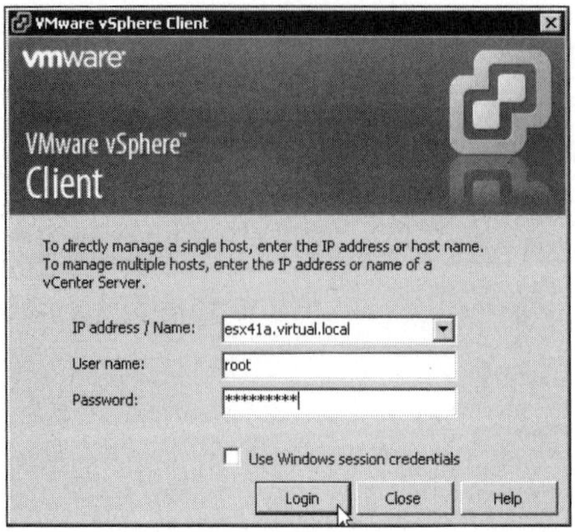

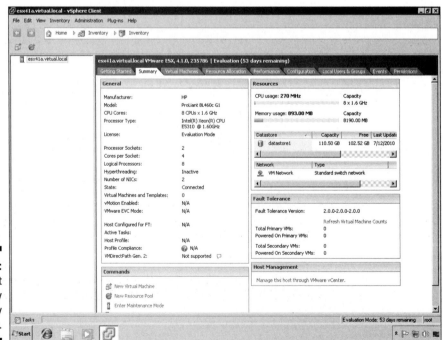

Figure 7-16:
vSphere
Client Login
page.

5. **Click Login.**

The ESX host inventory Getting Started window appears. If an SSL certificate warning appears, click Ignore to proceed.

6. **Click the Summary tab.**

The ESX host inventory Summary window appears, as shown in Figure 7-17.

7. **Verify the server specifications are as you expected.**

Figure 7-17:
ESX host
inventory
Summary
window.

Chapter 8

Building the vCenter Server

*V*Mware vCenter Server is a powerful platform that allows you to manage your ESX hosts and virtual machines (VMs) from a single console. vCenter Server adds a great deal of functionality that would otherwise be lost if you were to manage each ESX host individually. For example, vCenter Server gives ESX hosts the ability to make identical copies (clones) of VMs and then customize the cloned VM's operating system to give it a unique identity. vCenter Server ties into all the ESX hosts, making actions like live migration of VMs between interconnected hosts a reality.

This chapter guides you through building a new VMware vCenter Server. You discover how to choose the optimal specifications of a machine to host vCenter Server. You find out what needs to be loaded onto the machine before vCenter Server can be installed. Finally, this chapter walks you through the steps to install vCenter Server.

Placing vCenter Server in a Stable Home

Because it acts as the central command center for a farm of ESX hosts and their numerous VMs, vCenter Server needs to stay up and running. Having vCenter Server go down for a few minutes won't impact VMs running on ESX hosts, nor will it break high-availability services configured on ESX clusters. A vCenter Server outage will temporarily disable some of a vSphere administrator's most commonly used functions: VM cloning, ESX cluster management, and vMotion. vCenter Server is in no way a single point of failure in your vSphere infrastructure, but it's still important to make the right choices when selecting a suitable machine on which vCenter Server can run reliably.

Going virtual is the new Physical

Looking back to the days before VMware ESX and "x86" virtualization, a seasoned server administrator would automatically associate the concept of a highly available platform with a set of pricey, state-of-the-art, rack-mounted servers boasting component redundancy (multiple power supplies, network adapters, hard drives, and even memory). The introduction of the bare-metal hypervisor created the ability to put multiple machines onto a single physical server without an operating system underneath. Fast-forward to present day and consider all the high-availability functionality in vSphere. Excluding a few niche exceptions in very large environments, deploying vCenter Server in a VM makes more sense than installing it on a standalone physical server.

Putting vCenter Server in a VM gives you the benefits of running in a VMware vSphere Cluster:

- ✔ **Manageability:** Giving vCenter Server more computing power is as easy as dialing up the VM's resource shares. Need more disk space? Increase the size of the virtual disk by editing the VM using the vSphere Client, and the disk capacity in the VM will be available to the operating system instantly. Even better, if you're running Windows Server 2008, grow the Windows partition to include the new disk space, and the Windows volume will expand right before your eyes.

- ✔ **High availability:** Most people don't realize that once set up, vSphere High Availability will continue to function without vCenter Server, and in turn will protect your vCenter Server VM from hardware failure. If the ESX host running the vCenter Server VM fails, vSphere High Availability will bring that VM up on another host in the cluster.

- ✔ **Portability:** Using vMotion, you can move the running vCenter Server VM from one ESX host to another and even from one storage volume to another, allowing for host and storage maintenance without interruption.

- ✔ **Recovery:** Taking a snapshot of the vCenter Server VM before performing an upgrade allows you to roll back to a working snapshot of the VM. In the event things don't go as well as planned, connect to the ESX host directly using the vSphere Client, choose the snapshot to apply, and you're back up and running in no time.

- ✔ **Supportability:** VMware fully supports running vCenter Server inside a VM, as long as the VM meets the minimum requirements for CPU, memory, disk space, and database.

Right-sizing resources for vCenter

VMware vCenter Server is a powerful application, with the stated ability to manage up to 300 ESX hosts and 3,000 VMs with a single instance. At the opposite end of the spectrum, vCenter Server can also be used to manage five ESX hosts and 50 VMs.

Trying to figure out how much machine is needed to run vCenter may feel like an exercise in futility, but the grief it prevents in the long run makes it well worthwhile. You also need to consider database location and database storage when sizing the vCenter Server machine.

Database location

Putting the database on the vCenter Server machine increases the required disk space and compute power (by way of CPUs and memory). Using an external database server offloads the database server overhead, taking it out of the machine's sizing equation.

Database storage

The size of the vCenter Server database depends greatly on the size of the managed environment, but it is affected exponentially by the level of statistics collection being used. vCenter has four levels for statistics collection:

- ✔ **Level 1:** Basic metrics — average CPU, memory, disk and network utilization, along with system uptime, system heartbeat, and Distributed Resource Scheduler (DRS) statistics. No device statistics.

- ✔ **Level 2:** Everything from Level 1, plus summation and latest rollup types, but without minimum/maximum rollup types.

- ✔ **Level 3:** All metrics for all counters (including device metrics), but without minimum/maximum rollup types.

- ✔ **Level 4:** All metrics available in vCenter Server.

VMware provides two database sizing calculators on its Web site — one for Microsoft SQL Server and one for Oracle. Based on some assumptions about the infrastructure and its configuration, the calculator provides an estimated database size at the end of one year. As an example, use these values with the calculator:

- ✔ There is one ESX Cluster with five hosts, five datastores, and five resource pools.

- ✔ There are 50 VMs total.

- ✔ Each VM has one Network Interface (NIC), two vCPUs, and four disk devices (including CD-ROM, floppy disk, a storage controller, and a single virtual disk).

- ✔ Each host has two Network Interfaces (NICs), two physical CPUs, and ten disk devices (including CD-ROM, floppy disk, local storage controllers, and SAN HBAs and their associated disk volumes).

The calculator gives you an estimated database size after one year with 15 percent variance, plus temporary database space that will be needed while calculating rollup values. Using the example values, the results for each Statistics Collection Level are

- ✔ **Level 1:** Approximately 600MB for the database, with an additional 600MB for temporary space, for a total of 1.2GB, plus or minus 15 percent

- ✔ **Level 2:** Approximately 1.1GB for the database, with an additional 1.1GB for temporary space, for a total of 2.2GB, plus or minus 15 percent

- ✔ **Level 3:** Approximately 2.1GB for the database, with an additional 2.1GB for temporary space, for a total of 4.2GB, plus or minus 15 percent

- ✔ **Level 4:** Approximately 3.3GB for the database, with an additional 3.3GB for temporary space, for a total of 6.6GB, plus or minus 15 percent

Do not use the built-in Microsoft SQL Server 2005 Express database option for production deployments. Microsoft SQL Server 2005 Express has a database size limit of 4GB, and vCenter Server will eventually reach the 4GB limit. When the 4GB database limit is reached, vCenter Server will effectively be crippled and unable to run until the database is moved to a full version of Microsoft SQL Server, or Microsoft SQL Server Express is upgraded to a full version.

Because Microsoft SQL Server 2005 Express has a database size limit of 4GB, setting the Statistics Collection Level above Level 2, even in a small environment, can easily take the database beyond the 4GB limit. If you're using Microsoft SQL Server 2005 Express as the vCenter Server database, don't set the Statistics Collection Level above Level 2 unless instructed to do so by a VMware support engineer.

Going global and Multiple vCenter Instances

Deploying a single instance of vCenter Server to manage a vSphere environment is fairly straightforward. Many global organizations using vSphere are deploying multiple instances of vCenter Server in alignment with how the organization is divided: by geography. Using this approach addresses issues such as network latency and privacy laws, but it undermines the notion of deployment standards and uniform configurations.

A majority of global organizations also run a global directory service such as Microsoft Active Directory, giving users from all over the organization access to various resources around the globe. Giving a user from the UK access to a vCenter instance in India may be as simple as assigning permissions to that user's account on the vCenter Server in India, but doing so still requires the user to connect over a great distance, which spells trouble. VMware studied this and other related use cases and decided it was time to give vCenter Server the ability to communicate with its peer vCenter Servers. This feature is vCenter Server Linked Mode.

vCenter Server Linked Mode introduces individual vCenter Servers to each other so that they can collectively provide visibility across multiple vCenter instances. Linked Mode enables vCenter Server to pass along roles, permissions, and licenses to its peers so that you can simultaneously log in, view, and search the inventories of all the linked vCenter Servers.

Meeting the Prerequisites

Building a vCenter Server is more than just clicking the installer. First, you must meet a series of prerequisites to support the installation. You must have the vCenter Server installation media available. If you're not installing the bundled Microsoft SQL Server 2005 Express database engine, your new database must meet certain requirements. Microsoft Active Directory Domain membership is required by the server. These prerequisites and more must first be met before launching the actual installer.

Installing vCenter Server requires the following:

- ✔ vCenter Server installation media
- ✔ A Windows machine meeting the prerequisites for vCenter Server
- ✔ An Active Directory user account in the local Administrators security group on the vCenter Server machine
- ✔ A database with details on how to connect (unless you are installing the local Microsoft SQL Server Express 2005 database server as part of the vCenter installation)

Gathering information to meet the vCenter Server prerequisites can be a bit of a task of its own. Depending upon the size and nature of your organization, the details and resources needed to complete the installation may lie with an individual or with multiple people spanning the organization. Whichever the case, you need to know what each prerequisite is and why it's needed to install vCenter Server.

Operating system (OS)

VMware provides flexibility in which Windows Server OS versions are supported to install vCenter Server. You can install VMware vCenter on the following operating systems:

 ✔ Windows XP Pro 64-bit, SP2

 ✔ Windows Server 2003 Standard 64-bit, SP2

 ✔ Windows Server 2003 Enterprise 64-bit, SP2

 ✔ Windows Server 2003 R2 64-bit, SP2

 ✔ Windows Server 2008 Enterprise 64-bit, SP2

 ✔ Windows Server 2008 Standard 64-bit, SP2

 ✔ Windows Server 2008 Datacenter 64-bit, SP2

 ✔ Windows 2008 R2 Standard

 ✔ Windows 2008 R2 Enterprise

VMware Update Manager has slightly different OS requirements than vCenter Server. A 64-bit version of Windows Server 2008 SP2 is supported by both applications and allows you to install both applications on the same machine.

Hardware

The minimum hardware (physical or virtual) requirements to run vCenter Server are

 ✔ Two CPUs or one dual-core processor (64-bit required)

 ✔ 2.0GHz or faster Intel or AMD processor (64-bit required)

 ✔ 3GB RAM (4 GB when running vCenter Management Webservices)

 ✔ 2GB disk space (4 GB if installing SQL Server 2005 Express)

 ✔ Gigabit network connection (highly recommended)

These requirements are really the bare minimum needed just to get vCenter Server running. If the vCenter Server database is installed on the vCenter Server machine, increase processor speed, memory size, and disk capacity.

To make it a little easier, VMware provides some guidelines based on the size and scope of your vSphere deployment. The classifications are

> **Medium:** Up to 50 ESX hosts and 250 Powered-On VMs
>
> • Two CPUs
>
> • 4GB RAM
>
> • 3GB disk space

Large: Up to 200 ESX hosts and 2000 Powered-On VMs

- Four CPUs
- 4GB RAM
- 3GB disk space

Extra large: Up to 300 ESX hosts and 3000 Powered-On VMs

- Four CPUs
- 8GB RAM
- 3GB disk space

Real-world experience suggests you expect usability to decrease drastically when vCenter Server reaches about half the stated maximums of each classification, but your mileage may vary.

Microsoft Active Directory

Starting with version 4.1, vCenter Server added some requirements regarding the vCenter Server machine and Microsoft Windows Active Directory (AD). The vCenter Server machine must

- ✔ Be part of a Windows AD domain.
- ✔ Be able to communicate with one or more Windows AD Domain Controllers for authentication.
- ✔ Have its DNS name and actual computer name match.
- ✔ Be installed with a domain user account that does the following:
    - Is a member of the machine's local Administrators group.
    - Has permission to act as part of the operating system.
    - Has permission to log on as a service.
- ✔ *Not* be a Windows AD Domain Controller.

Database

vCenter Server supports Microsoft SQL Server, Oracle, and IBM DB2 databases. The vCenter Server installer provides Microsoft SQL Server 2005 Express Edition, but it's only intended to support up to five ESX hosts and 50 VMs. Larger deployments should use one of the supported database platforms, preferably hosted on a machine other than the vCenter Server itself, and ideally part of a highly available configuration (database cluster).

Here is the full list of supported databases and their requirements:

- ✔ Microsoft SQL Server 2005 Express:

    - Is included with vCenter Server installer.

    - Automatically installs if selected.

    - Is meant for small nonproduction deployments (five ESX hosts / 50 VMs)

- ✔ Microsoft SQL Server 2005:

    - Being hosted on a different machine is preferred.

    - vCenter Service Account must have DB_Owner (DBO) rights for the new database.

    - Requires a valid Open Database Connectivity (ODBC) Data Source Name (DSN) entry.

- ✔ Microsoft SQL Server 2008:

    - Being hosted on a different machine is preferred.

    - vCenter Service Account must have DB_Owner (DBO) rights for the new database.

    - Requires a valid ODBC DSN entry.

- ✔ Oracle 10g:

    - Being hosted on a different machine is preferred.

    - Requires patch 10.2.0.4 or later for client and server.

    - Requires patch 5699495 for the client.

    - Needs ojdbc14.jar file available from client.

    - vCenter Service Account must have DB_Owner (DBO) rights for the new database.

    - Requires a valid ODBC DSN entry.

- ✔ Oracle 11g:

    - Needs ojdbc14.jar file available from client.

    - Requires a valid ODBC DSN entry.

- ✔ IBM DB2 9.5 (new in vCenter 4.1):

    - Being hosted on a different machine is preferred.

    - Install IBM Data Server Runtime Client if database is not on the vCenter Server machine.

    - Install Hotfix 22318 on the vCenter Server machine.

    - Add `C:\Program Files\IBM\SQLLIB\BIN` to the vCenter Server machine's system path.

- vCenter Service Account must have DB_Owner (DBO) rights for the new database.
- Requires a valid ODBC DSN entry.

Networking

vCenter Server is very picky about its network configuration. For vCenter Server to properly interact with the ESX hosts it manages, the vCenter Server machine must have the following:

- A static IP address
- A host name registered in your network's Domain Name Servers (DNS)
- Unrestricted communication for the following network ports:

    - **Port 80:** HTTP Web access. Redirects to Port 443 for HTTPS.

    - **Port 389:** Directory Services for a vCenter Server group.

    - **Port 443:** vCenter Client access, vSphere Web Access Client, and the vCenter Web Services SDK.

    - **Port 646:** vCenter Server Linked Mode SSL connection.

    - **Port 902:** Communication between vCenter Server and the ESX hosts it manages. Also used by vSphere Client to connect to a VM's console.

    - **Port 903:** Another port used by vSphere Client to connect to a VM's console.

    - **Port 8080:** Web Services HTTP for vCenter Management Webservices.

    - **Port 8443:** Web Services HTTPS for vCenter Management Webservices.

    - **Port 60099:** Web Service change service notification.

The default installation of Windows Server 2008 comes with Windows Firewall enabled.

The ESX hosts being added to vCenter Server must be able to look up the vCenter Server's host name in DNS, and vice versa. While it is possible to add ESX hosts to vCenter Server simply by using their network IP addresses instead of their proper hostnames, doing so will make it nearly impossible to change the IP address of the ESX host in the future.

User account permissions

Installing vCenter requires the user running the installer to have local administrative rights on the machine. Using vCenter in Linked Mode (having interconnected vCenter servers) requires the installing user to have local administrative rights on all the vCenter servers.

Running vCenter Server as an AD domain account enables vCenter Server to use Windows Authentication when connecting to an external Microsoft SQL Server database, making the deployment inherently more secure.

Running the vCenter Server Installer

Installing vCenter Server is a relatively straightforward procedure. vCenter Server uses a wizard-based installer, with a clear explanation of the information you need to enter before moving to the next step. Before starting the installation, make sure that you've met all the prerequisites described in *Meeting the Prerequisites*, earlier in this chapter. Having all the information you'll need prior to launching the installer can help ensure a smooth installation process.

Follow these steps to install vCenter Server:

1. **Open the VMware vCenter Server installer media.**

    A menu of product installers appears. Figure 8-1 shows the menu of product installers.

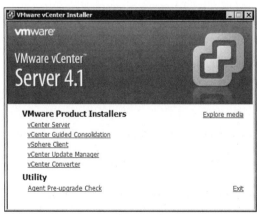

Figure 8-1:
VMware
vCenter
Server
Product
Installers
menu.

2. **Under VMware Product Installers, click vCenter Server.**

   The VMware vCenter Server installer launches. The Choose Setup Language page appears.

3. **Choose the appropriate language from the drop-down menu and then click OK.**

   The Installation wizard for VMware vCenter Server appears.

4. **Click Next.**

   The End-User Patent Agreement appears.

5. **Click Next.**

   The VMware Master End User License Agreement (EULA) appears.

6. **After you read the license agreement, choose I Agree to the Terms in This License Agreement and then click Next.**

   The Customer Information page appears (see Figure 8-2).

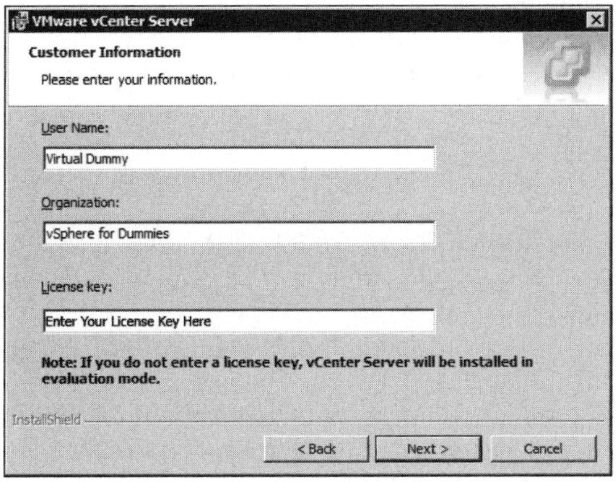

Figure 8-2:
Customer
Information
page.

7. **Enter a name in the User Name field.**

   If you're not sure which name to use, enter the name of your organization's VMware contact person.

8. **Enter a name in the Organization field.**

   If you're not sure which name to enter, use the name of the organization that purchased the vCenter licenses.

9. **Enter your vCenter Server license key in the License Key field.**

   The license key is specific to vCenter Server and can be obtained through the VMware support portal.

If you don't have the license key handy, you can still complete the installation without it. If no license key is provided during the install process, vCenter Server installs in evaluation mode and runs for up to 60 days. The permanent key can be applied before the evaluation period ends, by using the vSphere Client.

10. **Click Next.**

    The Database Options page appears.

11. **Select the appropriate database type.**

    Figure 8-3 shows the two available options.

    For a small deployment or simple testing, choose Install a Microsoft SQL Server 2005 Express Instance.

    For a normal or larger deployment, choose Use an Existing Supported Database; then choose the appropriate Data Source Name (DSN) for the database.

Figure 8-3:
Database
Options
page.

Using an existing supported database requires a 64-bit DSN to be created. If the vCenter Installer doesn't detect a suitable DSN, it will provide the option to create a new DSN. See the VMware vCenter Installation documentation for database-specific details.

12. **Click Next.**

    The vCenter Server Service page appears.

13. **Make sure the Use SYSTEM Account box is checked.**

    Figure 8-4 shows the default setting selected. Choosing the default setting will use your computer's Active Directory machine account to connect to the domain and to other servers (such as a database server). For greater security with Microsoft SQL databases hosted externally to the vCenter Server, enter the username and password for an AD domain account with sufficient privileges to access the remote Microsoft SQL database server.

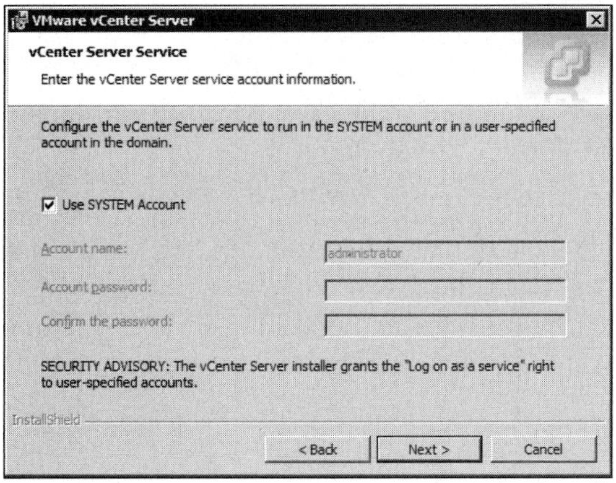

Figure 8-4: vCenter Server Service account page.

14. **Click Next.**

    The Destination Folder page appears.

15. **Click Next.**

    The vCenter Server Linked Mode Options page appears. Figure 8-5 shows the two available options.

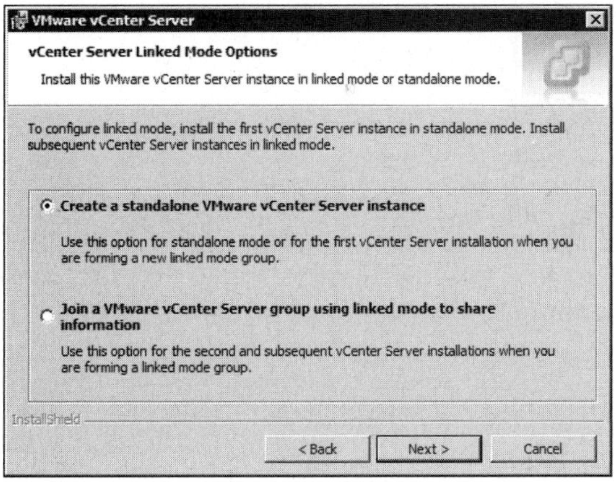

Figure 8-5: vCenter Server Linked Mode Options page.

16. **Choose the default setting to Create a Standalone VMware vCenter Server Instance and then click Next.**

    The Configure Ports page appears.

17. **Use the default settings and then click Next.**

The vCenter Server JVM Memory page appears. Figure 8-6 shows the three available options.

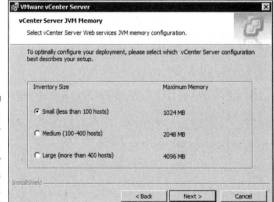

Figure 8-6:
vCenter
Server JVM
Memory
options
page.

18. **Choose the Inventory Size appropriate for your deployment and then click Next.**

The Ready to Install page appears.

19. **Click Install.**

VMware vCenter Server installs. After installation is complete, the Installation Completed page appears.

20. **Click Finish.**

Installation of the vCenter Server is now complete.

Chapter 9

Getting Started with the vSphere Client

In This Chapter

▶ Installing the vSphere Client onto your machine

▶ Discovering an alternative for simple operations

*T*he vSphere Client is your connection to the control center of vSphere. More than just a control panel, the vSphere Client is your dashboard into the operations of your vSphere infrastructure. It even allows you to control vCenter Server plug-ins for added functionality (such as physical-to-virtual migrations), all from the same interface.

This chapter guides you through installing the vSphere Client. You find out how to connect to vCenter Server using the vSphere Client. Finally, you see an alternative to the vSphere Client when you just need to do something simple (such as power on a virtual machine). Prepare to plug into the gateway to managing your vSphere world!

Installing the vSphere Client

Running the vSphere Client is a fundamental requirement for managing a vSphere environment. The vSphere Client connects you to vCenter Server for configuration and management of individual hosts, clusters, and advanced features. Alternatively, the vSphere Client connects to ESX hosts directly for localized configuration and to execute basic VM operations.

Reviewing the prerequisites

Installing the vSphere Client 4.1 requires the following:

- ✔ **OS:** Windows XP Pro (SP3 or 64-bit SP2), Windows Server 2003 (SP1 or SP2, Standard SP2, Enterprise SP2, or R2 SP2), Windows Vista (32-bit or 64-bit, Business SP2 or Enterprise SP2), Windows 7 (32-bit or 64-bit), Windows Server 2008 (Enterprise SP2 32-bit or 64-bit, Standard SP2 32-bit or 64-bit, Datacenter SP2) or Windows Server 2008 R2.

- ✔ **CPU:** 1 CPU.

- ✔ **Memory:** 1GB RAM.

- ✔ **Disk:** 1.4GB free for a complete installation (includes temp space for prerequisites).

- ✔ **Network:** Gigabit connection recommended.

- ✔ **Security:** Installing user must be a member of the local Administrators security group on the machine.

- ✔ **Internet:** The machine must have an Internet connection.

You can download the vSphere Client installer at `www.vmware.com`.

You can point your Web browser directly at your vCenter Server or a vSphere host and download the vSphere Client locally.

Running the installer

Follow these steps to install the vSphere Client 4.1 on your local machine:

1. **Launch the vSphere Client 4.1 installer executable.**

   The Choose Setup Language dialog box appears, as shown in Figure 9-1.

2. **Choose the appropriate language from the drop-down list and click OK.**

   The VMware vSphere Client Installation Wizard appears, as shown in Figure 9-2.

3. **Click Next.**

   The End-User Patent Agreement appears, as shown in Figure 9-3.

Figure 9-1:
The Choose
Setup
Language
dialog box.

Figure 9-2:
The
VMware
vSphere
Client
Installation
Wizard.

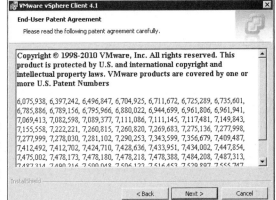

Figure 9-3:
The End-
User Patent
Agreement.

4. **Click Next.**

The License Agreement appears, as shown in Figure 9-4.

5. **Click the I Agree to the Terms in the License Agreement radio button and then click Next.**

This means you agree to the terms in the VMware Master End User License Agreement displayed in the text box.

The Customer Information page appears, as shown in Figure 9-5.

6. **Enter the name of the person who is the primary user of this computer in the User Name field.**

This value can be either the primary user of the computer where the vSphere Client is being installed or a generic name.

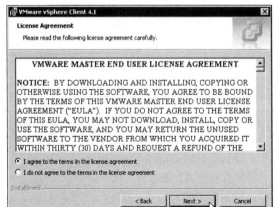

Figure 9-4:
The License
Agreement.

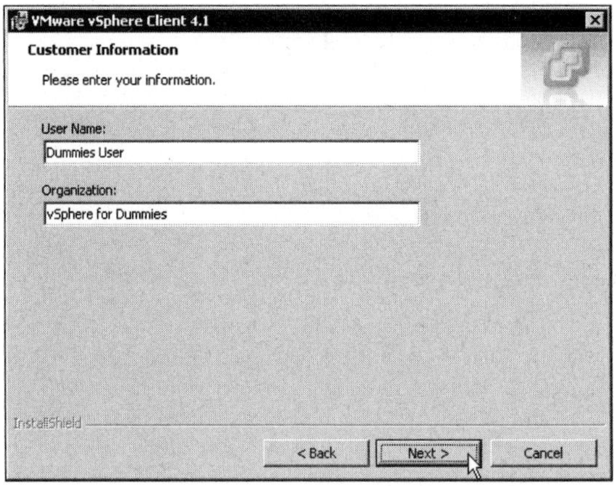

Figure 9-5:
Customer
Information
page.

7. **Enter the name of the organization that owns the vSphere licensing in the Organization field and click Next.**

   This value can be the name of the organization that owns the vSphere licensing or the name of the organization responsible for the computer where the vSphere Client is being installed.

   The Destination Folder page appears, as shown in Figure 9-6.

8. **Click Next.**

   The Ready to Install the Program page appears, as shown in Figure 9-7.

9. **Click Install.**

   The Installing VMware vSphere Client page appears, as shown in Figure 9-8.

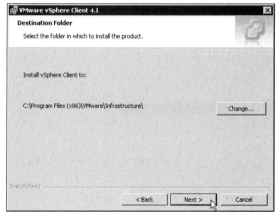

Figure 9-6:
Destination
Folder page.

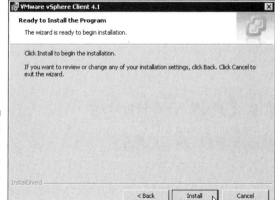

Figure 9-7:
Ready to
Install the
Program
page.

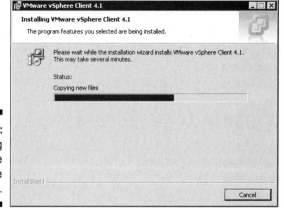

Figure 9-8:
Installing
VMware
vSphere
Client page.

When the installation process completes, the Installation Completed window appears (see Figure 9-9).

10. Click Finish.

The vSphere Client installation is complete.

Figure 9-9:
Installation
Completed
window.

vSphere Client's Less Famous Sister: vSphere Web Access

Standing in the shadow of your famous older sibling isn't easy, but that's just what vSphere Web Access has been doing since it was introduced. vSphere Web Access exists for people who either don't need all the capability of the vSphere Client or may need to manage vSphere from a location without access to the vSphere Client. vSphere Web Access contains a subset of capabilities, such as basic power functions, remote console access, managing snapshots, and creating, modifying, or removing virtual machines. To finish off what self-esteem was left, vSphere Web Access is disabled by default. In the following sections, we show you how to dust off this diamond-in-the-rough and put it to work for you.

Enabling vSphere Web Access

vSphere Web Access can reside on the vCenter Server and on each ESX host. In both cases, administrative privileges are required to enable vSphere Web Access and must be enabled prior to using them for the first time.

Follow these steps to enable vSphere Web Access on vCenter Server:

1. **Connect to the vCenter Server as an account with Administrator access.**

   You can connect using Microsoft Remote Desktop or with any other form of remote console access that gets you to the vCenter Server's desktop.

2. **Right-click My Computer and select Manage.**

   The Computer Management dialog box appears.

3. **Expand Configuration and select Services.**

   A list of Windows Services appears on the right-hand side of the dialog box.

4. **Locate VMware VirtualCenter Management Webservices and double-click it.**

   The VMware VirtualCenter Management Webservices Properties dialog box appears.

5. **Choose Automatic from the Startup Type drop-down list; then click Apply.**

   This step tells Windows to automatically start the service when Windows boots up.

6. **Click the Start button to start the service.**

   The VMware VirtualCenter Management Webservices service starts up. If the Start button is unavailable, stop the service with the Stop button; then restart the service with the Start button.

7. **Close the VMware VirtualCenter Management Webservices Properties window.**

   The VMware VirtualCenter Management Webservices service is now active.

Follow these steps to enable vSphere Web Access on an ESX host:

1. **Log in to the ESX host using root privileges.**

   You can connect by logging in directly on the ESX host's server console, or you can connect by using an SSH client and the additional admin account created at installation; then use the "su root" command to gain root access.

   vSphere Web Access is not available in ESXi.

2. **Check whether the vSphere Web Access service is running by entering this command:**

   ```
   service vmware-webAccess status
   ```

   A message appears stating whether the vSphere Web Access service is running.

3. **(optional) If vSphere Web Access is not running, use this command to start it:**

```
service vmware-webAccess start
```

vSphere Web Access should now be available from a Web browser.

If vSphere Web Access is running on your ESX host, but you're still unable to connect to it, there may be a firewall issue. Verify that the ESX host's Security settings allow connections to vSphere Web Access.

Connecting to vSphere Web Access

As suggested by its name, vSphere Web Access gives you a simple way to connect to vSphere using a Web browser. To get connected, you must be using a supported Web browser. vSphere Web Access formally supports the following browsers:

- ✔ Internet Explorer 6.0 or later for Microsoft Windows
- ✔ Mozilla Firefox 2.0, 3.0, or later for Microsoft Windows
- ✔ Mozilla Firefox 2.0, 3.0, or later for Linux

One factor limiting browser support has to do with VMware's Remote Console browser plug-in, which is used to provide native console access to a virtual machine. The plug-in has two flavors: one for Internet Explorer (Microsoft Windows only Web browser) and one for Mozilla Firefox (Windows and Linux). This combination of browsers and operating systems covers the majority of VMware administrators, while keeping support for the plug-in manageable.

Follow these steps to connect to vSphere Web Access:

1. **Connect to the vCenter Server using a Web browser.**

   The Welcome to VMware vSphere 4 page appears.

2. **Click Log In to Web Access.**

   The vSphere Web Access login dialog box appears.

3. **Enter the username of a vCenter Server Administrator in the Login Name field.**

4. **Enter the user account's password in the Password field.**

5. **Click Log In.**

   The vSphere Web Access window appears. You're now logged in.

Part IV
Configuring and Connecting vSphere

The 5th Wave · By Rich Tennant

Oh come on – how fatal can it be?

FATAL ERROR

In this part . . .

This part covers the setup of vCenter Server and configuration of VMware ESX hosts. Chapter 10 is a detailed guide to configuring vCenter Server. Chapter 11 explains connecting vSphere to your network. Chapter 12 shows how vSphere connects to shared storage. Chapter 13 goes through assembling a cluster of VMware ESX hosts.

Chapter 10

Configuring a New vCenter Server

*V*Mware vCenter Server is more than just the centralized management console for your virtual infrastructure. The vCenter Server also manages licensing, customizes cloned virtual machines, and allows configuration of each ESX host under its management.

This chapter guides you through setting up the basics for your vCenter Server. You set up a basic datacenter in vCenter and add ESX hosts to it. This chapter shows you how to load licenses into vCenter and apply those licenses to the hosts that vCenter manages. You also set up time synchronization for your ESX hosts using Network Time Protocol (NTP).

Laying the Foundation

Your vCenter Server is nearly ready for action. Getting the vCenter Server ready to be configured involves a few more steps to bring it into service:

- ✔ **Licensing:** Apply your permanent vCenter Server license to the vCenter Server.

- ✔ **Customization components:** Enable vCenter to customize cloned virtual machines requires that certain Microsoft Sysprep components are installed on the vCenter Server machine.

- ✔ **Initial datacenter:** Create an initial datacenter as a place to add ESX hosts in vCenter Server.

Adding licenses

In Chapter 8, you installed the vCenter Server using the built-in evaluation license. Part of bringing the vCenter Server online is adding your permanent vCenter Server license to the vCenter Server.

Follow these steps to install the permanent vCenter 4.1 license:

1. **Log into vCenter Server using the vSphere Client.**

    The VMware Evaluation License Notice appears, as shown in Figure 10-1.

Figure 10-1:
The
VMware
Evaluation
License
Notice.

2. **Click OK.**

    The vCenter Home Inventory window appears, as shown in Figure 10-2.

Figure 10-2:
The
vCenter
Home
Inventory
window.

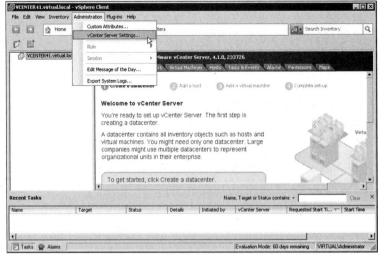

3. **Click Administration on the menu bar and select vCenter Server Settings from the drop-down menu.**

   The vCenter Server Settings dialog box appears, as shown in Figure 10-3.

Figure 10-3:
The
vCenter
Server
Settings
dialog box.

4. **Select the Assign a New License Key to this vCenter Server radio button in the vCenter License section.**

   The Enter Key button becomes active.

5. **Select the Enter Key button in the vCenter License section.**

   The Add License Key dialog box appears, as shown in Figure 10-4.

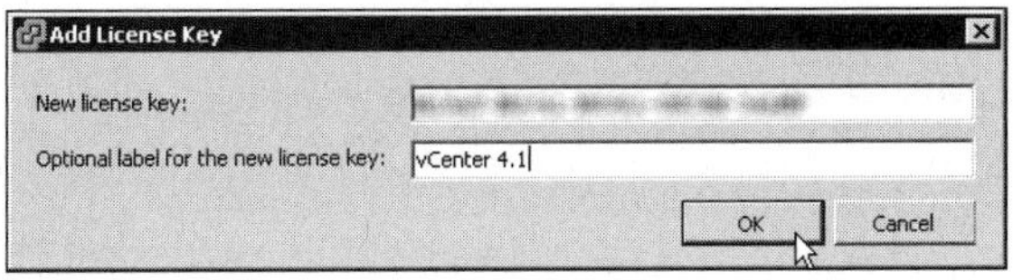

Figure 10-4:
The Add
License Key
dialog box.

6. **Enter your vSphere server license key in the New License Key field.**

   This value is a vCenter-specific license key provided by VMware. The license key is five sections, separated by hyphens, with each consisting of five alphanumeric characters.

7. **Enter a descriptive label for the license key in the Optional Label for the New License Key field and then click OK.**

   This step describes the license key entered. The description can refer to a specific purpose for the license or to any other helpful information.

   The vCenter Server Settings dialog box reappears reflecting the added license key, as shown in Figure 10-5.

Figure 10-5:
The vCenter Server Settings dialog box with added license key.

8. **Click OK.**

   The vCenter Server license key is now applied.

Adding your vCenter Server license key does not add licenses for anything other than vCenter Server. You add licenses for ESX using a different process, as described in the "Adding vSphere Licensing" section, later in this chapter.

Creating a new vCenter datacenter

Follow these steps to create the first datacenter in vCenter Server:

1. **Log into vCenter Server using the vSphere Client.**

   The vCenter Server Home Inventory window appears.

2. **Right-click the vCenter Server in the left pane and choose New Datacenter from the drop-down menu that appears.**

   This step creates a new vCenter datacenter, shown in Figure 10-6.

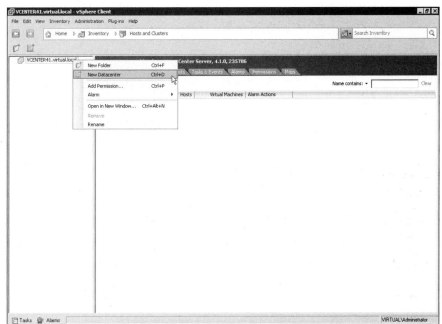

Figure 10-6: Adding a new vCenter Datacenter.

3. **Type a name for the datacenter and press Enter.**

   This datacenter contains a collection of hosts, clusters, and virtual machines. The datacenter name often reflects the geographic location of the hosts and resources associated with this datacenter.

   This step renames the datacenter from the default New Datacenter name to the name entered, as shown in Figure 10-7.

Figure 10-7:
The new
datacenter
with correct
name.

Adding ESX Hosts

During installation of ESX in Chapter 8, we skip over adding a license to the host. In this section, you add your vSphere license to your vCenter Server. After you add the license, it's applied to your ESX hosts as you add them to your vCenter Server. We also run through a few common tasks to make vSphere management a little easier.

Adding vSphere licensing

Although you can add ESX hosts to vCenter, you cannot use them until licensing is applied. The first step to licensing your ESX hosts is to add the license to the vCenter Server. Follow these steps to add a vSphere License to a vCenter Server:

1. **Log into vCenter Server using the vSphere Client.**

   The vCenter Server Home Inventory window appears.

2. **Click Home on the navigation bar at the top of the window.**

   The vCenter Server Home window appears.

3. **Click the Licensing icon in the Administration section.**

   The vCenter Server Licensing window appears, as shown in Figure 10-8.

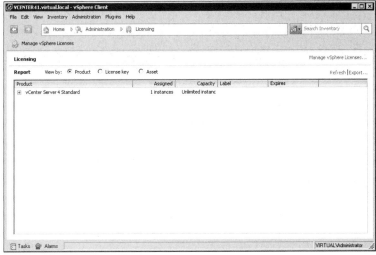

Figure 10-8:
The
vCenter
Server
Licensing
window.

4. **Click the Manage vSphere Licenses link.**

   The Add License Keys dialog box appears, as shown in Figure 10-9.

5. **Enter your vSphere license key(s) in the Enter New vSphere License Keys field.**

   This value is one or more license codes provided by VMware.

6. **Enter a description for the vSphere license(s) in the Enter Optional Label for New License Keys field.**

   This value is a one-line description of the licenses being added.

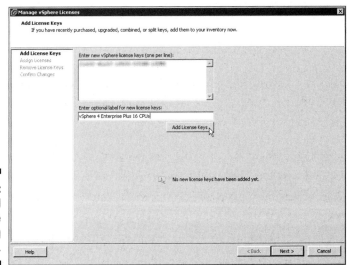

Figure 10-9:
The Add
License
Keys dialog
box.

7. Click Add License Keys.

The added vSphere license(s) appear at the bottom half of the dialog box, as shown in Figure 10-10.

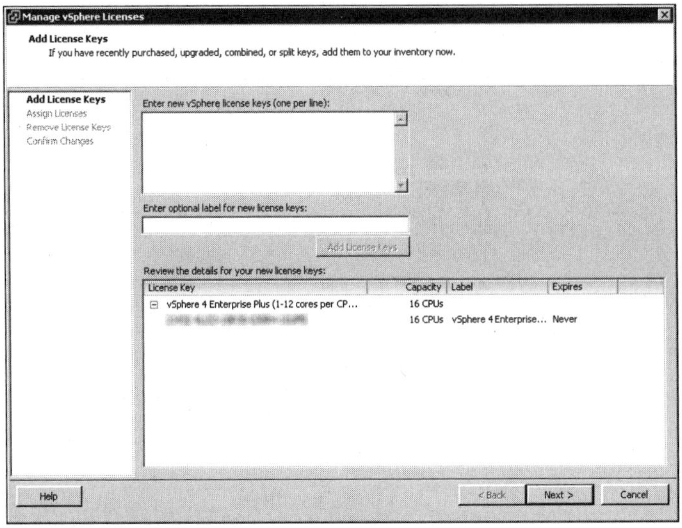

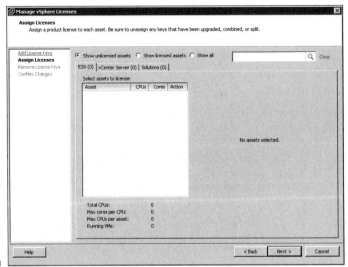

Figure 10-10:
Your added
vSphere
license(s).

8. Click Next.

The Assign Licenses dialog box appears, as shown in Figure 10-11.

Figure 10-11:
The Assign
Licenses
dialog box.

9. Click Next.

The Remove License Keys dialog box appears, as shown in Figure 10-12.

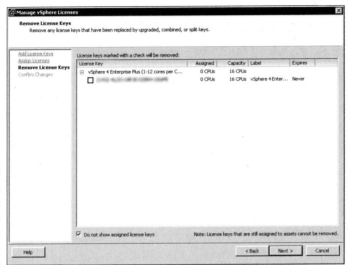

Figure 10-12:
The Remove
License
Keys dialog
box.

10. Click Next.

The Confirm Changes dialog box appears, as shown in Figure 10-13.

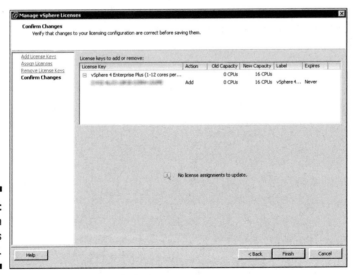

Figure 10-13:
The Confirm
Changes
dialog box.

11. **Click Finish.**

The vSphere license(s) are now successfully added to vCenter Server.

Telling vCenter Server about a new ESX host

vCenter Server is a powerful management tool, but because it can't read your mind, you must tell it about the ESX hosts you'd like it to manage.

Follow these steps to add an ESX host to vCenter Server:

1. **Log into vCenter Server using the vSphere Client.**

The vCenter Server Home Inventory window appears.

2. **Click the datacenter to which you'd like to add the ESX host.**

An ESX host must be added to a datacenter. If no datacenters are shown, add a new Datacenter as described in "Creating a new vCenter datacenter," earlier in this chapter.

3. **From the main menu, choose Inventory⇨Datacenter⇨Add Host.**

The Add Host Wizard dialog box appears, as shown in Figure 10-14.

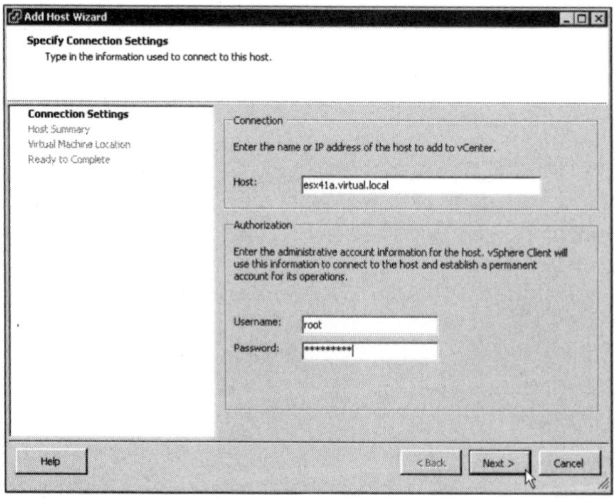

Figure 10-14:
The Add
Host Wizard
dialog box.

4. **Enter the fully qualified host name of the ESX host in the Host field.**

This value is the ESX host's host name followed by its domain.

5. **Enter a root administrator user account name in the Username field.**

   This value is usually provided as "root," but can also be the user name of the additional administrator account created during installation of the ESX host.

6. **Enter the password corresponding to the root administrator user name (provided in the previous step) in the Password field and click Next.**

   This value is the password that goes with the root administrator account provided in the previous step.

   A Security Alert window appears, as shown in Figure 10-15.

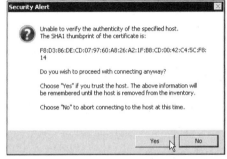

Figure 10-15:
The
Authenticity
Security
Alert
window.

   If the Security Alert window doesn't appear, the ESX host may be unreachable.

   If you're able to connect to the ESX host via a Web browser using the ESX host's IP address but can't connect by using its name, you probably have a DNS-related issue. If you can't connect to the ESX host using its IP address, something is preventing the vCenter Server from communicating with the ESX host. A newly built ESX host unreachable by an IP address usually points to a network configuration error during installation of the ESX host.

7. **Click Yes.**

   The Host Summary dialog box appears.

8. **Click Next.**

   The Assign License dialog box appears, as shown in Figure 10-16.

9. **Select the Assign an Existing License Key to This Host radio button.**

   The license key selection menu appears.

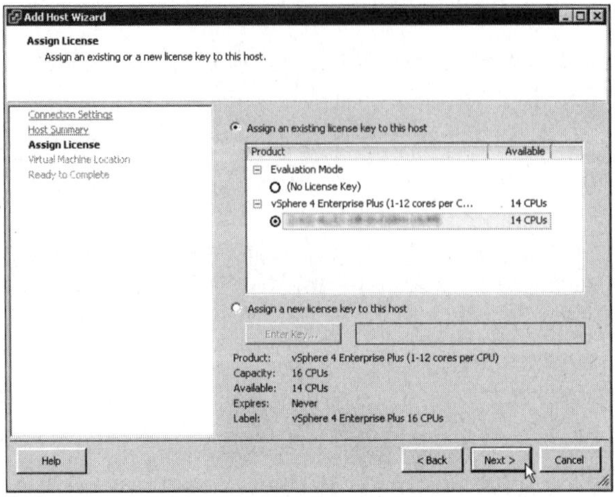

Figure 10-16:
Assign
License
dialog box.

10. **Select the appropriate license key to apply to the ESX host being added to vCenter Server and then click Next.**

    To choose the appropriate license key, select the radio button next to that license key's entry.

11. **In the Ready to Complete dialog box that appears, click Finish.**

    The ESX host is now successfully added to the vCenter server.

Setting up time synchronization on ESX hosts

Configuring each ESX host to automatically synchronize with a Network Time Protocol (NTP) server is another task that makes vSphere management life easier. Setting all your ESX hosts to the same time server ensures that the times and dates on log entries match, a must when trying to troubleshoot a multi-server issue.

Follow these steps to configure an ESX host to synchronize automatically with an Internet-based NTP time server:

1. **Log into vCenter Server using the vSphere Client.**

   The vCenter Server Home Inventory window appears.

2. **Click the ESX host to configure.**

   A series of tabbed pages appear toward the top of the window.

3. **Click the Configuration tab.**

   The ESX Server Configuration window appears, as shown in Figure 10-17.

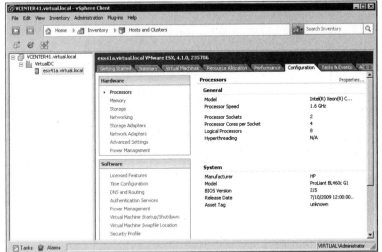

Figure 10-17:
The ESX
Server
Configuration
dialog box.

4. **In the Software submenu, select Time Configuration.**

   The Time Configuration window appears, as shown in Figure 10-18.

Figure 10-18:
The Time
Configuration
window.

5. **Click the Properties link in the Time Configuration section.**

The Time Configuration dialog box appears, as shown in Figure 10-19.

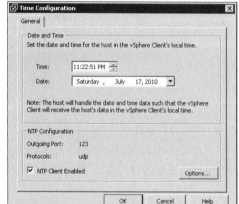

Figure 10-19:
The Time
Configuration
dialog box.

6. **Check the NTP Client Enabled check box in the NTP Configuration
   section.**

This setting activates the NTP client and opens the appropriate ESX
firewall port.

7. **Select the Options button.**

The NTP Daemon (ntpd) Options dialog box appears, as shown in
Figure 10-20.

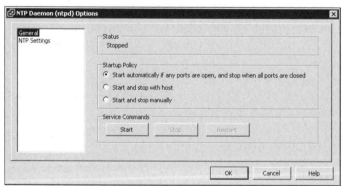

Figure 10-20:
The NTP
Daemon
(ntpd)
Options
dialog box.

8. **Choose NTP Settings from the list on the left side of the dialog box.**

   The NTP Servers list appears, as shown in Figure 10-21.

Figure 10-21:
The NTP
Daemon
(ntpd)
Options
Settings
dialog box.

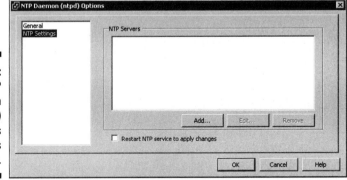

9. **Click Add.**

   The Add NTP Server dialog box appears, as shown in Figure 10-22.

Figure 10-22:
The Add
NTP Server
dialog box.

10. **Enter the name of an NTP server and click OK.**

    This value is the fully qualified name of an NTP server. The server may reside internal to your infrastructure, or it may be external on the public Internet.

    A popular NTP server is `pool.ntp.org` because of its single host name that automatically selects a different NTP server from a pool of NTP servers each time you connect.

    When you click OK, the NTP Daemon (ntpd) Options dialog box reappears, showing the added NTP server.

11. **Click OK.**

    The NTP Client activates and immediately updates the system time. NTP Configuration is complete.

Chapter 11

Wiring Up vSphere to the Network, Virtually

*V*Mware vSphere networking design is one of the most critical architectural decisions you need to make when planning your deployment. In most traditional server implementations, networking is a relatively simple affair. In vSphere, although networking is significantly more involved, with a couple simple tips, it's something that you can do.

This chapter explains several important concepts in networking and illustrates differences between traditional server networking and vSphere networks. You also find out about options in network design and best practices.

Creating a vSwitch

A vSwitch is a logical entity in vSphere that aggregates network traffic and makes the network traffic available to a virtual machine (VM). In past versions of VMware products, only one type of vSwitch was available. In vSphere, now vNetwork Standard Switches (vSS) and vNetwork Distributed Switches (vDS) are available. Standard Switches are individually set up and managed and are available in all editions of vSphere. Distributed Switches are available only in the Enterprise Plus edition, but have many enhancements over Standard Switches.

Creating a vSS using the vSphere Client is easy. In fact, usually the installation automatically creates one for you. Most enterprise installations of vSphere require you to create one or more additional Standard Switches.

To create the vSS, follow these steps:

1. **Connect and log in to the vSphere Client and navigate to the host on which you want to create the vSwitch.**

2. **Choose the Configuration tab and then choose Networking in the Hardware section of the content pane.**

   Figure 11-1 shows the Networking configuration.

3. **Select Add Networking.**

   The Add Networking Wizard appears.

4. **Select Virtual Machine or the appropriate Connection Type in the Add Networking Wizard and click Next.**

   The wizard displays the network adapters and existing vSwitches.

Figure 11-1:
Networking
configuration
of a host.

5. **Ensure Create A Virtual Switch is checked; uncheck any selected network adapters or vSwitches and click Next.**

   The Virtual Machines — Connection Settings wizard page appears. Figure 11-2 shows the Virtual Machines — Network Access page.

6. **In Virtual Machines — Connection Settings, leave the selections at the default settings.**

   The wizard shows information on port groups, which we discuss later in the chapter. The wizard shows the Ready to Complete page and a diagram of the vSwitch configuration.

7. **Click Finish to complete creating a vSwitch.**

Now you have your first vSphere switch, but it's internal to the host. If you connect this vSwitch to two VMs, those two VMs can communicate, but this vSwitch isn't able to communicate with any other devices on the network. Nevertheless, internal vSwitches aren't restricted to a particular speed, so two hosts can communicate over them at speeds in excess of the individual Network Interface Cards (NICs), making them a very useful tool in datacenter configurations such as multi-tiered applications or with firewalls.

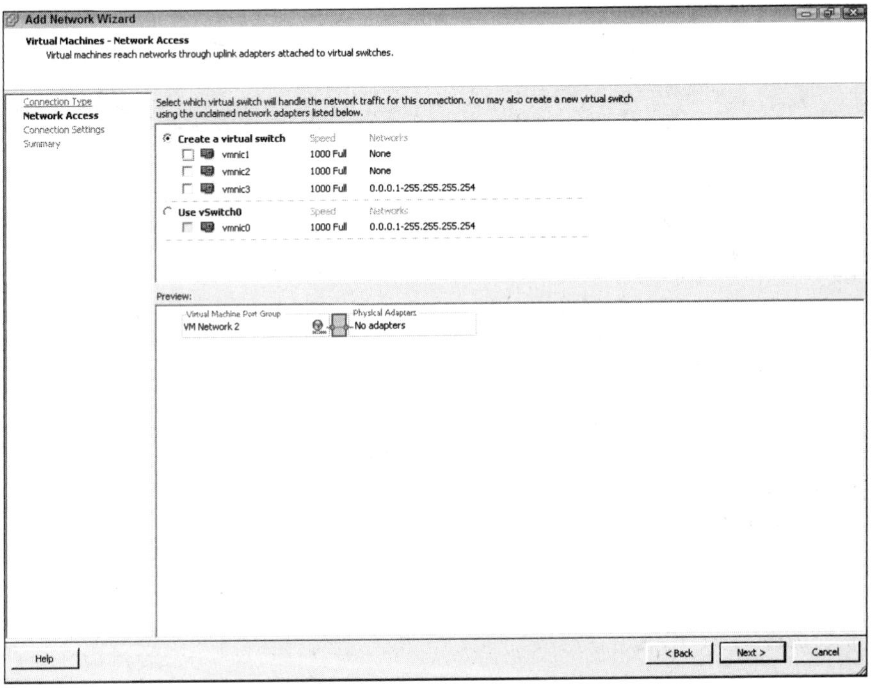

Figure 11-2: The Network Access page shows the physical adapters of the host.

Associating physical NICs to the vSwitch

Internal vSwitches are useful for communication between VMs, but most vSwitches are connected to the physical network to allow communication with other servers and systems. To connect the vSwitch to the physical network, you need to associate a physical NIC to the vSwitch, also called *uplinking*.

To add an uplink to the vSwitch, go to the Networking section of the Configuration tab in the vSphere Client and follow these steps:

1. **Click Properties for the vSwitch you just created (likely named vSwitch1).**

   The Properties window appears.

2. **Choose the Network Adapters tab and click the Add tab.**

   The Add Adapter Wizard appears.

3. **In the Add Adapter Wizard, choose the physical adapter you want to use as the uplink and click Next.**

   The adapters not in use are in the Unclaimed Adapters section, along with information on their speed and which networks they can see according to Cisco Discovery Protocol (CDP), if CDP is available from the connected physical switch. Unless you're doing a major reconfiguration, choose one of these adapters. Figure 11-3 shows the Add Adapter Wizard.

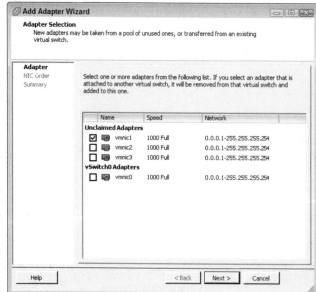

Figure 11-3: The Add Adapter Wizard shows unclaimed physical adapters.

If you choose a physical adapter already in use, it will be removed from the other vSwitch, so be careful here. Removing the uplink that the Service Console uses renders the vSphere host unreachable!

In the Policy Failover window, you can define an order in which the uplinks are used. This is especially important if the adapters are different speeds, as you might want the faster one to be primary.

4. **Click Next.**

5. **In the Summary window, review your selections and click Finish.**

   You now have a vSS that can communicate with the outside world, or at least with the network outside your host!

Configuring NIC teaming and failover

NIC teaming is when two or more NICs team up to provide more bandwidth. NIC teaming allows vSphere to provide more bandwidth into the vSwitch, and it can also provide fault tolerance.

Because users may run ten or more VMs on a single physical server and want the additional bandwidth and availability that teaming can provide, almost all vSphere implementations use NIC teaming. However, depending on your requirements, teaming can also be difficult to set up properly. Your network administrator may be unfamiliar with the unique requirements that vSphere usually requires, so testing in your environment is important.

To configure NIC teaming, you need to add a second uplink to a vSwitch. Follow the instructions in the Associating physical NICs to the vSwitch section to add the second uplink to the vSwitch you created in the Creating a vSwitch section. After you add it, there should be two uplinks attached to that vSwitch, and you next need to configure the teaming.

1. **Choose the vSwitch and click Properties.**

   The Properties window opens.

2. **Click the vSwitch item in the configuration list; then click Edit.**

   A window opens displaying the properties of the vSwitch.

3. **Click the NIC Teaming tab.**

   The window displays the NIC Teaming settings. The Policy Exceptions settings are where most configurations on NIC teaming takes place.

   Load Balancing is where you specify what a vSwitch does with outbound traffic. You can't configure inbound load balancing here, because that must be done at the upstream physical switch, usually by your network team.

4. Choose one of the four options for load balancing.

Which one to use is a very common point of contention among vSphere administrators, network administrators, and occasionally server administrators. The right answer is usually determined by the capabilities of the physical switch hardware and the type of communication you'll usually see between the VMs and other systems. Here are your four options:

- **Route Based on the Originating Port ID:** This option is the default and works with any upstream switch. It simply round-robins based on the virtual port that originated the outbound traffic. This option makes good use of the uplinks, but does not provide a benefit to a VM that talks to many external systems.

- **Route Based on IP Hash:** This option is often used with switch-based inbound load balancing and selects the uplink based on a hash of the source and destination addresses of the packet. It's generally considered the best all-around configuration if the upstream switch can handle it. This option lets a single VM spread across all the uplinks and should not be used with standby uplinks.

  The upstream switch needs to be able to perform the same computation so that the inbound and the outbound traffic flow over the same physical link. Most systems don't like it when they see traffic go out one link and the reply come in through another link.

- **Route Based on Source MAC Hash:** This option is also usually used with switch-based inbound load balancing and selects the uplink based on a hash of the source Ethernet address of the packet. This option behaves similarly to the Route Based on the Originating Port ID option, but you can have an upstream switch perform a similar calculation on inbound traffic. This option is not frequently used.

- **Use Explicit Failover Order:** This option uses the uplink that is at the top of the list until it fails. This option is generally considered the least attractive and provides no performance enhancement.

For all of these choices, vSphere uses the physical NIC only if it is functional. If the physical NIC stops working, vSphere uses another adapter. The Network Failover Detection setting determines how to determine whether an adapter has failed. The default is Link Status Only, which simply relies on the NIC to detect the connection. Link Status Only detects bad cables and down ports on the physical switch, but cannot detect misconfigurations and other upstream issues. Beacon probing sends out periodic probes on the link and listens for replies on the other NIC. Beacon probing can be helpful, especially if you have three or more uplinks. Beacon probing doesn't work reliably when you use the Route

Based On IP Hash load balancing setting, because the upstream switch may not deliver all the packets to all the other NICs. Figure 11-4 shows the NIC Teaming tab with the default selections.

5. **Leave Notify Switches and Failback options, which are simple Yes/No settings, at the default.**

Notify Switches simply tells vSphere to send a message to the upstream switch if a VM's virtual NIC has moved from one physical adapter to another. This option allows the physical switch to update the switching tables and results in the fastest failover. It should be left at the default Yes unless you use a specific host-based load balancing, such as Microsoft Network Load Balancing in unicast mode. Failback is just whether vSphere should move traffic back after a failed link comes on line. While the default of Yes may seem like a no-brainer, many administrators choose to set it to No to ensure that they investigate any failover event and prevent an uplink going between failed and active in the event of an issue that keeps occurring.

The last section on this window is the Active and Standby Adapters.

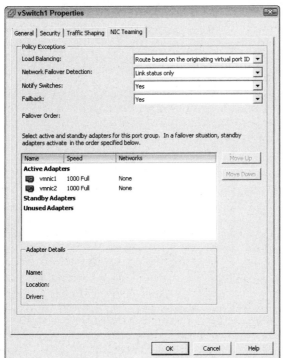

Figure 11-4:
The NIC Teaming tab in the vSwitch properties.

6. **Configure the Active and Standby Adapters to use one as Active and one as Standby.**

   This section lets you set the order of the adapters and whether the adapter should be used all the time or only if an active adapter fails. Most enterprises configure all uplinks to be active, but if you have different speed adapters, you may never want a slower adapter to be used except when a primary fails.

Confirming the connection

After all the wiring, you can step back and see how you're doing. Luckily, in the virtual world, you don't need a wiring permit, and you're unlikely to get electrocuted! The best way to confirm the connections is to connect a VM to the new vSwitch and give it a shot. You can use the same troubleshooting tools you do for a physical server in the VM.

When discussing vSwitches with a network team new to vSphere, often the first concern raised is bridge loops. vSphere networking is a single layer, so you can't create a bridge loop in vSphere by itself. The vSwitches don't participate in Spanning Tree Protocol (STP) and can't be connected to one another. However, if you connect two vSwitches to a VM and do a host-based layer 2 bridge, you can create a bridge loop. A bridge loop is not something that can occur by accident, and in this regard, vSphere is no different from any physical host with more than one NIC.

Creating Port Groups on a vSwitch

Most companies use Virtual Local Area Networks (VLANs) to separate broadcast domains and organize the network. In vSphere, it's common to have a single vSwitch for VM traffic and have multiple VLANs use it, which is accomplished by using port groups. In fact, the moment you create the vSwitch (see the section "Creating a vSwitch," earlier in this chapter), vSphere automatically creates a port group!

To create another port group:

1. **Click Properties for the vSwitch you want to create the port group on and click the Add button.**

   The Add Network Wizard window appears.

2. **Choose the connection type of Virtual Machine and click Next.**

   The Virtual Machines — Connection Settings page appears.

3. **Name the Port Group.**

   If you're using vMotion or Distributed Resource Scheduler (DRS), which is detailed in Chapter 13, make this name consistent across a cluster.

4. **In the VLAN ID (Optional) setting, enter the VLAN number, usually assigned by your network administrator, and click Next.**

   This number, referred to as Virtual Switch Tagging (VST), must match the one on the physical switch and is the most common way of using VLANs with vSphere.

5. **Review the changes on the Ready To Complete page and then click Finish.**

6. **Close the properties window of the vSwitch to which you added the port group.**

Associating port groups with VLANs

Each port group can be associated with only one VLAN. You can change the VLAN number by choosing the port group in the vSwitch properties and editing it. Keep in mind that doing so can disrupt network traffic if a VM uses that port group.

A common naming convention is critical when using a vSphere cluster. When you move a VM from one host to another, vSphere expects names to match. A live migration using vMotion isn't possible if the appropriate vSwitch or port group doesn't exist on the destination host.

Using a port group without VLAN tagging

Port groups are most often associated with VLANs, but they don't have to be. In some environments, all tagging is done in the external switch so that they are all configured to use VLAN 0. This is called *External Switch Tagging* (EST), and in this case, you need many network adapters because not each vSwitch participates in the tagging.

Another option is Virtual Guest Tagging (VGT), which relies on the guest to add the VLAN in the network properties. To use VGT, you must set the port group that the VM uses to VLAN 4095. This mode is useful if you already use host-based VLANs on the physical network and want to continue doing so with vSphere.

Adding a Management Network Port

The management network connection, also known as the Service Console connection in ESX, is pretty important. All service console connections are a type of management network, so we use the term management network to mean both. It's how you manage the vSphere host, so you may want to make sure that it doesn't go down. Also, when using High Availability (HA), the management network port is especially important, because it's used to keep track of whether the host is up. So, having redundancy for your host management is important.

Most of the same methods you employed for VM Network changes work for the management network. It's wise to ensure that there are two uplinks from the vSwitch to the physical switch for the vSwitch that the management network uses. Additionally, many administrators like to create an additional management network port to another physical switch. Doing so enables you to protect host management from an upstream switch failure, and even to put a second management network connection on a completely different VLAN. To put the management network on a completely different VLAN, complete the following steps:

1. **In the vSphere Client, go to the Configuration tab and choose Networking.**

2. **Click Add Networking.**

   The Add Network Wizard appears.

3. **Choose the appropriate connection type and click Next.**

   If you're running ESX, you must choose Service Console. If you're running ESXi, you don't have the option to choose Service Console. Choose the VMkernel connection type if you're using ESXi.

4. **In the Network Access page, select Create A Virtual Switch.**

5. **Choose an appropriate uplink based on your network configuration and click Next.**

6. **In the Connection Settings page, enter a label for the port group and VLAN ID, if necessary, and click Next.**

7. **Enter the appropriate IP settings on the IP Connection Settings page.**

   Note that while you can put the Management Network on a different VLAN, you can have only a single default gateway for the connection. Figure 11-5 shows the IP Connection Settings window of the additional management network connection.

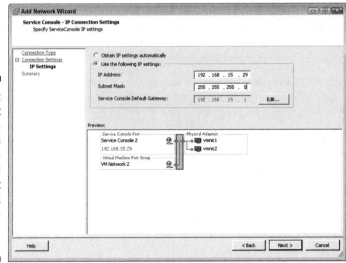

Figure 11-5:
You must enter the IP settings for the additional management network connection when you create it.

In ESX, the Service Console virtual Ethernet adapter is called a `vswif`. If you use the command line, each Service Console virtual Ethernet adapter begins with `vswif`, starting with `vswif0`. ESXi uses a VMkernel connection for management.

8. **Test connectivity by attempting to connect to the new IP address you have set for the management network using the vSphere Client.**

Also, on ESX, if you're familiar with command-line interfaces, you can log in to the host console and use the ping command. This is a standard implementation of the common networking troubleshooting tool, ping.

Adding a VMkernel Port

A VMkernel port is used for several functions, including vMotion, Network File System (NFS) connectivity, and software iSCSI connectivity. VMkernel ports are logical connections that reside right in the base hypervisor.

To add a VMkernel port, in the vSphere Client, go to the Add Network Wizard and follow these steps:

1. **In the Connection Type page, select the VMkernel option and click Next.**

2. **In the VMkernel — Network Access page, choose an existing vSwitch or create a new one and click Next.**

   You'll want to choose one that has external connectivity, as almost all VMkernel connections need access to other devices on the network.

3. **Label the Port Group and choose a VLAN in the VMkernel — Network Settings Wizard page and click Next.**

Enabling vMotion

One of the most common uses of a VMkernel network adapter is for vMotion. To enable vMotion, you can select the Use This Port Group for vMotion check box in the VMkernel — Network Settings dialog box.

The Use This Port Group for Fault Tolerance Logging check box is for setting up a host to be able to use VMware Fault Tolerance (FT). While you can enable both vMotion and FT on the same port group, doing so can cause problems. Both vMotion and FT are intensive network consumers, so they ought to have a minimum of a dedicated 1 gigabit per second (Gbps), connection. In most cases, for any more than a single FT VM, you want to dedicate a 10 Gbps Ethernet link for FT logging. Figure 11-6 shows the settings where you can enable vMotion on a VMkernel connection.

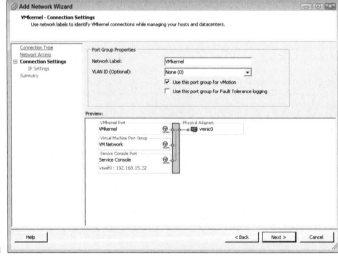

Figure 11-6: Check the vMotion check box to allow a port group to be used for vMotion.

To configure the network settings, in the VMkernel — IP Connection Settings dialog box, enter the appropriate IP address information. Often, VMkernel connections are for special use, so you may not need to assign a default gateway if the traffic should not be routed.

To confirm a VMkernel connection, connect a laptop or other machine to the network segment and ping other addresses you expect you should be able to, such as a default gateway or other highly available address.

Another option is to log in to the host console if you're using ESX, and use the vmkping command. This vSphere-specific command lets you do a standard ping test from the VMkernel port. It differs from the ping command you used to test the Service Console in that it exclusively uses the VMkernel port.

Adding a vNetwork Distributed Virtual Switch

A vNetwork Distributed Switch is a new feature in vSphere that is available only in the Enterprise Plus edition. vDS have several enhancements over vNetwork Standard Switches. A vDS is designed to be on multiple hosts and also provides more fine-grained control over traffic, better VM state management, and the ability to control how much bandwidth each connection type can use.

Most of the action in this chapter has been at the host level, but you define a vDS in vCenter at the datacenter level. By defining it at the datacenter, you can assign the VDS to any host in the datacenter.

Here's how you create a vDS:

1. **In the vSphere Client, choose Home➪Networking to go to the networking page in the Inventory group of icons.**

2. **Right-click the datacenter in which you plan to create the vDS and choose New vNetwork Distributed Switch.**

    The Create vNetwork Distributed Switch Wizard appears.

    If you're using vCenter 4.1, the wizard prompts you for which version of vDS to use.

3. **If all the hosts to which you'll connect the vDS are running vSphere 4.1, choose the vNetwork Distributed Switch Version: 4.1.0 option; otherwise, choose the vNetwork Distributed Switch Version 4.0.**

   Version 4.1 vDS support Network I/O Control and Load-Based Teaming, new features that allow much more control over the bandwidth allocation that individual port groups can use. You can always upgrade the vDS, but you can't downgrade it.

4. **Click Next.**

5. **In the General Properties page, name the vDS, set the maximum number of uplink ports the vDS can have, and then click Next.**

   Not all of the hosts attached to the vDS need to use the same number of ports.

   The Add Hosts And Physical Adapters appears.

6. **Choose either to assign physical adapters to a vDS or do it later and then click Next.**

   Choosing to do so later can be valuable if you have not yet configured the physical uplinks or if you have multiple vDS to create.

   The Ready to Complete page, which shows you a diagram of the vDS, appears.

7. **Leave the Automatically Create A Default Port Group check box selected and click Finish.**

   This option is useful for simple configurations. However, because many enterprises that use the vSphere Enterprise Plus edition have more complicated requirements, most of the time, you'll uncheck this option. But for the purposes of this set of steps, you leave this option checked.

Attaching hosts to the vDS

A vDS must be attached to a host before the VMs on that host can use it. When you attach a vDS, you'll need to select which physical adapters will be the uplinks for the vDS.

To attach a host to a vDS, follow these steps:

1. **Choose Home⇨Networking to change the vSphere Client to focus on networking and then click the switch name in the navigation pane at the left of the window.**

2. **In the Getting Started tab, under Basic Tasks, click Add A Host.**

   The Add Host To vNetwork Distributed Switch Wizard appears. This page provides a consolidated list of hosts and physical adapters, as shown in Figure 11-7. Similar to assigning a physical adapter from one vSwitch to another, choosing an adapter already in use removes it from the existing switch and attaches it to the target vDS.

3. **Select the hosts and which physical adapters to use for uplinks.**

   When you have many hosts, you may not know which adapter you need to use. For details on the physical adapter, click View Details.

4. **After selecting the host and the adapters you need to use, click Next.**

   The Network Connectivity page appears, allowing you to migrate the virtual adapters to the new vDS.

   Be careful if you are changing the Service Console adapters, which begin with `vswif`. If the uplinks don't work and you don't have multiple adapters to the Service Console, you can render the host unmanageable until you fix it from the console command line. Because often they don't need the advanced features of vDS for these connections, many administrators keep management network and VMkernel connections on standard vSwitches.

5. **Select the virtual adapters to migrate and then click Next.**

   The Virtual Machine Networking page appears, enabling you to migrate virtual machines to the new vDS.

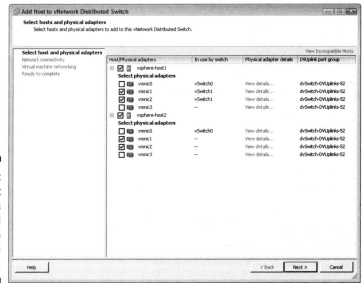

Figure 11-7:
Select which hosts and physical adapters to attach to the vDS.

Completing a vDS migration

Now that we've teased you about how to do a standard vSwitch to vDS migration without downtime, here's how you do the migration: If you have a standard switch with two uplinks, you can grab one of the uplinks from the vSS when you assign the vDS to the host. Then you can migrate the VMs over to the vDS. You'll probably lose a packet or so, but any traffic over Transmission Control Protocol (TCP) will handle minimal packet loss gracefully. After you've vacated the standard switch, you can move the uplink to the vDS and destroy the standard vSwitch. Naturally, this migration is something to perfect in the lab first!

6. **After choosing the virtual machines to migrate, click Next.**

   This migration window is helpful in cases where you're confident in your networking configuration team; however, in most cases, we recommend that, if you choose to migrate a VM here, you choose a test VM. Later, after you're confident in the networking implementation, you can do a migration, often without downtime!

7. **The last page of the wizard appears, where you review your choices and see a graphical presentation of the configuration you have created.**

   vDS are more complex than standard switches, so you should review this window carefully. A simple configuration is shown in Figure 11-8.

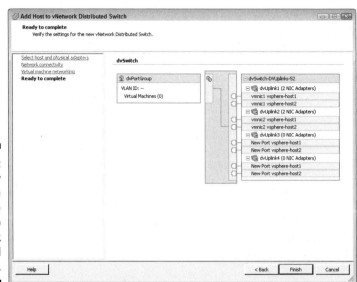

Figure 11-8: The Ready to Complete page of the Add Host to vNetwork Distributed Switch.

Configuring VLANs

VLANs in vDS work the same as a standard switch. You create a port group in the vDS by clicking Create a New Port Group in the Getting Started tab. The wizard is similar, but you have a couple of new options on VLAN Type:

- **None** is used if there is no VLAN information associated with the port group.

- **VLAN** is a similar setting to VST tagging on standard vSwitch port groups. You need to enter a number that matches the VLAN used on the physical switch.

- **VLAN Trunking** is similar to VGT and is used when you tag the VLANs inside the guest VMs. If you select this option, enter all the VLAN numbers for which you expect the vDS to forward traffic.

- **Private VLAN** is a setting used for security conscious environments that want to implement a layer 2-based security so that two VMs on the same vDS can't communicate with each other.

Configuring Network I/O Control

Network I/O Control (NetIOC) is a new feature in vSphere 4.1 that allows an administrator fine-grained control over different traffic all flowing over the same vDS. While you can use this feature with any sort of uplink, its real intent is for servers that have few high bandwidth connections, such as a server with two 10 Gbps links. This capability enables an administrator to carve up the link and still ensure that the different needs are provided for.

Like most performance guarantees in vSphere, NetIOC doesn't come into play until a network link is saturated. Once the link is saturated, NetIOC uses shares to determine the splits.

NetIOC characterizes traffic into six different Network Resource Pools, as shown here:

- FT Traffic
- iSCSI Traffic
- vMotion Traffic
- Management Traffic
- NFS Traffic
- Virtual Machine Traffic

If you have three Network Resource Pools, and one, Virtual Machine Traffic, has 100 shares and the other two have 50 each, when the network becomes saturated, the vDS will allocate 50 percent of the bandwidth to the virtual machines and 25 percent to each of the other Network Resource Pools.

You can enable NetIOC by going to the vDS and clicking the Resource Allocation tab. If that tab isn't present, you likely have a vNetwork Distributed Switch Version 4.0. You can upgrade it by selecting the Summary tab and clicking Upgrade. A wizard opens and checks compatibility, and you can follow it to finish the upgrade.

If the vDS is at version 4.1, you click Properties in the Resource Allocation tab and select the Enable Network I/O Control On This vDS check box.

After NetIOC is enabled, it has a default set of share values set. To modify them, right-click the Network Resource Pool and choose Edit Settings. Enter the appropriate settings for the physical adapter shares and host limit into the dialog box, as shown in Figure 11-9.

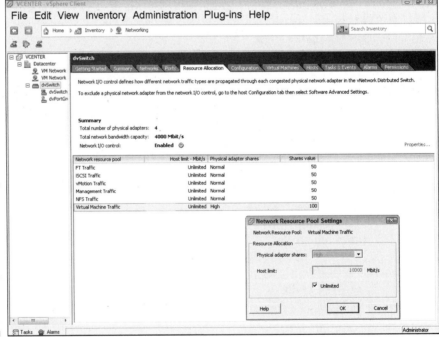

Figure 11-9:
The vSphere Client showing the Resource Allocation tab and Network Resource Pool settings.

Troubleshooting vSphere Networking

vSphere networking is much more complex than networking traditional servers, so making an error is easy to do. Luckily, many of the wizards used in this chapter ensure that you can't do anything outright wrong, but some areas can still sneak up on you.

Many of the common configuration mistakes happen when typos occur in VLAN settings or vSwitch names. These mistakes are especially common in situations where many servers are in a cluster and they're configured with vSS. Because they all must match to allow DRS and vMotion to function, you must ensure accuracy when creating the vSS.

Many problematic issues are related to the uplinks. If you forget a configuration setting, such as configuring the physical switch to trunk the appropriate VLANs, the problem can be especially confusing to troubleshoot.

You need to make sure that you can test the network aggressively before putting production traffic on the vSphere host. We highly suggest using a test VM that you can put on a VLAN and then test each host. Then move the VM from host to host and confirm all of them. You may need to test several VLANs, because it's not uncommon for large enterprises to use dozens of different VLANs.

vSphere is able to tell you if a link is up or down, so as you create the network design, it's good to pay attention to the vSphere Client. The client provides information if a physical adapter is down or set to the wrong speed.

Chapter 12

Connecting vSphere to Shared Storage

*V*Mware vSphere Storage is the foundation of your virtualized environment. Like vSphere Networking, vSphere places unusual burdens on storage because multiple virtual machines (VMs) all must share the same physical connections. Storage for vSphere can be local to an individual host, or it can be shared across several hosts. Most organizations use shared storage to hold the VM data files. With shared storage, multiple vSphere hosts can access the same data, allowing many killer app features of vSphere, such as vMotion. This chapter explains the many different options you have when setting up shared storage and the advantages and disadvantages of each.

Getting Familiar with vSphere Storage

After installing vSphere, a partition is often automatically created on the local hard drives that can be used for VM storage. Many vSphere administrators don't use this partition because they use shared storage and implement policies that all VMs should reside on shared storage.

If administrators go through all that trouble, then shared storage must be pretty great, right? Well, only if you want to be able to take advantage of almost any of the major features regarding performance or availability that vSphere provides!

Interpreting vSphere storage device naming

vSphere has to keep track of a lot of storage. In a large configuration, a single host can have access to 256 VMFS volumes and 64 NFS volumes! So, to manage this, vSphere assigns names to the storage devices. These names are complex, but unique. When you create a volume or connect to an NFS export, you can also name the storage. Make sure that you have a good naming convention before you start, because it can get confusing fast!

Whenever you deal with storage, remember that storage is usually absolute. When you make changes at a low level to disks, there is no Recycle Bin that provides recovery. Be careful here, as most of the configuration in this chapter can profoundly modify data; if you perform an operation on an unintended target, you may not be able to recover from the damage.

vSphere storage options include

- ✔ Virtual Machine File System (VMFS)
- ✔ Network File System (NFS)

VMware Virtual Machine File System

In many operating systems, such as Microsoft Windows, you can't natively share a file system across multiple hosts. Special configurations, such as clusters, create unique file system filters to allow multiple servers to see the same disk, but even then they usually don't allow multiple servers to read and write to the same disk. vSphere uses Virtual Machine File System (VMFS), a proprietary clustered file system that allows many hosts to mount the same disk and use it. Any volume mapped to an ESX or ESXi host is called a datastore.

VMFS is used by many companies running vSphere. Custom-designed by VMware for virtualization, VMFS provides the best performance and features for storage and execution of VMs and snapshots of VMs.

VMFS allows up to 64 hosts to access the same volume. In practice, 64 hosts would be very unlikely because the hosts must contend with one another when performing some operations, such as power on and changes to a VM, so you usually don't want so many hosts to have access to the same volume.

VMFS doesn't have to actually lock the file system often. When it does, VMFS uses something called a Small Computer System Interface (SCSI) reservation. A *SCSI reservation* is a brief time when a single host has complete control of the volume — for example, vSphere issues SCSI reservations when you power up a VM or create, delete, or change the name or size of a file. Because thin-provisioned files grow, using thin provisioning can increase the amount of SCSI reservations. SCSI reservations can reduce performance, so it is wise not to put too many VMs on a single datastore. In vSphere 4.1, some arrays provide a plugin called a vStorage API for Array Integration (VAAI). A VAAI improves performance by offloading several functions to the array, and also reduces the need for SCSI reservations.

Because VMFS was designed for holding whole virtual machines, it supports large files and large volumes. Volumes can be up to 64TB , but they're never that big because of performance and some limits by the SCSI protocol. The file size limit in VMFS is 262,144 blocks, and a block can be either 1, 2, 4, or 8MB. This translates to maximum file sizes of 256GB, 512GB, 1TB, and about 2TB. The 2TB size is very slightly less than 2TB, because 512 bytes is used by some metadata and the SCSI command set.

When you create a VMFS, you must choose the block size. Once you choose, you can't change it without destroying and reformatting the volume, so choose wisely. There are no performance advantages or penalties to any particular size. The block size is usually dictated by the size of the volume you are creating and the size of the Virtual Machine Disk Format (VMDK) files you plan to put on the volume. For example, if you're creating 750GB volumes, you may choose a 2MB block size or even a 4MB size, but an 8MB size would be unnecessary. However, you can grow the VMFS, so you may want to consider growth in your plans.

In older versions of VMFS, choosing a big block size had a serious disadvantage. Any small file would take up a whole block. So, with a 1MB block size, a tiny configuration file would take up 1MB. In the version of VMFS that is included with vSphere 4, sub-block allocation is performed, meaning that small files are stored in 64K sections of the disk. So, you can safely choose an 8MB block size, and small files will be stored in the special small file area of the file system.

VMware administrators can spend hours debating the block size question. There are almost no disadvantages to using one of the larger block sizes, so we recommend that you simply go with the maximum. Doing so gives you the greatest flexibility in the future, and you'll be prepared for the rapid adoption of vSphere that most organizations experience.

Network File System

Network File System (NFS) is a protocol developed by Sun Microsystems for sharing files over the network. NFS is usually used by UNIX and UNIX-like systems, but it's defined in Internet Request For Comments (RFCs), so many platforms and products can use it. This flexibility is why a growing number of administrators use NFS for their primary VM storage.

Also, NFS can be easier to manage than other storage technologies. Usually, for complex storage designs, an organization will need a dedicated storage administrator, but NFS is often managed by the server administrators. NFS can also be a great way to try out the capabilities of vSphere because it works with vMotion, Distributed Resource Scheduler, and most of the other vSphere features.

The NFS protocol doesn't specify the underlying file system, but rather how it is accessed over the network. Originally, use of NFS was seen as a lower performance option for nonproduction systems and desktop VMs, but now it's commonly used for production server VMs. Servers providing NFS access often have other powerful features, such as advanced replication and the ability to deduplicate data, making NFS a welcome option to the vSphere suite of protocols.

NFS is also often called Network Attached Storage (NAS). Almost all NFS implementations use the network, so they're limited by that network's throughput. In many cases, the bandwidth can be less than competing technologies, but with 10Gbps Ethernet, that gap is closing. In vSphere, you can have 64 NFS mounts (volumes) per host, and the size of the NFS volume is determined by the NFS server that provides the export.

Deciding on Disk

There are several options for disks that you can use for a VM, and it is important to understand how you can use them. VMs usually have one or more hard drives, but they can be mapped to different locations:

- ✔ **VMDK:** VMware Disk Format (VMDK) files are disks attached to the VM, and are files that reside on a VMFS datastore. The VMDK can be up to about 2TB, and VMDKs support snapshots, a copy on write technology that vSphere provides, as well as allows migration of the VMDK amongst datastores and hosts using vMotion.

✔ **Raw Device Mapping:** RDM allows a VM to connect to a SAN LUN directly. Originally, that meant that you had to give up all the goodness that a VMDK provides, such as vMotion and snapshots, but that is no longer the case. RDMs come in two types:

- *Physical compatibility mode RDMs* provide access to the hardware directly, without any involvement from vSphere. With physical compatibility mode, also known as pass-through RDMs, the storage array sees the VM like any other physical server, and any applications that must communicate to the array will work. Features such as snapshots, clones, or vMotion don't work with physical compatibility mode RDMs, although your array may be able to provide some of those services.

- *Virtual compatibility mode RDMs* abstract the raw device a bit and allow the advanced features of vSphere, such as cloning, snapshots, and vMotion. Virtual compatibility RDMs are also known as non-pass-through RDMS.

All RDMs use a mapping file, usually stored on the disk with the VM configuration file. This mapping file contains the data that the VM uses to keep track of the associated RDM disks.

When VMware first introduced RDMs, they often had to be used for high performance I/O workloads. Now, the performance characteristics of RDMs are indistinguishable from the performance of VMDK files. The choice is usually based on individual preference, but we recommend using VMDK files in almost all situations. Situations that require RDMs are often related to guest based clustering, specific storage environments, or cases where an existing SAN LUN was already present, and it does not make sense to copy the data into a VMDK.

Sizing Up vSphere Storage Options

vSphere supports so many options for storage that making sense of what is best for you can be difficult. Luckily, vSphere also has several ways to ease migration of VMs across storage platforms and technologies if you need to migrate from one technology to another:

✔ **Local storage:** *Local storage* is the internal disk attached to the server. Usually, this disk contains the Service Console but no other VMs. In many cases, this disk can be quite small, as the local disk is often a small mirrored drive, often as small as 50GB. In some standalone installations, a large, dedicated Redundant Array of Inexpensive Disks (RAID) is used, and all disks inside the server is considered local storage. When you install ESX or ESXi on the host, the installer automatically creates a local VMFS volume. Most of the time, you don't need to configure or modify anything on local storage, so we don't elaborate too much on local storage.

✔ **Fibre Channel (FC):** FC is a storage protocol that extends the SCSI command set over longer distances. For some time, it was the de facto standard of SANs, and it continues to be widely used.

FC is complex to configure and supports many physical form factors and topologies. It can signal at 1, 2, 4, and 8 gigabit per second (Gbps), with faster versions on the roadmap for the future. FC SANs are connected to FC Host Bus Adapters (HBAs), and servers commonly have at least two HBAs to allow for redundant pathways.

✔ **Internet SCSI (iSCSI):** iSCSI is a newer protocol that allows the SCSI protocol stack to travel over basic IP connections. iSCSI allows a lower cost alternative to FC solutions, while preserving many of the FC protocol features. iSCSI SANs are growing in market share every year and have become the standard in smaller to mid-range deployments.

✔ **Network-attached storage:** NAS is popular with organizations of all sizes and eliminates several of the limitations of SAN protocols. Best of all, it's often easier than SAN to configure! NAS solutions are also valuable because they can greatly simplify the backup design.

Mounting a NAS export on another device is easy, and then you can use any backup solution that supports open files to back it up. Easy backups of NAS volumes can increase the efficiency and reliability of your environment.

SANs versus NAS

Is NAS just SAN backwards? No, these are different terms for different access methodologies. SAN is *block-based,* meaning the storage is presented as a disk like any other storage device, such as a traditional internal disk. The operating system must put a SAN volume to use with a file system of some sort. NAS differs from SAN because in NAS, the key access unit is the file. The file system is behind the scenes, but not controlled by the operating system. So, both FC and iSCSI are SAN technologies, because they're both block-based, and NFS is a NAS technology. Got It? Good, because to confuse things further, there are also NAS gateways, where you use SAN to present FC or iSCSI volumes to a device. That device puts a file system on a SAN volume, and makes it available to the network as NAS!

Configuring Fibre Channel SAN Storage

Fibre Channel is considered one of the more complicated storage technologies to configure, but most of that complexity is in the SAN network, also known as a fabric. The connection to vSphere is relatively straightforward, but setting up a working, redundant SAN is a daunting task, not covered in this book. For more information on SAN design and concepts, please reference *Storage Area Networks For Dummies,* 2nd Edition (Wiley) by Christopher Poelker and Alex Nikitin.

Because FC was the first shared storage protocol supported by VMware, you'll find that the other protocols follow the same basic constructs.

In Fibre Channel parlance, the host uses an HBA to connect to a port on the array, also called a *target.* The host ports are called *initiators,* and generally, in the FC fabric, an administer configures the SAN so that a single initiator can see only a single target on the SAN. Configuring the SAN in this way is called *zoning.*

Every device connecting to a SAN has a hardware address called a World Wide Name (WWN).

Attaching the Logical Unit Numbers to vSphere hosts

A *Logical Unit Number* (LUN) is a designation of an exported volume from an array. It's not exactly a number — it's more like a complex identifier — but it's considered synonymous to an exported disk. So, a storage administrator might say, "I'll carve the array into some LUNs for you." Each LUN is specific between the array and the host, so for an array with 10 hosts, each with one LUN, the array will usually export 10 LUNs each as LUN ID 1.

When building a cluster, each of the vSphere hosts should have access to the same storage. Although not strictly necessary, each vSphere host should also have the same LUN ID so that each volume is presented consistently to each of the hosts.

To present a disk, first make sure that it's presented by the array to the host. Then complete the following steps after logging into the vSphere client:

1. **Go to the host Configuration tab, Storage Adapters, and click Rescan All in the upper-right corner of the Storage Adapters panel**.

    The Rescan dialog box, shown in Figure 12-1, appears.

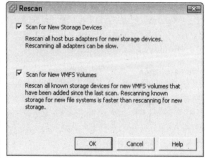

2. **Ensure that both the Scan for New Storage Devices and Scan for New VMFS Volumes check boxes are selected and then click OK to begin the rescan.**

   The rescan can take several minutes. When the host finds the FC LUN, the LUN appears in the Details panel.

3. **Ensure that the Devices button is selected and then click the LUN column to sort.**

   If the LUN you were expecting does not show up, ensure that the zoning is correct and the array is presenting the LUN to the host.

After the disk is seen by the host, you need to format it as VMFS to make it usable. Formatting as VMFS is covered later in the chapter in the "Preparing LUN-Based SAN Storage for First Use" section.

Setting the path selection policy

Fibre Channel is almost always set up with redundant connections. A connection may go through several FC switches before reaching the array, and the way the traffic flows is called a *path*. Often, but not always, there is one FC path per connection to the fabric.

When setting up a datastore, you need to choose a *path selection policy*. Path selection policies are contained in Path Selection Plugins (PSP). Three PSPs are available in vSphere, and third parties can create them as well:

✔ **VMW_PSP_MRU — Most Recently Used Path Selection:** This PSP is used for Arrays that aren't Active/Active. Active/Active arrays can service any request from any node on the array. Active/Passive arrays cannot service requests from any node on the array, so this PSP is ideal for Active/Passive arrays. Most Recently Used PSP will continue to use a particular path until that path is unavailable. If a path becomes unavailable, Most Recently Used switches to an alternative path, and will always use that until that path becomes unavailable. Most Recently Used doesn't failback automatically.

✔ **VMW_PSP_FIXED — Fixed Path Selection:** This PSP is commonly used on Active/Active arrays. Fixed Path Selection uses a preferred path if one has been configured; if one hasn't been configured, Fixed Path Selection uses the first discovered path. It will use this path until it becomes unavailable and then will randomly choose an alternate working path. When the original path becomes available again, the Fixed Path Selection PSP switches back to it.

With a Fixed Path Selection, you can manually create a load balance for your vSphere hosts, allowing fine-grained control over the I/O profile for a host, but you must manually configure the paths.

✔ **VMW_PSP_RR — Round Robin Path Selection:** In vSphere 4.0, VMware introduced Round Robin path selection in a fully supported way to reduce the manual configuration associated with Fixed Path for Active/Active arrays. Round Robin rotates across all working paths, enabling load balancing to the storage array. You can also use Round Robin with Active/Passive arrays, and it will round robin through all paths connected to the active node. Round Robin is not supported by VMware for use with Microsoft Clusters because clusters are very sensitive to the changing storage performance that a Round Robin path selection may have.

VMware maintains a list of certified arrays, and vSphere will automatically choose Most Recently Used or Fixed Path selections when the array is connected. If you have multiple hosts accessing a datastore, you must configure all of them with the same Path Selection Policy.

Selecting the wrong path policy can have a disastrous effect on your environment. It can result in poor performance or even cause array nodes to fail. Discuss any change to path selection in depth with the array vendor and the person or team administering it before making changes.

To use Round Robin or change from what vSphere has selected, follow these steps:

1. **Open the vSphere Client and choose the host on which you want to manage paths.**

2. **Click the Configuration tab; then in the far-left panel, click Storage Adapters.**

   The Storage Adapters Configuration view appears, as shown in Figure 12-2. This view lists all the storage adapters accessible to the host.

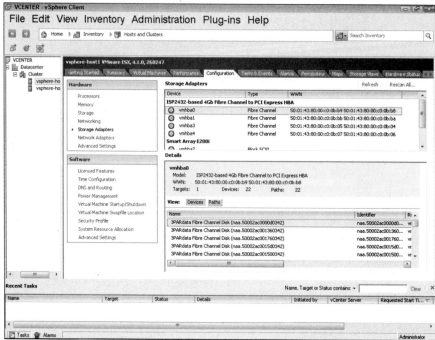

Figure 12-2:
Fibre
Channel
storage
adapters.

3. **Click the adapter name.**

   The content pane shows information such as the HBA model, the WWN, and how many devices and paths the adapter can see.

4. **Choose the Devices view in the Details panel.**

   This step accesses the disk devices the adapter can communicate with.

5. **Choose the LUN for which you want to change the Path Selection Policy.**

   You can sort by LUN number to easily find the exact volume.

6. **Under the Name heading, right-click the device name and choose Manage Paths.**

   The Manage Paths window opens, as shown in Figure 12-3. At the top, under Policy, you see the Path Selection drop-down menu.

7. **Choose Round Robin (VMware) and click Change.**

8. **Click Close to exit the Manage Paths dialog box.**

The change you just made changes the Path Selection Policy for one datastore on one host. To take advantage of the change, the policy should be the same for all host/path combinations. A host can use more than one path selection policy, but each datastore should have only one policy that is the same for all hosts that access it.

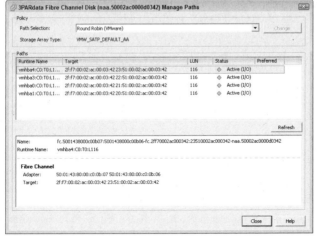

Figure 12-3:
The Fibre
Channel
Manage
Paths
window.

Optimizing FC SAN performance

To optimize FC SAN performance, often you'll want several connections into the fabric. Where a single traditional server may never need more than the usual two FC connections, a vSphere host may often require more FC connections. Disk performance is often critical to the performance of the vSphere environment, so it's best to build a LUN with many disk drives backing it.

Often, for best performance, the Round Robin Path Selection Policy can meet your needs. Sometimes, with an Active/Active array, the Fixed Path Selection may be better with manual preferred path selection.

To change the preferred path, follow Steps 1 through 6 in the preceding section, "Setting the Path Selection Policy." These steps open the Manage Paths window. With the Path Selection to Fixed, right-click the path you want to make preferred and choose Preferred from the menu that appears. Remember that this changes one host, and when setting paths manually, you need to consider the load profile of the VMS and balance the preferred paths across the ports of the array as well as the host HBAs. Usually, on a big environment, it is wise to draw a detailed diagram to plan the paths accurately.

You can add more FC SAN space to a vSphere host by adding datastores, as shown in the earlier section, "Attaching the Logical Unit Numbers to vSphere hosts." Because vSphere allows up to 256 LUNs per host, many designs use dozens of LUNs.

Avoiding common configuration errors

Most configurations regarding FC storage are in the fabric, rather than the vSphere host. Zoning is complex, and most arrays have other security built in, such as LUN masking, which allows only the hosts that are defined in the array to see a particular LUN. Generally, if you can't see a volume you expected, begin with the fabric and the array.

Many vSphere hosts may have several HBA ports, but not all of them may be connected. Be sure you're looking at the correct HBA, as sometimes the one you're looking at isn't connected.

Configuring Internet SCSI SAN Storage

iSCSI is becoming more and more common in large datacenters. This type of storage can provide similar performance as FC, but at a lower cost. Because both FC and iSCSI are rooted in the SCSI protocol, they share similar features, with one important difference — iSCSI runs on top of standard Transmission Control Protocol (TCP) traffic and can share the same IP network as the data.

Just because iSCSI can run over the same network as data doesn't mean it's a good idea. Most iSCSI implementations use a dedicated set of physical switches, which are often managed jointly between the network and storage administrators. iSCSI is often more demanding than standard network traffic and may require special design consideration. Many failed implementations of iSCSI result simply from putting it on the same network as the data traffic.

Understanding Internet SCSI Naming

iSCSI uses many of the same concepts and names as FC, such as initiator and target. However, because iSCSI is going over normal IP networks, it uses specific names for the connections, called *iSCSI Qualified Names* (IQN).

An IQN has a bunch of information so that it is unique, and it usually looks a bit funny to humans. An example of an IQN is `iqn.1998-01.`

`com.vmware:localhost-60fc871a`, and it contains the reversed domain name of the authority using the iSCSI connection, here `com.vmware`, the date the authority registered the Domain Name System (DNS) name, such as `1998-01`, as well as some information defined by the naming authority, often including a number designed to be unique.

Comparing hardware versus software iSCSI initiators

vSphere supports both hardware- and software-based initiators. A hardware initiator makes the connection to the iSCSI target outside the vSphere software. Software initiators are inside the vSphere hypervisor. Generally, like most things, performance of the hardware initiators can be better, but they aren't as easy to configure. The performance gap has almost closed in vSphere, however, because it can take advantage of any hardware acceleration built into the Network Interface Card (NIC).

So why use a hardware initiator? So that you can boot your host from the iSCSI SAN or, if you don't or can't configure the vSwitch, to allow iSCSI VMkernel traffic. Hardware initiators show up as storage adapters and are configured just like the software initiator.

Enabling the iSCSI initiator on a vSphere host

The first thing you need in order to use the iSCSI software initiator is a VMkernel port attached to a working vSwitch with an uplink. For information on how to do so, refer to Chapter 11.

Usually, you want to dedicate physical NICs for iSCSI traffic, because like all storage, vSphere isn't very tolerant of dropped connections.

To configure the iSCSI initiator:

1. **Click the Configuration tab of the host you want to configure in the vSphere Client; then click Storage Adapters, located in the Hardware panel to the left in the content pane.**

2. **In the Storage Adapters panel, select the iSCSI Software Adapter device and click the Properties link in the Details panel.**

   The iSCSI Initiator (iSCSI Software Adapter) Properties window appears, as shown in Figure 12-4.

3. **Click Configure.**

   A General Properties dialog box appears, as shown in Figure 12-5.

4. **Choose the Enabled check box in the Status frame and then click OK.**

   It takes a moment for vSphere to compute an IQN. You can change this IQN by clicking Configure. You can also change the iSCSI Alias, which is an informational name used to describe the connection.

The iSCSI software initiator is now enabled on the host.

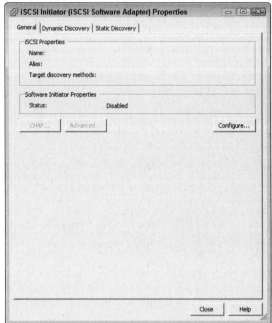

Figure 12-4:
iSCSI
software
initiator
properties.

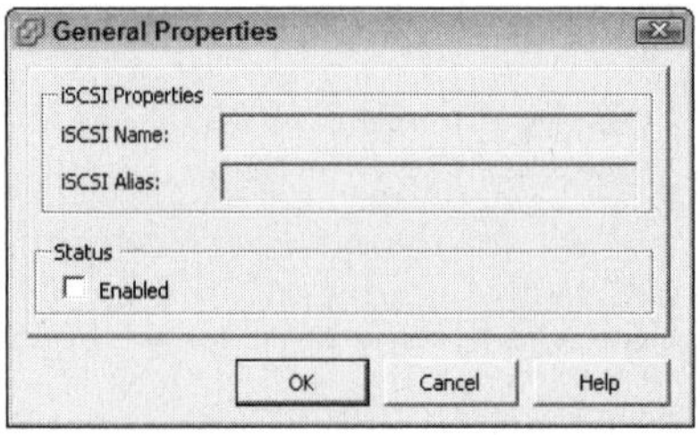

Figure 12-5:
The iSCSI
General
Properties
dialog box is
where you
can enable
iSCSI.

Configuring Dynamic Discovery of an iSCSI server

Most implementations use Dynamic Discovery. *Dynamic Discovery* is when the initiator asks the target server what disk targets are available. This feature allows for a dynamic implementation of iSCSI that behaves very similar to FC.

1. **Click the Configuration tab of the host you want to configure in the vSphere Client; then click Storage Adapters, located in the Hardware panel to the left in the content pane.**

2. **In the Storage Adapters panel, select the iSCSI Software Adapter device and click the Properties link in the Details panel.**

   The iSCSI Initiator (iSCSI Software Adapter) Properties window appears (refer to Figure 12-4).

3. **Click the Dynamic Discovery tab.**

4. **Click Add.**

   The Add Send Target Server dialog box opens, as shown in Figure 12-6, where you can configure the iSCSI server.

5. **Enter the DNS name or the IP address of the iSCSI server.**

   Keep in mind that the DNS name may not work if the iSCSI solution operates on a dedicated separate network.

6. **Click OK to close the dialog box and enable dynamic discovery.**

7. **Click Close in the iSCSI Initiator Properties window.**

8. **If the vSphere client prompts you to rescan the host bus adapter, click Yes.**

   The discovered target appears in the Details panel of the iSCSI Software Adapter device.

Figure 12-6:
The Add Send Target Server dialog box and the iSCSI Initiator (iSCSI Software Adapter) Properties window.

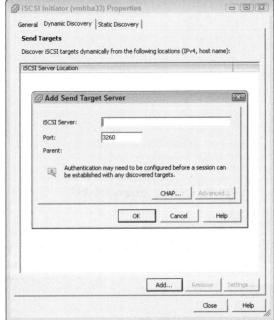

After the Dynamic Discovery is set up, to rescan, follow the steps in the section, "Attaching the Logical Unit Numbers to vSphere hosts," earlier in this chapter. Because iSCSI and FC are both based in the SCSI protocol, the steps are the same and should work the same.

Adding more iSCSI storage is similar to adding more FC storage. Remember to rescan after you make the target available, and you should see it in the Details panel when the iSCSI Software Adapter is selected in the Storage Adapters panel of the configuration tab.

Avoiding common configuration errors

Most configuration errors are related to the actual configuration of the array. If you don't see the disk you expected to see, be sure the array is making it available and check any iSCSI security settings.

Because iSCSI can run over the normal network, there could be port filtering or firewalls. For maximum performance, it's best to ensure that the initiator and target are on the same subnet so that the traffic doesn't need to traverse a router.

Preparing LUN-Based SAN Storage for First Use

LUN-based storage is a disk that is attached to vSphere. vSphere doesn't know whether it's on the storage network or local disk. To use any LUN-based storage, you need to format it with VMFS before you can use it.

The vSphere Client shows the storage in the Details panel when the HBA is selected in the Storage Adapters panel. To view the actual disk, make sure that the Devices button is selected in the Details panel. You may see several devices, so vSphere allows you to sort by several items, including Type or LUN.

Creating a new VMFS volume

Simply confirming that the vSphere host sees the storage isn't likely to get you where you need to go. In order to actually use the datastore, you need to format it with the VMFS file system:

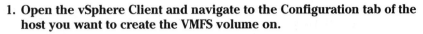

1. **Open the vSphere Client and navigate to the Configuration tab of the host you want to create the VMFS volume on.**

   Most of these steps in this chapter must be done on each host that you want to use with the storage. Some operations, such as actually formatting the LUN, should be done from only one of the hosts. If you format and reformat the LUN and don't put any VMs on the datastore, no data will be lost. However, if you do a format after you place VMs on the datastore, they will be erased and unrecoverable.

2. **Go to the Storage panel and click Add Storage.**

   The wizard that appears guides you through creating the datastore.

3. **Choose Disk/LUN and click Next.**

   The Select Disk/LUN page opens. Disk/LUN is used with VMFS. The other option, Network File System, is used with NAS devices.

4. **Select the Disk or LUN you want to use and click Next.**

   The Current Disk Layout page opens. To prevent loss of data, by default, vSphere shows only LUNs that don't already have a VMFS on them, as shown in Figure 12-7.

5. **Review the proposed layout and click Next.**

   The Properties page opens. Here, you must enter a datastore name.

6. **Enter a datastore name and click Next.**

   The datastore name should identify the target and disk. Keep in mind that even if you start small, you'll likely have a bunch of datastores as your vSphere footprint grows. After you click Next, the Disk/LUN Formatting page appears.

7. **Choose a block size and click Next.**

   Here, use the drop-down menu to choose 2048GB, Block Size: 8MB, as shown in Figure 12-8. Ensure that Maximize Capacity is selected so that vSphere uses the whole LUN for VMFS. After clicking Next, the Ready to Complete page appears.

8. **Review your selections and click Finish.**

The new datastore is shown in the Datastores view of the Storage panel. If you have multiple servers that have access to the LUN, you may need to click Rescan All on those hosts so that they see the datastore.

The Storage panel lets you easily test access to the new volume. You can right-click the name of the datastore and choose Browse Datastore. The Datastore Browser, which lets you see the objects on the datastore, opens. Because you just created the datastore, you'll find the new datastore should be empty. You can click the folder icon on the menu bar to create a new folder and confirm that you have read and write access to the volume.

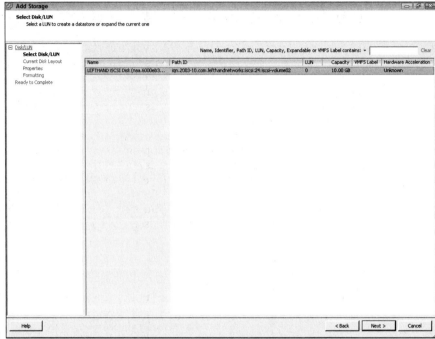

Figure 12-7:
Only LUNs
that don't
have a
VMFS are
shown in
the Select
Disk/LUN
page.

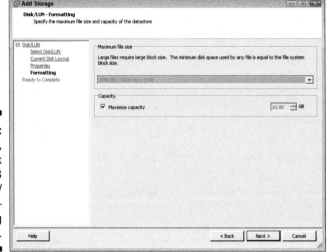

Figure 12-8:
Generally,
use a block
size of 8MB
in the Disk/
LUN —
Formatting
page.

Enabling Storage Input/Output Control

In vSphere 4.1, for LUN-based storage, you can enable Storage Input/Output Control (SIOC). This new feature allows better performance management at the datastore level by ensuring fair access to the disk. Before SIOC, you could configure shares so that one VM couldn't monopolize the storage, but this was a per-host configuration. If two hosts thrashed the same LUN, the existing shares method wouldn't help.

SIOC looks at the LUN, and if a certain performance threshold is reached, SIOC begins leveling out access. SIOC is customizable, but most of the time, all you need to do is enable it with the default settings to gather the benefits.

SIOC operates at the LUN level, so if you do enable SIOC, it will affect all VMs and hosts connected to the LUN. Make sure that you know the impact before you enable SIOC.

To enable SIOC:

1. **Log in to the vSphere Client and navigate to the Datastores view.**

   The Datastores view is located in the Inventory panel of the Home page. The Datastores view contains information about all the datastores that vCenter is aware of.

2. **Choose the datastore you want to enable SIOC on.**

   The datastore must be a local, iSCSI, or FC device with VMFS on it.

3. **Click the Configuration tab of the datastore.**

   The Configuration tab displays various details of the datastore in the content pane of the vSphere Client.

4. **Click Properties in the Datastore Details.**

   The datastore Properties window appears, as shown in Figure 12-9. The name of this box will depend on what you named the datastore.

   Note that the Properties link is located mid-page on the right of the content pane.

5. **Under Storage I/O Control, choose Enabled.**

6. **Click Close.**

   These steps enable SIOC with the default congestion threshold value of 30 milliseconds, which means that if a LUN starts to service requests at 30 milliseconds or more, SIOC will level out the access so that one VM cannot monopolize the LUN.

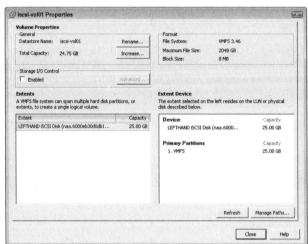

Figure 12-9:
The
datastore
Properties
window has
information
about the
datastore
and allows
you to
enable
SIOC.

Configuring Network-Attached Storage

NAS Storage is one of the most popular configurations now because it is less expensive and easy to set up. In this section, you configure NAS so that you can put VMs on a remote NFS server.

NFS uses the terms *NFS Clients* and *NFS Servers*. A NFS Client is the device that is making use of the remote resource, such as the vSphere host. The NFS server makes a directory available to the network called an export, and the client device (often another server) mounts the export.

Like iSCSI, you need to have a working VMkernel connection with access to an outside network. While iSCSI is often run on a dedicated set of physical network switches, NFS often is not. To ensure maximum performance, place the VMkernel connections you plan to use for NFS on the same subnet as the NFS Server.

Additionally, DNS is commonly used for NFS connections and is required for some security settings. vSphere utilizes NFS version 3 over TCP and must mount the NFS export with root access.

Since vSphere requires root access to NFS, you need to configure root access on the server providing the export. By default, root access to NFS is not enabled on most platforms. In most UNIX-like systems, you need to flag the export with the `no_root_squash` parameter.

Mounting NFS exports in vSphere

On a system that can host an NFS export, you'll need to choose the directory you want to export and follow the instructions for the particular operating system. NFS uses an IP address-based security, so it's wise to restrict the export to only the VMkernel IP addresses that you will use to access the NFS from.

After the directory is exported, you need to mount it on each of your vSphere hosts, which you do by following these steps:

1. **Open the vSphere Client and navigate to the Configuration tab of the host you want to add storage to.**

2. **Go to the Storage panel and click Add Storage.**

   The Add Storage wizard appears. As with creating a datastore on a LUN, this wizard guides you through creating the datastore.

3. **Choose Network File System for the storage type and click Next.**

   The Locate Network File System wizard page is displayed. Here, you enter the location and name of the NFS storage you're going to use.

4. **Enter the server name in the Server field.**

   In Figure 12-10, note that the wizard provides some examples of valid notations. Either a DNS or an IP address will work, depending on your environment and conventions.

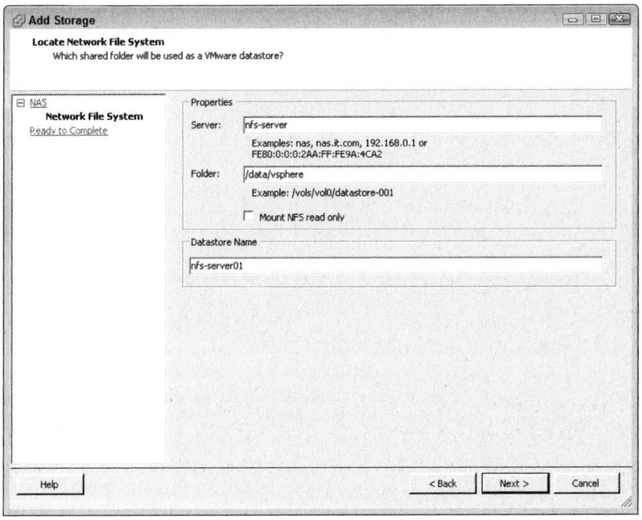

Figure 12-10: The Locate Network File System page of the Add Storage wizard.

5. **Enter the export name in the Folder field.**

   This name must start with a forward slash and should be the complete path to the export. This path must allow root mounts and be case-sensitive. Like iSCSI and FC, naming is important in NFS. It's best to choose a descriptive, yet short, name. Because with NFS you may have multiple servers exporting filesystems, it is a good idea to note the server that is providing the export and a volume number.

6. **Leave Mount NFS Read Only deselected.**

7. **Name the datastore and click Next.**

8. **Review your settings and click Finish.**

   The wizard connects the vSphere host to the datastore, which may take several minutes.

You can have up to 64 NFS datastores in a cluster. NFS datastores don't have the file system limitations of VMFS, so the datastores can be larger. However, it's wise to separate them a bit so that you can troubleshoot datastores independently. To add an additional datastore, simply follow the same steps as you did above.

Avoiding common configuration errors

The most common issue when setting up NFS is an incorrect export path. When entering the folder information, it must be exact. Because export paths are case-sensitive, typos can be common. To ensure accuracy, work hand in hand with the person who administers the NAS systems in your organization.

NFS also uses some peripheral services in order to function, such as portmapper and Remote Procedure Call services. Ensure that these are enabled and aren't being blocked by any network devices.

Chapter 13

Assembling an ESX Cluster

*Y*ou can place VMware ESX hosts into a cluster configuration when managed by vCenter Server. ESX clusters are the foundation of vSphere's availability capabilities, such as High Availability (HA), Distributed Resource Scheduler (DRS), and Fault Tolerance (FT). Sharing resources (such as storage and network) among vSphere ESX hosts is key to VMware ESX clustering and, when done correctly, makes building a VMware ESX cluster easy work.

This chapter guides you through setting up an ESX cluster. You discover the importance of keeping things consistent across the hosts in a cluster. You create an ESX cluster in vCenter Server. After you create the cluster, you add ESX hosts to it.

Keeping Consistent Configurations

A *cluster* is a logical grouping of hosts with common resources such as shared datastores and network connections. The most important point to remember when configuring an ESX cluster is consistency. Ideally, a virtual machine can relocate to any other host in a cluster without configuration changes. This condition can occur only when the attributes of a virtual machine's new home match its previous one.

Network naming

Each virtual network interface (vNIC) on a virtual machine must be associated with a port group. When an administrator chooses the port group, the port group's label, or network name, is displayed in a drop-down list. This name is then stored in the virtual machine's configuration file. When a virtual machine is relocated to another ESX host, the ESX attempts to match up the network name in the virtual machine's configuration file with a port group of the same name on the new ESX host. If no match is found, the virtual machine's network interface is left disconnected until an administrator manually associates it with a new network name.

Because virtual machines rely on just the name of a port group, it's critical to have consistent naming and configuration of port groups across all the ESX hosts in a cluster.

Each port group may be associated with or without a Virtual LAN (VLAN). While configuring each port group, make sure that both the network name *and* the VLAN ID are the same on every host in a cluster.

Same datastore, same name

Whenever vSphere creates a new VMware File System v3 (VMFS-3) volume on shared iSCSI or Fibre Channel storage, it writes a unique identifier to the datastore. Upon adding the volume to an ESX host in a cluster, the volume is automatically added to the other hosts in the cluster, provided that each host is configured to access the storage array containing the volume.

You add an NFS share to an ESX host manually, and you must repeat this process for each ESX host in a cluster. Similar to the way vSphere maps virtual machines to networks by name, vSphere also maps ESX hosts to NFS datastores by their host name and their friendly name. Even if two different ESX hosts in a cluster have access to the same NFS volume, their friendly names and host names must match, or they are considered to be different volumes.

To avoid this situation, follow these steps:

- ✔ **Host name:** ESX asks for the host name or network address of the NFS storage device when adding an NFS datastore. Use the same value for every host in the cluster and don't mix IP addresses with host names, or the datastores will be considered different.

> ✔ **Datastore name:** While adding an NFS datastore to an ESX host, you're prompted for a name to call the mounted volume. This name must be the same on every ESX host in the cluster, or each variation is considered different from the next.

Same access, different hosts

Just because ESX hosts are configured the same doesn't guarantee that they all can access the same networks or storage resources. In an ideal world, the hosts that make up an ESX cluster would be deployed and configured all at once. Each host's switch ports would be configured at the same time, and all the shared storage would be made available to the hosts simultaneously. Unfortunately, not everyone has that luxury, and hosts are added to ESX clusters as demand for virtualization grows. Each time an ESX host is added, it's possible that this host's network switch port connections or storage settings may differ from the other hosts. To prevent this possibility, always confirm the following:

> ✔ **VLANs:** All the VLANs presented to the other ESX hosts in the customer are also presented to the new ESX host.

> ✔ **Storage ACLs:** Most network-based storage arrays set their default Access Control List (ACL) to deny access from all sources. Confirm that the new ESX host's network address is included in the "accept" list.

> ✔ **Network Adapters connected to the correct switch ports:** This may seem like common sense, but you can easily accidentally swap network connections. Some blade server network interconnects aren't very intuitive and make it even easier to map a blade server's network adapter to the wrong connection.

Inviting ESX Hosts to the Cluster Club

Because all the member hosts in a cluster are alike, a virtual machine residing on that cluster can run on any host in the cluster. This condition lets administrators relocate VMs to other hosts to redistribute workloads or restart VMs elsewhere when their original host is unavailable.

Creating a cluster

Clustering is a vSphere feature managed by vCenter Server. A host cluster must be defined in vCenter Server before any ESX hosts can be added to it.

Follow these steps to create a new host cluster in a vSphere datacenter:

1. **Connect to vCenter Server with the vSphere Client.**

   The Inventory panel of the Home page appears with the Summary tab showing.

2. **In the inventory tree, right-click the appropriate datacenter and then choose New Cluster.**

   The New Cluster Wizard appears, as shown in Figure 13-1.

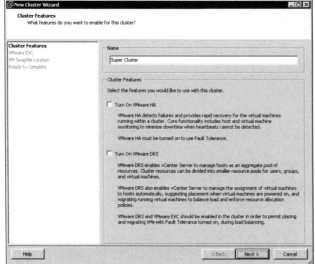

Figure 13-1:
The New Cluster Wizard — Cluster Features.

3. **Enter the new cluster's name in the Name field.**

   This value appears in the vCenter Server inventory tree.

4. **Click Next.**

   The VMware Enhanced vMotion Compatibility (EVC) settings page appears, as shown in Figure 13-2.

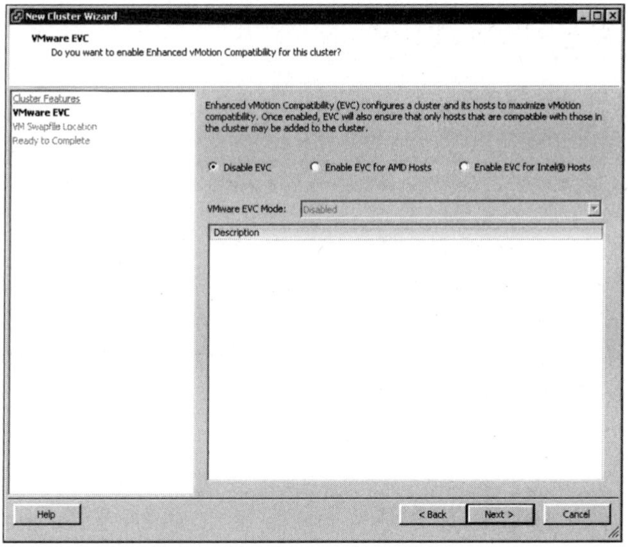

Figure 13-2:
The
VMware
EVC settings
page.

5. Click Next.

The Virtual Machine Swapfile Location dialog box appears, as shown in Figure 13-3.

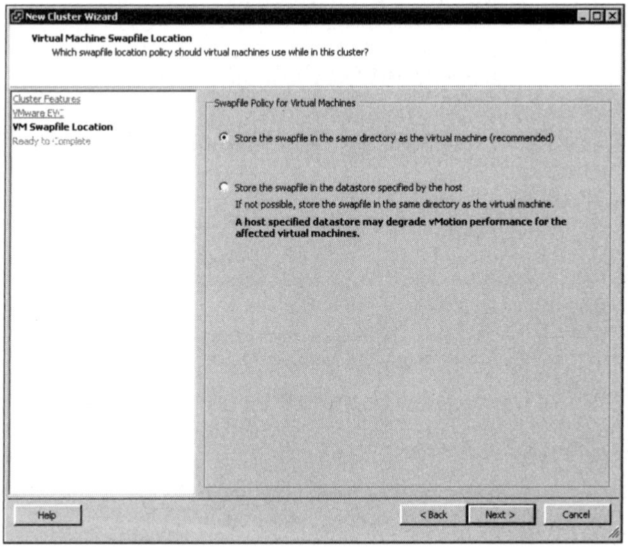

Figure 13-3:
The Virtual
Machine
Swapfile
Location
page.

6. **Click Next.**

The New Cluster Wizard summary page appears, as shown in Figure 13-4.

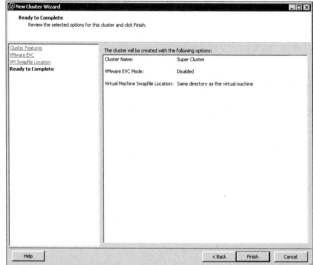

Figure 13-4:
The New
Cluster
Wizard
summary
page.

7. **Click Finish.**

The new cluster is now created.

Adding an ESX host to a cluster

After you create the cluster, you can add ESX hosts. Follow these steps to add an ESX host to a cluster:

1. **Connect to vCenter Server with the vSphere Client.**

The Inventory panel of the Home page appears with the Summary tab showing.

2. **Select the ESX host you want to add to the cluster.**

A summary of the selected hosts appears in the Summary tab.

3. **To add the ESX host to the cluster, click and drag it onto the cluster.**

An ESX host must be in maintenance mode to be removed from a cluster.

When you're adding ESX hosts with existing resource pools to a cluster with DRS enabled, vCenter asks how you want to map them to the resource pools defined in the cluster. vCenter asks this question because resource pools defined for a cluster map to all hosts in the cluster, whereas resource pools defined for an individual host do not account for the resources of other hosts.

Sharing the Load with Distributed Resource Scheduler (DRS)

Another feature of vSphere is the Distributed Resource Scheduler (DRS). This feature allows administrators to set rules defining the placement and precedence of VMs in the cluster. DRS brings intelligence to an ESX cluster through features such as load balancing and affinity rules. These features are designed to help you optimize your vSphere environment, while giving consideration to operational policy.

DRS offers three levels of automation:

- **Manual:** vSphere makes recommendations regarding the best host in the cluster to power on a VM. vSphere makes recommendations for virtual machine migrations among cluster members to balance the load across the cluster hosts.

- **Partially automated:** vSphere automatically selects the best host in the cluster on which to power on a VM. vSphere makes recommendations for virtual machine migrations among cluster members to balance the load across the cluster hosts.

- **Fully automated:** vSphere automatically selects the best host in the cluster on which to power on a VM. vSphere automatically executes virtual machine migrations based on its recommendations.

Automation levels may be set on a per-VM basis, overriding the cluster setting, which is useful for VMs that don't fit within the level of automation configured for the cluster.

Keeping VMs separated

Modern computing regularly uses the concept of availability through redundancy by using two or more systems capable of the same task, but with each having a unique identity. The most common example is a Windows Active

Directory (AD) domain controller, which is used to authenticate users logging into domain-related resources. Two or more AD controllers regularly synchronize their data, allowing Windows-based systems to authenticate users against any one of the domain controllers. This redundancy is built on the assumption that at least one domain controller is available at all times.

While highly unlikely, consider a scenario where all the domain controllers are virtual machines running on a single ESX host in a cluster. In the event the ESX host were to fail, the domain controllers running on the ESX host would also fail, leaving users in the domain unable to log in to their machines. The way to mitigate this risk is to keep the domain controllers on separate hosts, limiting the impact of an ESX host failure.

DRS loves to optimize workloads across ESX hosts. Unfortunately, it doesn't know the importance of keeping certain VMs (such as domain controllers) on different hosts to mitigate risk. When DRS is running in fully automatic mode, the administrator is never prompted to determine what might happen if two specific VMs are placed together. In order to reap the benefits of DRS without the risk of introducing a single point of failure, DRS offers a set of rules to indicate which VMs should be kept together and which VMs should be kept apart. These rules are known as VM-VM affinity rules.

ESX hosts and VMs, hand-in-hand

Setting rules to keep redundant VMs on separate hosts is a good way to mitigate risk of a single host failure. This configuration is sufficient for most ESX hosts, but doesn't take into account an event that impacts a group of servers. Blade servers share a common power source in a blade chassis, meaning a chassis failure will take down all the blade servers in the chassis simultaneously.

You can limit the impact of a major failure, such as a blade chassis going down, by using VM-Host affinity. VM-Host affinity allows the administrator to keep a VM assigned to a specific host. If the ESX cluster spans hosts in more than one chassis, DRS can keep the VMs attached to hosts in more than one chassis, eliminating another single point of failure.

Enabling DRS on a cluster

According to VMware best practices, DRS should be enabled on a cluster after the hosts are added. Follow these steps to enable DRS on a cluster:

1. **Connect to vCenter Server with the vSphere Client.**

   The Inventory panel of the Home page appears with the Summary tab showing.

2. **In the inventory tree, right-click the appropriate cluster and then choose Edit Settings.**

   The Super Cluster Settings dialog box appears, as shown in Figure 13-5.

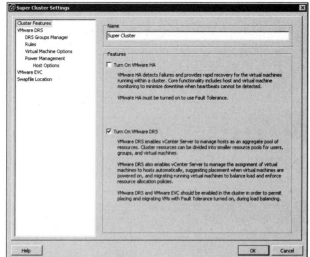

3. **To enable DRS on the cluster, select the Turn On VMware DRS check box.**

4. **In the left-hand menu, choose VMware DRS.**

   The Cluster Settings Automation Level dialog box appears, as shown in Figure 13-6.

5. **Choose Partially Automated and click OK.**

   This mode automatically places VMs on the best host in the cluster when the VM is powered on and suggests virtual machine migrations that would improve the cluster's load balance.

   DRS is now enabled for the selected cluster.

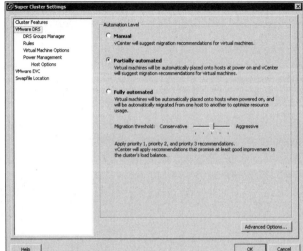

Figure 13-6:
The Cluster
Settings
Automation
Level dialog
box.

To get the most out of DRS, configure the ESX hosts in your cluster to use vMotion. This allows DRS to rebalance virtual machines across hosts without powering them off.

Part V
Administering and Maintaining vSphere

The 5th Wave   By Rich Tennant

"It appears a server in Atlanta is about to go down, there's printer backup in Baltimore and an accountant in Chicago is about to make level 3 of the game 'Tomb Pirate.'"

In this part . . .

This part covers the administration and ongoing maintenance of your vSphere environment. Chapter 14 introduces you to creating virtual machines (VMs) and cloning VMs from templates. Chapter 15 shows you how to leverage vCenter Server to organize your vSphere resources. Chapter 16 gets into vSphere events and monitoring the environment using alarms in vCenter Server. Chapter 17 is a quick review of your vSphere virtual infrastructure. Chapter 18 covers configuration of VMware ESX hosts using the Host Profiles feature.

Chapter 14

Creating, Cloning, and Converting VMs

*V*irtual machines (VMs) are why you have a vSphere infrastructure. While VMs can do some amazing things, in the end, they're just a set of files. This chapter explores the files that make up a VM, as well as other types of files that you may run into.

The Makings of a Virtual Machine

So, what makes a VM? First, several files work together. The files make up everything that you might see in a physical form if you were to take apart a computer. One file is the computer itself; another one may be the hard drive. Even things like the basic input/output system (BIOS) are there in file format. In some cases, vSphere puts multiple physical devices into a single file for simplicity, such as virtual floppy disks and virtual network adapters.

Configuration

The vSphere configuration file is usually named the same as the vSphere VM name. All configuration files have the .vmx file extension and are text files with all the settings of the VM. Information, such as how many CPUs and how many virtual Ethernet adapters the VM has, is stored in the configuration file. This configuration file is similar to the actual computer in the physical world.

Coscheduling

Sometimes, a VM with 1 vCPU is as fast or faster than one with 2 vCPUs, because an operating system with multiple CPUs expects to run instructions on both of them simultaneously. vSphere must then schedule the VM to have control of 2 CPUs or CPU cores simultaneously, which is called *coscheduling*. Coscheduling adds a small penalty as the hypervisor waits for all of the physical CPUs that the VM needs to free up. So, a VM with 1 vCPU may get two turns at the physical CPU, while the VM with 2 vCPUs waits its turn. This gets worse as you go up in the vCPU count, so keep the vCPUs to a minimum!

When you create the VM, the configuration file matches the name of the VM. If you change the name of the VM, the configuration file is not automatically changed. If you need to locate the configuration file or virtual disk, you can go to the settings of the VM and view the properties to see the path to the VM files.

Virtual disks

The configuration file has entries for all devices in the VM, including disks. However, the disk entries simply note the type of disk and the size, but don't contain data, which is stored in the VMDK file. A VMDK file is used on both NAS and SAN storage systems, and it contains the data that resides on the VM's disk. (SAN and NAS configuration is discussed in detail in Chapter 12.)

When looking at a file list of a VM, usually two files have VMDK in the name. One is the actual disk data and is named `*.vmdk-flat`, and the other is just named `*.vmdk`. The vmdk file contains the disk geometry and other pertinent information about the vmdk-flat file. They work together and should usually not be separated.

The flat file has the data in it, so if you lose it, you need to rely on a backup. However, you can create the metadata VMDK file from the flat file if you do lose or corrupt the flat file. You can find more information on how to regenerate the metadata on VMware's Web site at `http://kb.vmware.com/kb/1002511`.

Virtual hardware

If you edit the virtual machine properties of the VM, you can see the virtual hardware. The virtual hardware that is available and chosen by default depends on your operating system. Every VM has at least a couple of components.

- **Memory:** Memory is the amount of Random Access Memory (RAM) assigned to the VM. In vSphere, the maximum amount of memory is 255GB. Some OS versions allow you to hot-add memory without even a reboot.

- **CPU:** A VM must have at least 1 CPU. In vSphere, the CPUs allocated to a VM are called Virtual CPUs (vCPUs). Depending on your edition of vSphere, you can have up to 8 vCPUs in a VM, in increments of 1.

- **Video card:** Every VM has a single video card. Most of the time, you can leave the video card at the defaults. Depending on the operating system you configure in the VM properties, the video card will have different settings.

- **VMCI device:** The Virtual Machine Communication Interface (VMCI) device is a high-speed connection that is used in order for the host and the VM to communicate. In vSphere, two VMs can use this device for high-speed communication on the same host, without going through the VM networking stack. The default setting is to allow communication only between VM and host.

  You can have other devices in the Hardware tab of the virtual machine properties. Some of these are added to every VM, but aren't required. Only a single VMCI device can be on a VM.

- **SCSI controller:** The SCSI controller lets you attach a hard disk to the VM. While you don't need an SCSI controller, most implementations should include it. In vSphere, you can use an IDE hard disk, but for maximum performance, SCSI controllers and disks are recommended.

  Four types of SCSI controllers are available in vSphere: BusLogic Parallel, LSI Logic Parallel, LSI Logic SAS, and VMware Paravirtual. For the most part, the BusLogic and LSI Logic controllers offer indistinguishable performance, and usually the selection is based on native driver availability in the operating system used in the VM. The Paravirtual SCSI (PVSCSI) controller behaves differently. For VMs with extreme disk performance demands, PVSCSI can be faster than the other SCSI adapters. However, PVSCSI works only with a couple of operating systems, and unless you drive a large amount of data from a VM, it does not help. A VM can have up to four SCSI controllers, and the standard SCSI rules apply, so there is a maximum of 15 SCSI devices per controller.

- ✔ **Hard disk:** Most systems today require a hard disk, but a vSphere doesn't require one. If you are testing a live CD, for example, you might remove the hard disk. You can add several disks to each SCSI controller.

- ✔ **Ethernet adapter:** All newly created VMs have Ethernet adapters, but they don't need one. vSphere supports six types of Ethernet adapters, and you can have up to ten adapters in a Virtual Machine.

- ✔ **Vlance:** Vlance is an older adapter that emulates an AMD Network Interface Card (NIC). Older operating systems have drivers for vlance, but this adapter doesn't perform as well as the other available adapters. This adapter is available only for x86 systems.

- ✔ **E1000:** This adapter looks to the VM operating systems as an Intel E1000 adapter. The Intel E1000 is a very common adapter, so many recent operating systems support it.

- ✔ **VMXNET:** This adapter is designed for VMware and is optimized. It's faster than the Vlance adapter. To use VMXNET, you must install VMware Tools, so you have the appropriate driver.

- ✔ **Flexible:** This adapter identifies itself as a Vlance adapter, but if VMware Tools are installed, it functions more like a VMXNET. The Flexible adapter eliminates the need to install the Vlance adapter, install the operating system, and then replace Vlance with VMXNET.

- ✔ **VMXNET 2 (Enhanced):** This adapter is a newer version of the VMXNET adapter. It's available only for the most common operating systems and requires VMware Tools. This adapter supports hardware checksum offloads and jumbo frames.

- ✔ **VMXNET 3:** This adapter is the highest performing adapter available to a VM and is a superset of VMXNET 2. It supports additional performance features, such as Receive Side Scaling and additional checksum offloads. Like all VMXNET adapters, VMXNET 3 requires the VMware Tools to be on the operating system and is supported only for a few operating systems, namely Microsoft Windows and some Linux distributions.

- ✔ **CD/DVD drive:** The CD/DVD drive is the optical disk that you can use to install an operating system or an application. If you have a CD/DVD drive on a VM, you can choose to connect it to a physical drive device. In cases where you have the CD or DVD data as an image, you can connect that to a VM and the VM will see it as a native CD/DVD device. You can connect the CD/DVD drive at the host or the client using the vSphere Client. The CD/DVD drive is a read-only device and cannot write CDs or images. The drive is a standard IDE device, and a VM has one IDE controller and a maximum of four IDE devices.

Paravirtualized hardware

Virtual Hardware is contained within the configuration file. However, even VMware knows that some functions are best served by hardware. To accommodate, vSphere supports paravirtualized hardware. Paravirtualization is when a device is provided to a VM in a way consistent with virtualization, but the device is also able to take advantage of the underlying hardware capabilities. An example is in the VMXNET 3 adapter. Many current NICs have acceleration chips to allow better throughput, and the VMXNET 3 adapter allows a VM to utilize some of those features, such as TCP checksum offloading.

It's always wise to configure a VM to have only the devices it really needs, but you should also connect only removable devices, such as CD/DVD drives and floppy devices, when you need them. Leaving a drive connected can impact the ability to move the VM in the vSphere cluster, impacting DRS and maintenance mode.

The following devices aren't used as much as the preceding devices, but they are possible to configure in cases of specific need.

- ✔ **Floppy drive:** For some reason, this is still a default device in every VM, although most physical servers don't have floppy drives today, and this device is rarely used. Floppy drives can still be useful, but many vSphere administrators remove this device. A VM can have one floppy controller and up to two floppy drives. A floppy device can come in handy to install drivers early in the OS install process, but many administrators simply add the appropriate drivers to the install media.

  Similar to a CD/DVD drive, you can connect it to the physical device or an image, which is done from the server or from the client. Unlike a CD, the floppy drive is read/write.

- ✔ **Parallel port:** This allows you to map a VM to have access to a physical parallel port on a host, or output the data to a file. This option is rarely used, but it can be helpful if you have an application that needs access to a parallel port. You can configure a VM with up to three parallel ports.

- ✔ **Serial port:** Like the parallel port, use of the serial port is also uncommon in most organizations. A serial port can be handy if you must map a device such as a UPS to a VM. You can map it to a physical port on the host, a file, a named pipe, or even over the network to a Virtual Serial Port Concentrator (VSPC). Like most physical PCs that were equipped with serial ports, a VM can have up to four serial ports.

✔ **USB Controller:** The Universal Serial Bus (USB) Controller is required for a VM to connect to a USB device. This controller has no configuration items, but must be present if you want to map a VM to have access to a USB device attached to the host. A VM can have only a single USB controller.

✔ **USB device:** This is a connection to a physical USB device on the host. You need a USB Controller to connect a USB Device and you can connect up to 20 devices to the controller. With appropriate components, USB devices can be redirected so that a VM using USB still can be moved using vMotion, which is especially useful for programs that require hardware based USB license dongles.

✔ **SCSI device:** This allows a VM to directly access a SCSI device attached to the host.

✔ **PCI device:** VMDirectPath is a very advanced capability of vSphere that allows a VM to directly access a Peripheral Connect Interface (PCI) device. To use it, a host must support special virtualization extensions in the CPUs, and the host must configure the device for pass-through. It is a new feature that may be helpful for very specialized applications, such as offloading encryption processing.

Many of these less common devices are less common for a reason: They often reference physical devices. Mapping a VM to these physical devices can result in issues moving the VM between hosts, so use this device sparingly. So, use these devices only as a last resort, as they can negatively impact the design and benefits of a virtualized infrastructure.

Filling Up the Virtual Container

You can create a VM and then install an operating system on it, or because a VM is simply a group of files, you can make a copy of an existing VM.

Building a VM from scratch

Organizations of all sizes benefit from copying a VM, but before you can do that, you need a VM to copy. To do that, you need to create your base VM. To create the VM, follow these steps:

1. **Open and log in to the vSphere Client and navigate to Hosts and Clusters.**

2. **Right-click an object that can contain a VM, such as a host, cluster, or datacenter, and choose New Virtual Machine.**

   The Create New Virtual Machine wizard opens. This wizard guides you through the creation of the VM.

3. **Choose Typical and click Next.**

   The Create New Virtual Machine wizard prompts you to choose a Typical configuration or a Custom configuration. Typical has VMware's recommendations and is generally where to start. Custom lets you override suggestions and is good to tailor a VM to an application's need. With a custom configuration, you can set up a VM that won't function, so it's wise to make sure that you have researched the settings you choose with operating system and application vendors.

   The Name and Location page appears.

4. **Name the VM, select the location, and click Next.**

   Ideally, you want the VM name and the computer name to match, but they don't have to. Generally, you choose the default location, but if you have many datacenters, you may need to select the appropriate datacenter in the Inventory Location panel. If you have resource pools or VApps defined in the cluster, the Resource Pool page appears. If not, the Datastore page appears, and you can skip to Step 6.

5. **Choose the resource pool that you want to contain the VM and click Next.**

   The Datastore page appears.

   The Resource Pool page lets you choose which resource pool you want to put the VM in. Resource pools govern access to CPU and memory and can impact performance of the VM. Chapter 19 covers resource pools in depth.

6. **In the Datastore page, choose the datastore that you want to store the VM on and click Next.**

   The Guest Operating System page appears.

   The Datastore page lists all the available datastores that you can use for the VM. You can sort by the headings at the top of the window, and often administrators will sort on the Free heading, which shows the datastore with the most space. Pay special attention to the Type field so that you know whether you're using NFS or VMFS.

7. **Choose the Guest Operating System and click Next.**

   The Create a Disk page appears.

The Guest Operating System is important because in it, you determine the hardware that the VM can use and how vSphere interacts with the VM. After you choose the operating system, be sure to use the drop-down menu to choose the Version, as shown in Figure 14-1. For this exercise, use Microsoft Windows Server 2003, Standard Edition (32-Bit).

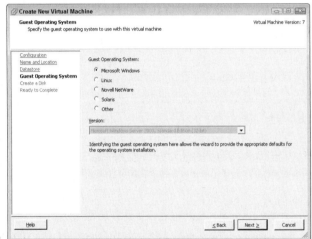

Figure 14-1: The Guest Operating System page of the Create New Virtual Machine wizard.

8. **Specify the virtual disk size, set the Thin Provisioning or Fault Tolerance settings, and click Next.**

   The Ready To Complete page appears.

   Because most modern operating systems need a hard disk, here, you can set the size. Usually, the disk you're creating here becomes the boot disk. On VMFS volumes, you can choose the Allocate and Commit Space on Demand (Thin Provisioning) option to reduce the disk space the VM initially occupies. In this way, a thin-provisioned 10GB disk won't initially use 10GB on disk. Alternatively, you can choose Support Clustering Features Such As Fault Tolerance. This feature is necessary for Fault Tolerance, but results in a fully provisioned virtual disk. So, if you choose 10GB for this disk, it will begin at 10GB used on disk. More information on these settings is discussed in the section, "Virtual machine disks of all shapes and sizes," later in this chapter.

9. **Review your settings and click Continue or Finish.**

   As shown in Figure 14-2, you can review the settings and choose to edit the settings before completion. Choosing the Edit The Virtual Machine

Settings Before Completion check box and clicking Continue automatically opens the Virtual Machine Properties box, where you can add additional disks and remove unnecessary items like the floppy drive.

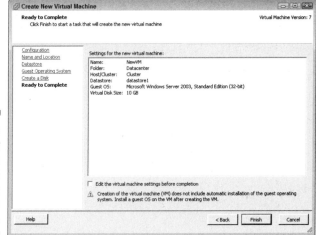

Figure 14-2:
The Ready to Complete page where you can review your choices.

What's a worker without VMware Tools?

Much of the hardware that a vSphere host presents to a VM is industry-standard, but to really make the VM run great, you need to install VMware Tools. The VMware Tools package is available for several common operating systems, including Windows, Linux, Netware, FreeBSD, and Solaris.

On supported operating systems, VMware Tools provides the following:

- ✔ Customized drivers for the VM allowing better video and network performance
- ✔ Tuning parameters for the guest operating system
- ✔ Enhanced timekeeping in the VM
- ✔ Memory management enhancements tailored to the unique requirements of a VM
- ✔ Functionality such as shrinking VM disks
- ✔ Communication with the host so vSphere is aware of guest OS information such as name and network address

If an operating system is supported by VMware Tools, vSphere will prompt you to install it after the OS is installed. To do it manually for a Microsoft Windows VM:

1. **Open the vSphere Client, navigate to the VM, right-click the VM you want to install VMware Tools on, and choose Guest⇨Install/Upgrade VMware Tools.**

   A warning box appears telling you that the guest operating system must be running.

2. **Click OK.**

   This step mounts the appropriate installer to the CD drive of the VM. In the VM, you complete the installer. The exact steps on how to complete the installer vary depending on the operating system of the VM.

   If the guest is Microsoft Windows, in most cases, the installer begins automatically. If it does, you can skip Step 3.

3. **If the installer does not run automatically and you're using Microsoft Windows, open the CD drive in the guest operating system and double-click the `setup.exe` file.**

   The Welcome page appears.

4. **In the Welcome page, click Next to begin.**

   The VMware Tools installer displays the Setup Type page.

5. **Ensure that Typical is selected and click Next.**

   The Ready to Install the Program page appears.

   Typical is used in most installs, as shown in Figure 14-3. The Complete install is useful if you plan to move the VM between VMware products. Custom is used in rare cases where you want only a subset of tools installed.

6. **Click Install in the Ready to Install the Program page.**

   The installation begins.

7. **If you see a prompt that hardware acceleration is not enabled, click Yes to set the hardware acceleration.**

   The installer opens the Display Properties control panel and a Notepad file with instructions on how to set the hardware acceleration. Meanwhile, the installer may finish.

8. **Review the instructions displayed on screen in the Notepad file on how to set hardware acceleration and click back to the Display Properties control panel.**

9. **To make changes to the Windows VM display hardware acceleration, click the Advanced button.**

   The Standard VGA Adapter Properties dialog box opens.

10. **Click the Troubleshoot tab, slide the Hardware Acceleration all the way to Full, and click OK.**

    The Standard VGA Adapter Properties dialog box closes. The Display Properties control panel is still shown.

    VMware Tools makes a big difference in performance, but making sure that the hardware acceleration is on is key. Not doing so makes the console of the VM sluggish and difficult to use.

11. **Click OK in the Display Properties control panel to close it.**

    The Display Properties control panel closes.

12. **In the Install Complete dialog box, click Finish.**

    The installer prompts you to reboot.

13. **Click Yes.**

    The reboot occurs, and the VMware Tools is loaded on boot.

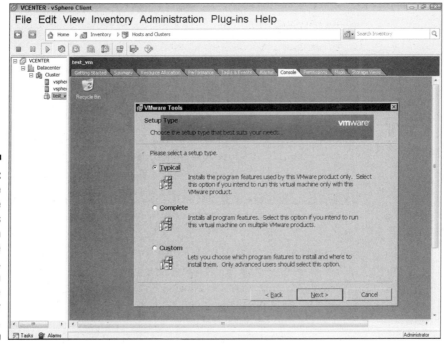

Figure 14-3:
The
VMware
Tools
Installation
Setup Type
screen,
which
installs the
drivers for
the VM.

A Computer in a File

A VM is a collection of files, and as a group, they make up a whole computer. Often, the most important part of the VM is the disk because it contains data.

Disks can range from 1MB to just shy of 2TB, depending on the settings of the datastore. When creating a disk, the Create New Virtual Machine wizard asks whether you want to allocate and commit space on demand, if the datastore supports it. Committing space on demand is called *thin provisioning* and is a useful feature that requires careful planning. In VMware ESX, the predecessor to vSphere, you couldn't use thin provisioning, and ESX always fully allocated the disk upfront. Other VMware products could grow on demand, but ESX didn't in order to maintain high performance. Today's disk arrays are much faster than yesterdays, and VMware now sees thin provisioning useful in certain circumstances.

Over-allocation is possible with thin-provisioned disks. You can have a 100GB VMFS datastore with five VMs each with a 25GB thin-provisioned disk. As long as those 25GB disks don't all grow at the same time, each one can grow slowly. However, if the OS tries to grow a file and VMware is unable to, both the VM and other VMs on that datastore can fail. Thin provisioning is useful only if you have an appropriate plan to monitor the environment and a predictable disk growth curve. You can set up alerts for disk space in the vSphere Client. (See Chapter 16 for more on alerts.)

Fully allocated disks are often called thick provisioned. If you don't select Allocate and Commit Space on Demand, you create a thick-provisioned disk. To do so, vSphere allocates the space on the datastore, but doesn't zero it out. If you select the Support Clustering Features Such As Fault Tolerance option, vSphere zeroes the entire virtual disk file, which is called an eager zeroed thick. This process can take a long time for ESX to complete and is often used only when required by clustering or fault tolerance.

Importing an existing virtual machine disk

You can create a VM that uses an existing disk file by creating a new VM and choosing Custom Configuration in the Create New Virtual Machine wizard Configuration page , which is the first page of the wizard. When you get to the Select a Disk dialog box, you can choose to Use an Existing Virtual Disk. This choice is helpful if you have a virtual disk and want to build a VM around it or in specialized situations such as clustering.

Thinning out an existing virtual disk

Thin provisioning is a powerful feature that can save disk space by consuming only what is written on a disk. What if you have a server that once was large but now doesn't consume as much disk? You can *thin out* a disk and free up space on the underlying datastore.

To thin out a disk, you simply perform a migration of the disk to a different datastore and choose it to be a thin-provisioned disk at the destination.

 After thinning out the disk, it may be larger than you like. Keep in mind that the virtual memory pagefile, also called a *swapfile,* may still be there, and many operating systems don't fully delete data off the disk when deletes occur. They, instead, only remove it from a master file table, leaving it on the disk. To get the best results, you should zero the empty space first. Every operating system has a different way for zeroing the empty space, but on Microsoft Windows, most people use the free SDelete utility, from Microsoft Sysinternals. SDelete is available at `http://technet.microsoft.com/en-us/sysinternals/bb897443`.

Bring in the Clones

When you need to make an identical copy, or *clone,* of a physical server, you usually have a very complex set of tasks. To make this clone, you'll need identical hardware, a hard disk imaging program, appropriate disk or network communication with which to move the data over, and a way to change the identity or segment from the rest of the network. In most cases, with vSphere, this week-long effort to create a clone is reduced to seconds!

When creating a clone, the most important thing to be concerned about is network communication. Even if you rename an operating system, the application may not see the system renamed and may communicate over the network with the source server's identity.

Also, cloning can use a lot of disk space, so use it appropriately. The clone will have a similar resource footprint, but you can adjust the virtual hardware by editing the virtual machine's properties.

Making a clone of a VM

To create a clone, you just right-click the VM in the vSphere Client and choose Clone. The Clone Virtual Machine wizard appears, as shown in Figure 14-4.

1. **On the Name and Location page of the wizard, provide a name for the VM and click Next.**

   The Host/Cluster page appears.

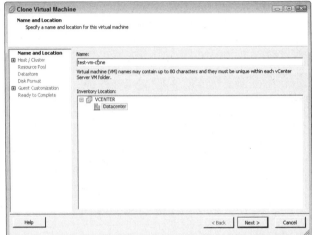

Figure 14-4:
The Clone
Virtual
Machine
wizard
guides you
in making
a copy of a
VM.

If you create a clone of a production VM and don't segment it on the network or customize it before boot up, it will likely knock the other production system off the network. This situation can impact your organization and isn't a great way to demonstrate the power of vSphere cloning!

Remember that this name is not the operating system name, but the name of the VM to vSphere. Ideally, this name matches the name within the operating system, so use the name you plan to use for the server.

2. **Choose where the clone will reside and click Next.**

   You may want to move the clone to another cluster, and if so, you can select that here. Moving a clone to another cluster is especially helpful if you have a production and a nonproduction cluster and you want to clone from a production to a nonproduction location.

   If you have resource pools or vApps defined in your cluster, the Resource Pool page appears. If you do not, the wizard displays the Datastore page.

3. **Choose the resource pool that you want to contain the clone and click Next.**

   The Datastore page appears.

Like with a new VM, the Resource Pool page lets you choose which resource pool you want to put the VM in.

4. **Choose the Datastore and click Next.**

The Disk Format page appears.

Remember to check how much free space a datastore has whenever you put a new VM on it. The easiest way to do so is to click the Free column, as shown in Figure 14-5.

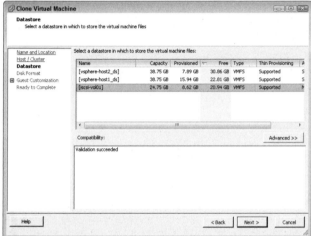

Figure 14-5: The Datastore page of the Clone Virtual Machine wizard.

5. **Choose the type of disk and Click Next.**

The options in the Disk Format page are similar to when you created a VM, but there is an additional option named Same Format As Source. This option simply keeps the disk in the original design and is a good choice if you don't know which format to use for the clone.

6. **In the Guest Customization dialog box, choose Do Not Customize and click Next.**

This page may not allow you any other option if the files needed to customize the operating system aren't on the vSphere server. In this case, all the options on the page are disabled. You add them later in this chapter.

7. **Review your selections and click Finish.**

Don't select the Power on This Virtual Machine After Creation or Edit Virtual Hardware (Experimental).

The options to power on the VM can be useful if you're confident that the clone won't interfere with other systems and want it to come up right away. Edit Virtual hardware can be really handy if you need to segment the VM from other traffic. If you have a testing Virtual Local Area Network (VLAN), you can modify the clone to use that VLAN while still in the wizard.

Deploying from a template

Clones are helpful for troubleshooting, but what about deployment? Making copies is a fast way to provision a new system. *Templates* are special source VMs that are designed for deployment. When you deploy a VM from a template, vSphere clones the template and makes it available as a VM. Desktop and server engineers have been building "golden images" for platforms for years, which is exactly what a template is.

When creating a template, it's wise to build a new VM and configure it just for the template. Do so only with software that you use on every system. Often, management agents and antivirus programs are included in a template. Like with any golden image, all agents may need to have a special setting to allow them to be cloned, so make sure that you work with your vendors for any of those products.

Configure the hardware to be representative of what you expect the template to be used for. Generally, configure the template to be a bit smaller than you might usually use, as you can always add more resources later if the VM needs it. You can clone templates, so many organizations have multiple templates.

You have two options when you're ready to transform the VM into a template:

- ✔ **You can Clone to Template.** Clone to Template leaves the source intact. This is useful if you've built a template for one use and then want to add onto it for another use. You can build the VM, clone to template, and then keep building on the source.

- ✔ **You can Convert to Template.** Convert to Template modifies the VM to become a template in place. This means that the VM has data noted in the configuration file to make it a template without making a clone first. This is usually used for established templates that are converted to a VM to be modified, and then converted back to a template.

To create a template, navigate to the VM in the vSphere Client and Right-click it. Choose Template⇨Convert to Template. The disk is automatically converted to thin format to reduce space.

Automatically Customizing Clones

We mention several times how dangerous it can be to clone a system with the same name. So, what do you do about that?

vSphere has the option to customize commonly deployed systems at clone time. This option enables you to modify Windows or Linux systems, thus speeding the clone or deployment operation.

To customize many Windows-based systems, you need to get some files from Microsoft. If you've created golden images in the past, you may be familiar with these files. For vSphere, you need to place the files in the correct location in the vCenter server. The files are located in the `deploy.cab` file and must be placed in the following locations on the vCenter server, depending on the operating system vCenter is running on:

- **Windows Server 2008:**

    `%ALLUSERSPROFILE%\VMware\VMware VirtualCenter\sysprep`

- **All other supported Windows operating systems:**

    `%ALLUSERSPROFILE%\Application Data\VMware VirtualCenter\sysprep`

In the `deploy.cab` file, the critical file is `Sysprep.exe`. This Microsoft tool is used to reset a system's identity, redetect hardware, and prepare the installed Windows installation to be copied.

VMs running Microsoft operating systems after Windows Server 2003 don't need `Sysprep.exe` on the vCenter server to be able to be customized. These operating systems have the customization capabilities built in.

Cloning with customization

Begin by following the steps that you used to do the clone in the section "Making a clone of a VM," earlier in this chapter. When you get to the Guest Customization page in the wizard, choose Customize Using the Customization Wizard and click Next. The vSphere Client Windows Guest Customization wizard launches, as shown in Figure 14-6.

To clone with customization:

1. **Type the name and organization registration information for the guest operating system in the Registration Information page of the wizard and click Next.**

    The Computer Name page appears.

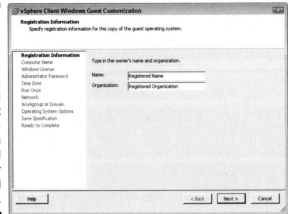

Figure 14-6:
The
Registration
Information
page of the
Windows
Guest
Custom-
ization
wizard
prompts for
name and
organization.

2. **Choose Use the Virtual Machine Name and click Next.**

   On the Computer Name page, you can enter a name for the system. This is the name that the guest operating system will go by, so make it unique. You can have the wizard automatically add a numeric value or have the deployment wizard prompt you later.

   Note that the Generate a Name Using the Custom Application Configured with vCenter Server option is disabled unless you set it up. Use this option when you need a specific custom name generation. Because it's best practice to match the names in vSphere and the operating system, we recommend using the virtual machine name.

   The Windows License page appears.

3. **Enter the Microsoft Product Key and the server license information if the guest being customized is a server and click Next.**

   Make sure that you get the product key correct. This wizard collects the information, so it's unable to validate the key.

   The Administrator Password page appears.

4. **Enter the password for the administrator account; if you need the guest to log on automatically, choose how many times it should do so.**

   If the VM you started with has renamed the administrator account, the password to that account is changed. The customization utility Sysprep references the administrator account by the security identifier number, so the name of the original administrator account does not matter to Sysprep. Like the product key, the wizard cannot validate that a password entered meets the requirements set in policy, so be careful with this field. The wizard encrypts the password when storing it for Sysprep.

5. **Choose the appropriate time zone from the drop-down list and click Next.**

   The Run Once page appears.

6. **In the Run Once page, enter custom commands and then click Next.**

   If you have custom-engineered scripts or configuration tools, you can put them in this section.

   The Network page appears.

7. **Choose Typical Settings in the Network page and click Next.**

   Here, you can set all sorts of network configurations. Often, it's easier and faster to configure them at the VM after the clone is complete.

   The Workgroup Or Domain page appears.

8. **Enter information about a workgroup or domain and click Next.**

   The Operating System Options page appears.

9. **Ensure that Generate New Security ID (SID) is selected and click Next.**

   An SID is a key identifier of Windows systems that should be unique. It's important for communication between Windows systems and the Active Directory Domain.

   The Save Specification page appears.

10. **In the Save Specification page, deselect Save This Customization for Later Use and click Next.**

    The Ready To Complete page appears.

11. **Review your settings in the Ready to Complete page and click Finish.**

    This completes the customization, and the vSphere Client Windows Guest Customization wizard closes, returning to the Clone Virtual Machine wizard Ready to Complete page. Click Finish in the Clone Virtual Machine wizard Ready to Complete page to begin the clone operation.

Customization specifications

Each time you customize an operating system using Sysprep, you need to provide information such as time zones, licensing information, and product keys.

Microsoft made it possible to automate the Sysprep, and vSphere goes a step further, by storing these settings as Customization Specifications that you can save and reuse.

The easiest way to create a customization specification is to save it when prompted in the Save Specification page. Make sure that you enter appropriate information in the Description field so that you know what settings are contained in the customization specification.

To create a Customization Specification before a clone operation, click vSphere Client and on the Home page, choose Customization Specifications Manager.

Click the New button, as shown in Figure 14-7.

The vSphere Client Windows Guest Customization wizard appears. The first page, the New Customization Specification page, asks which operating system the customization specification is for, after which the wizard is the same as in the previous section.

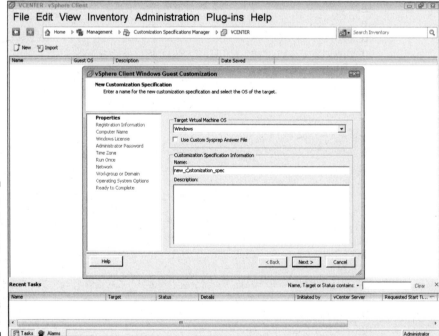

Figure 14-7:
The vSphere Client, showing the Customization Specifications Manager.

Things That Don't Clone Very Well

Cloning a VM is really handy, but sometimes cloning a VM is a bad idea. If you're planning on cloning a VM, it's usually a good idea to research and test it in advance, because often issues may not be readily apparent.

Applications with identities

Most applications take their identities from the operating system. So, when you clone, you simply need to update the operating system's identity, and then the application will derive its identity from that identity. However, some applications have a significant amount of identity information at the application level. This situation is quite common with mail applications and directory services, such as Microsoft Exchange and Microsoft Active Directory Services. These applications may also communicate on the network, causing issues for the source VM that may be in production.

For many applications with identities, you can still clone them, but you may need to perform several actions before bringing the cloned server up on the network. Often, you can work with the application vendor to determine the steps to do so. Even if you are confident in the steps, it's often wise to consult vendors to ensure that your process is complete.

Licensing tied to hardware

Some applications' licenses are based on a particular hardware configuration. Many of the applications can see only the virtual hardware, but a clone may have differences, such as internal Universally Unique Identifiers (UUID), similar to hardware serial numbers in physical servers. Because a clone will change that number, some applications will not function if they're tied to a unique identifier. It's possible to create an exact copy of a VM, but you should not run two VMs with the same UUID in a vSphere Cluster. Other applications often are linked to the Ethernet Media Access Control (MAC) address, and having two VMS with the same MAC address can cause issues as well.

Just because cloning works doesn't make it okay. Many application End User License Agreements (EULA) prohibit cloning operations without purchase of appropriate licenses. Before cloning, check with your software vendor regarding technical and licensing issues.

Chapter 15

Organizing vSphere Resources

- -

- -

*Y*ou're likely to quickly find that your view of the virtual infrastructure is messy. Virtual infrastructures grow rapidly, so you'll want to start off organized and continue that way. This chapter covers the ways you can group VMs and helps you implement features that let you perform operations on the groups, such as startup and shutdown commands.

The Client Perspective: Four Views, One vSphere

The vSphere Client is a handy tool designed expressly for the administration of your vSphere environment. When looking at the Home page, shown in Figure 15-1, you see several different panels, each with numerous icons.

You manage objects in vSphere in the Inventory panel of the vSphere Client. Besides a search icon, four other icons are located here: Hosts and Clusters, VMs and Templates, Datastores, and Networking. These icons each lead to a view, and this section of the book explains what the views do.

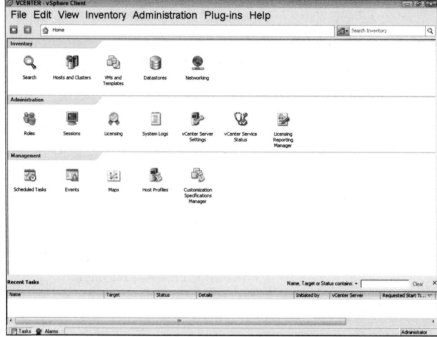

Figure 15-1:
The vSphere
Client Home
page is a
great place
to start
your day.

Focusing on the vSphere hosts: The Hosts and Clusters view

When setting up a new vSphere environment, you primarily work in the Hosts and Clusters view, shown in Figure 15-2. As you might guess, this view focuses on the hosts and clusters, but by default, it also shows the VMs and the resource pools. Many administrators prefer operating the vSphere Client from this view.

When you have a configuration setting to make on a host, you do so from this view. While you can access a VM from almost any view, hosts are most commonly managed from here.

The Hosts and Clusters view has several other important functions. You can

- Create a cluster
- Add a host to a cluster
- Create a resource pool
- Create a vApp

Figure 15-2:
The Hosts
and Clusters
view of the
vSphere
Client.

In large environments, you may have dozens of hosts and hundreds of VMs. To organize the VMs, you might think that you can simply place them into resource pools, but don't! Resource pools dramatically modify key performance characteristics and are covered in depth in Chapter 19.

vApps are logical groups of VMs used to keep several VMs together. We discuss them in more detail in the section, "All Together Now: vSphere vApps," later in this chapter.

Virtual machines on the brain: the VMs and Templates view

With the same level of obviousness, the VMs and Templates view focuses on VMs, as shown in Figure 15-3. Although you can create and manage VMs from the Hosts and Clusters view, you can't arbitrarily organize them from there. All VMs show up in the VMs and Templates view in folders that you can create. You can nest these folders, and they don't change performance characteristics like resource pools do. The VMs and Templates view is also a common starting point for any vSphere administration.

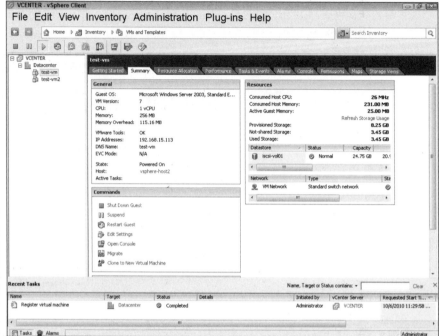

Figure 15-3:
The
VMs and
Templates
view of the
vSphere
Client.

Thinking capacity — a storage perspective: The Datastores view

The previous two views in the vSphere Client have been part of the client for several versions, but the Datastores and Networking views (see next section) are new as part of vSphere 4.

The Datastores view gives you a consolidated view of all datastores in the cluster, as shown in Figure 15-4. This view is handy because you often need to get an idea of the storage situation, and this view lets you get that high-level view. Perfect for planning, you can view both shared and local storage.

While you can create VMs in the Datastores view, mostly what you do is browse datastores and add datastores. While individuals responsible for storage may start here, this view is not used as frequently as Hosts and Clusters and VMs and Templates.

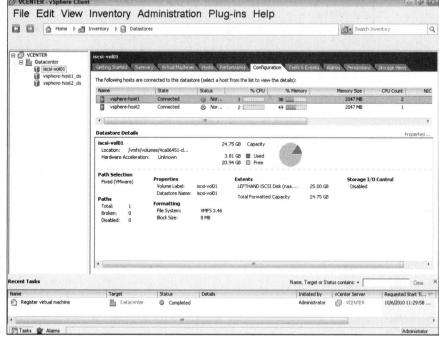

Figure 15-4:
The
Datastores
view
focuses on
the storage
volumes of
vSphere.

Networking, and whatever it connects: Networking view

The last important view is Networking, shown in Figure 15-5. This view is similar to the Datastores view because it shows a consolidated inventory of all networks known to the cluster. This consolidated inventory can be helpful when you need to troubleshoot a network or are looking to confirm that all your networks are on all the hosts in the cluster. You can click a network name on the navigation pane on the left of the vSphere Client and then click the Hosts tab to see which hosts are connected to that network. To see a summary of networks, click the datacenter object on the left navigation pane and then click the Networks tab.

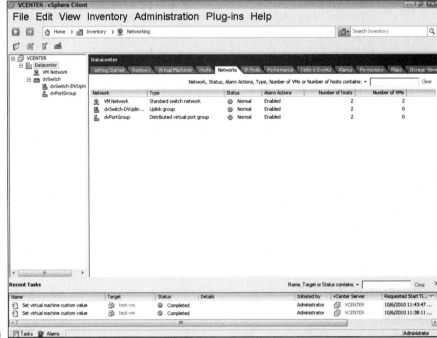

Figure 15-5:
The
Networking
view, show-
ing all the
networks
in the
datacenter.

Using Logic to Place a New Virtual Machine

When you create a VM, whether it's a complete new VM or from a clone or template, you're always asked which datastore you want to put it on. Instead of just placing it on the first datastore you see, it makes sense to consider the use and expected size of the datastore.

Considering storage growth

Growth is often the first thing that an administrator considers when placing the VM. You can sort the list of datastores in new VM wizards to easily see which datastore has the most free disk space, and you can place the VM on that one. If you use thin provisioning, keep in mind how much the VMs can grow. While it's unlikely that all of them will grow simultaneously, if you have an automated patch solution deploying files or if they get infected with a worm, it is possible.

Another aspect of growth is related to performance. It's wise to consider what else is using the datastore. If you have several high-throughput database servers, you may not want all of them to be on the same datastore. Even if your array can handle it, putting all of your high-throughput VMs on the same datastore often has significant performance penalties at the ESX host level.

Creating a common sense folder structure

There's an old adage that common sense is not so common. This saying is true for vSphere as well. The clearly sensible folder structure of grouping VMs based on the cat-breed preference of the application owner may not work for others in the organization. Like VM names, it's best to stick with the basics.

vSphere generally manages the folder structure on the datastores, but you need to do it in the client for organization of the VMs:

1. **To create your first folder, open the vSphere Client and navigate to the VMs and Templates view.**

2. **Right-click the Datacenter object in the navigation pane on the left and choose New Folder.**

   The client creates a new folder object and allows you to edit the folder name.

3. **Edit the folder name and exit the folder edit by clicking somewhere else in the client.**

   The folder name is no longer highlighted.

4. **To create a nested folder, right-click the folder you just created and choose New Folder.**

   You can nest folders dozens deep, but doing so can make the client refresh more slowly, so it's wise not to go overboard. The vSphere Client can become slower as your environment contains more objects, so keep in mind that simple can be better here.

5. **To add a VM to a folder, simply drag and drop the VM into the folder.**

Drag and drop is an easy way to quickly organize your vSphere objects.

Assigning ownership through Custom Attributes

In large organizations, administrators begin to wonder how they got so many VMs and who owns them. While the permissions and the access to a VM may be limited to administrators, often a business owner needs to be contacted to arrange downtime and other necessary upgrades. You want to store this information in vCenter, but where?

Custom Attributes are the answer. With Custom Attributes, you can define an attribute and set the Type to either Virtual Machine, Host, or Global. Global attributes apply to both Virtual Machine or Host objects.

These Custom Attributes let you define these important values and easily view them from the summary tab of the object.

To define an owner Custom Attribute for your VMs:

1. **In the Hosts and Clusters or VMs and Templates view, click the VM you want to modify in the left navigation pane.**

   The vSphere Client content pane displays information on the VM.

2. **Click the Summary tab in the content pane.**

   Summary information about the VM appears in the content pane.

3. **In the Annotations panel, click the Edit hyperlink.**

   The Edit Annotations dialog box appears, where you can add or remove Custom Attributes, as well as enter notes on the VM.

   Removing an attribute deletes it and all of the values on all the objects it applies to, including other VMs. As with any delete operation, make sure that you're confident before clicking Remove.

4. **Click the Add button in the attributes frame.**

   The Add Custom Attribute dialog box appears in front of the Edit Annotations dialog box. The Add Custom Attribute dialog box, shown in Figure 15-6, prompts for the Name, Type, and Value.

5. **Enter** Business Owner **for the Name and set the type to Virtual Machine.**

6. **Type an appropriate entry for the value and click OK.**

   The name of the attribute is saved and available to all objects of the attribute type. The value of the attribute is linked to this Virtual Machine object.

7. **Click OK again to exit the Edit Annotations dialog box.**

Figure 15-6:
The Add
Custom
Attribute
dialog box.

This attribute is now attached to every VM in your vCenter environment, but the attribute value is blank for the other VMs. You can easily populate this information by editing the Annotations for the VMs and adding the value in the Edit Annotations dialog box. Now that the attribute exists for all your VMs, you can click in the cell under the Value heading and type the value. This shortcut makes it unnecessary to enter the Custom Attribute dialog box for each VM.

The new custom attribute is easy to see when you look at the VM Summary tab, shown in Figure 15-7.

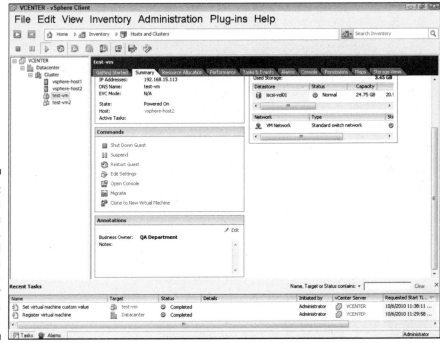

Figure 15-7:
With a
custom
attribute,
you can add
information
specific
to your
organization
to a VM.

Giving permissions to the new owner

Custom attributes are a nifty way to annotate a VM with a business owner, but what if the business owner in your organization needs to have access to his VM? The custom field you just created is merely a useful piece of information, but it really has nothing to do with security.

To give this business owner access, first you must either give the business owner an account in the Active Directory that the vCenter authenticates against or create a local account on the vCenter server. Then, follow these steps to add that account to a VM:

1. **From the navigation pane of the Hosts and Clusters or the VMs and Templates view, right-click the VM on which you want to modify the permissions and, from the pop-up menu, choose Add Permission.**

   The Assign Permissions dialog box opens, as shown in Figure 15-8. The dialog box is split into two frames, Users and Groups and Assigned Role. Users and Groups is where you select the users and groups from the local server or Active Directory you want to work with. The Assigned Role is where you set what they can do.

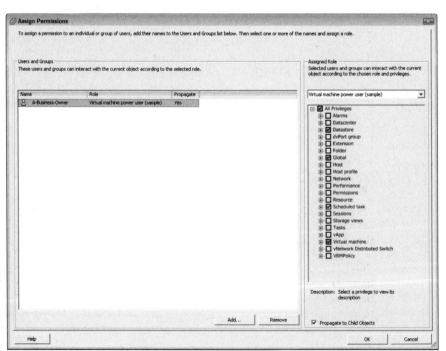

Figure 15-8:
The Assign Permissions dialog box.

2. **Click Add.**

   The Select Users and Groups dialog box opens on top of the Assign Permissions dialog box. In the Select Users and Groups dialog box, you can select the user or group you want to add. If you can't find the user you're looking for, check the Domain drop-down list at the top of the dialog box. The client occasionally chooses the local server, noted as (server) in the drop-down list.

3. **Choose a user that you want to give permissions to and click Add.**

4. **Click OK to exit the dialog box.**

   The Select Users and Groups dialog box closes, and you return to the Assign Permissions dialog box.

   The user you selected in Step 3 is now in the Users and Groups list in the Assign Permissions dialog box. By default, the user has Read-Only permissions.

5. **Select the Virtual Machine Power User (sample) role and click OK.**

   This role is created by vSphere to serve as an example of a role that can be copied and modified to meet your organization's specific needs.

The user and role are added to the virtual machine. When logging in, all the user can see and do is what the Virtual Machine Power User (sample) role permits.

If you want to remove a permission, just follow the preceding steps backwards, right? Not really. If you go into the Assign Permissions dialog box, you'll find that the Users and Groups panel is probably empty. To remove permissions, go to the Permissions tab of the VM, right-click the name of the user or group, and choose Delete.

All Together Now: vSphere vApps

vSphere vApps let you group virtual machines in a container that focuses on management and performance. Applications may require multiple VMs so that a vApp can group them.

The most common use for a vApp is when you have several systems that must be managed as a group. A simple example is a Web server and a database server that always work together. With a vApp, you can link them together so that they can be powered on or off together or even cloned together. You can define a strict power on/power off order for a vApp to ease maintenance.

Defining a vApp in vSphere vCenter

vApps aren't terribly complex and, like everything else in vSphere, are managed from the vSphere Client. Follow these steps to create a vApp:

1. **In the vSphere Client, go to the Hosts and Clusters view, right-click a cluster, and choose New vApp.**

   The New vApp wizard appears.

2. **Enter a name, choose an inventory location for the vApp, and click Next.**

   The Resource Allocation page appears.

   Usually, with DRS enabled, the location is just the datacenter in which you create the vApp.

3. **Leave the Resource Location set at the defaults.**

   As shown in Figure 15-9, this page allows you to set exactly how many resources the vApp can use and the vApp's priority in a low-resource situation. We discuss resource allocations in detail in Chapter 19.

4. **Click Next.**

   The Ready to Complete page appears.

5. **Review the settings in the Ready to Complete page and click Finish.**

   To add a VM to the vApp, from either the Hosts and Clusters view or the VMs and Templates view, drag and drop the VM onto the vApp.

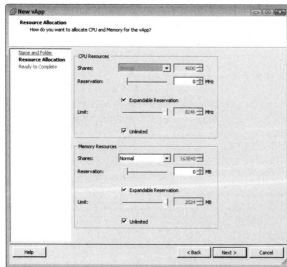

Figure 15-9:
The Resource Allocation page prompts for resource allocation.

Bringing order to virtual machines

For most applications on multiple servers, it's critical to start and shut them down in the correct order. vApps make that easy, because you can set those rules within the vApp:

1. **To set a Start Order for the VMs in a vApp, right-click the vApp in the navigation pane of the Hosts and Clusters or VMs and Templates views and choose Edit Settings.**

    The Edit vApp Settings dialog box opens with two tabs: Options and Start Order.

2. **Click the Start Order tab.**

    The Start Order tab appears, as shown in Figure 15-10. Here, you can modify the order of the individual VMs, change the delay between groups, and define actions for startups and shutdowns. By default, the vApp does a Power Off operation on the VMs, which is similar to a hard power button press. Be sure to change the Operation to Guest Shutdown if you have VMware Tools installed in the VM to ensure a graceful shutdown.

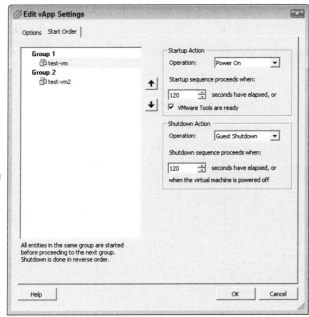

Figure 15-10: vApps allow you to define a specific startup and shutdown order.

Chapter 16

Events, Alarms, and Monitoring

*A*fter you set up your environment, you need to keep track of what's going on. vSphere is a capable system that provides a wealth of information for your administrative purposes, and it can even send alerts when thresholds are reached. These valuable features mean that you can monitor the vSphere environment without additional tools.

Using Events to Track Activity

vSphere makes use of events to inform you and other administrators of activities in the vCenter environment. *Events* are records of activities that administrators or the system initiate. Events are entered into the various logs and are shown in the vSphere Client as they occur.

At the bottom of the vSphere Client is the Recent Tasks pane. This pane shows you what is going on in the vSphere solution. When another administrator creates a VM, for example, an event is shown. In this way, everyone in the loop knows what is going on, which is important because, in a large environment, several administrators may be working on different things at once.

vCenter also performs actions without administrator involvement. When it does, vCenter raises an event, too. If you have Distributed Resource Scheduler (DRS) enabled in an automated mode (and you should), it will move VMs around to maximize performance. All these events appear in the Recent Tasks pane.

Spotting the events that matter

With so many events going by, which ones should you pay attention to? You can sort the columns in the Recent Tasks pane if you're looking for a particular task, such as a Clone Virtual Machine event, and you can sort by the name column. You can also sort on the status for completed tasks.

In some cases, sorting is not good enough. In that case, you can search. At the top of the Recent Tasks pane is a text field where you can enter a value and define what fields to search, which lets you filter the recent tasks so that you can see what you're looking for.

When you're in the vSphere Client, it's usually a good idea to keep an eye out for anomalies. If a vMotion is stuck at 10 percent for ten minutes or a Rescan All HBAs goes on for 15 minutes, you need to investigate. You may also watch for changes by other administrators or the system to avoid making duplicate changes to the same object.

Finding an event related to a failure

The Recent Tasks pane is great, but what about something that occurred earlier than recent? How do you find out what happened an hour ago?

To do so, the vSphere Client has a Tasks & Events tab on just about every object that you can view. If you open the Tasks & Events tab for a host, you can see all the events that have occurred on the host, as shown in Figure 16-1.

Even when looking at a single host, you can find a lot of events. If you have a sharp eye, in Figure 16-1, you may notice a search box in the upper-right corner of the tab. To filter for iSCSI-related events, for example, you simply enter Internet SCSI in the text box. All the items with Internet SCSI in the name, target, or status appear. You can change the fields to search for by clicking the down arrow at the left of the text box.

...ms in vSphere

...t you can set to bring various conditions to your atten-
...may want an alarm that warns you when a datastore
...acity.

...l. vSphere supports two states:

...re relatively minor events intended to inform you about an
...ing situation. You should check these warnings within a reason-
...able time.

✔ **Alerts** are more serious. Alerts occur when a counter is reached that
requires immediate attention. Usually, you want to address an issue
raised to alert state as the alerts come in. Organizations that operate on
a 24 x 7-schedule may want the alert to go to someone who is on call and
available.

Exploring the default alarms

If you do want a datastore alarm that is triggered at 75 percent capacity, you're in luck! vSphere has dozens of default alarms, and datastore at 75 percent capacity is one of them.

The alarms are defined at the vCenter level and affect all objects below that level. Many of the default alarms are set to useful levels, but it's helpful to understand what they're set to and how to change them.

To view the default alarms, follow these steps:

1. **Open the vSphere Client, log in, open the Hosts and Clusters view, and navigate to the vCenter object.**

   The vCenter object is the topmost item in the navigation pane, and all the objects in the navigation pane are contained within the vCenter object.

2. **Choose the Alarms tab of the vCenter object.**

   By default, the Triggered Alarms view of the Alarms tab appears. This view lists any alarms that are active and require action.

3. **Click Definitions.**

   The Definitions view shows the alarm definitions. Here, you can view, edit, add, or delete alarms.

To view the details of an alarm, double-click the alarm name. You see a dialog box similar to the one shown in Figure 16-2 with information on the alarm as well as what it's monitoring.

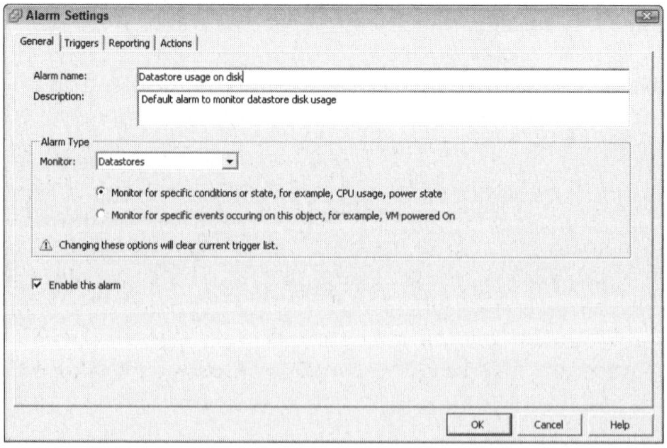

Figure 16-2: The Alarm Settings dialog box for default alarm Datastore Usage on Disk.

In the General tab, under Alarm Type, you see the Monitor drop-down list, which has all the objects that vSphere can monitor, including Hosts, Virtual Machines, and Datastores. Below this drop-down list is a set of radio buttons:

- ✔ **Monitor For Specific Conditions Or State, For Example, CPU Usage, Power State:** Use this option for things that need active polling, such as memory consumption and datastore usage. Datastore Usage on Disk is an example of a default alarm based on conditions. Only Hosts and VMs can be monitored for conditions.

- ✔ **Monitor For Specific Events Occurring On This Object, For Example, VM Powered On:** Use this option for transient events that can be captured. With this monitor type, you can raise alarms when the monitored actions occur. The Host Error alarm, which is created by default, is an example of an event alarm type. You can monitor all objects this way.

To actually see when the alarm is triggered, click the Triggers tab. This tab shows the events or conditions that must be met to raise the alarm. If the alarm type is condition-based, the Triggers tab will look like Figure 16-3.

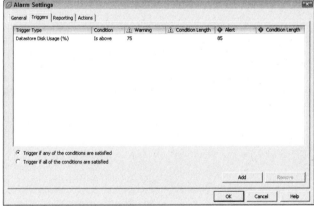

Figure 16-3: Triggers tab of the default alarm Datastore Usage on Disk.

The Trigger Type attribute in the Triggers list is what you're actually looking for to key off of and raise the alarm. Depending on the Alarm Type settings, the Trigger Type allows you to choose from a drop-down list. The condition attribute is either Is Above or Is Below, depending on what condition you want to alert on. The Warning and Alert attributes are the values that vSphere will compare the metric of the Trigger Type to. The unit of the number is often noted in the actual name of the Trigger Type. The condition length attributes are how long the condition must occur before the alarm fires off.

Event alarms are somewhat different. With event-based alarms, you aren't constantly sampling for an exact threshold, so the alarm just watches for the event. In Figure 16-4, you can see that the alarm Triggers tab looks different for an event-based alarm. When an event is seen, vCenter flags the alarm based on the status you set. This condition lets you watch for events that are minor or major.

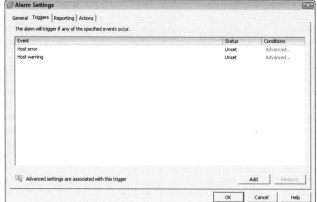

Figure 16-4:
Triggers
tab of the
default
alarm Host
Error.

In both alarm types, you can have multiple triggers. If the Alarm Type is a condition-based trigger, you can choose whether all the triggers must occur or whether any one of them can trigger the alarm (the latter is the default). Event-based triggers are always set to fire off if any trigger events occur.

Calming vSphere alarm paranoia

Every vSphere environment has alarms that are active at some time. If you get an alarm, don't panic. You can log in, see what the alarm is, and address it. After you address the issue that triggered the alarm, the alarm will usually disappear. If the alarm is an event-based issue, you may need to manually acknowledge the alarm to make it go away:

1. **Open the vSphere Client and navigate to the alarm.**

   If a warning occurs, you see a yellow triangle with an exclamation point on the object. If an alert occurs, you see a red diamond with an exclamation point on the object.

2. **Click the object in the navigation pane and then click the Alarms tab in the content pane.**

   The Alarms tab opens to the Triggered Alarms view by default, so you should see the alarm there.

3. **Right-click the alarm and choose Acknowledge Alarm.**

The alarm you acknowledged turns grey, showing that the alarm is acknowledged, but it doesn't get rid of the alarm if the condition or event that triggered it is still happening. With lots of administrators on a team, acknowledging an alarm can be an easy way to make sure that the other administrators know someone is working on an issue. Acknowledged alarms show when it was acknowledged and who acknowledged it.

You can also further restrict the triggering of a condition-based alarm by changing the values on the Reporting tab in the alarm settings. You have two options: Range and Frequency. Range is a tolerance above or below the trigger value that allows additional flexibility.

Using the Range settings, you don't alarm on a minor condition change. For example, when an amount is exactly at the threshold, it may go over by one and under by one repeatedly. This might occur if you have a setting to 85 percent, and the setting fluctuates between 84 and 86 percent. By setting a tolerance range of 2, you can make it so that the alarm stays on, and you don't get inundated with messages as it fluctuates within the tolerance range.

By setting a time during which vCenter will not send multiple identical alerts, you can use Frequency to prevent sending too many alerts. After the time you set expires, vCenter raises the alert again if the conditions are still met.

Tweaking alarms to understand "normal"

The default definitions can be a bit aggressive, especially some of the percentage-based alarms. On all datastores, for example, the default warning occurs at 75 percent capacity. This alarm is good in some cases, but if you use large 2TB datastores, you may not want to be alerted when a mere 500GB is left!

You can modify the alarms, but before you do, it's a good idea to get a baseline in your environment. Every organization is different, so what works in the default configuration may not work for you. Run with the stock definitions for a bit before you modify any of them.

Putting Alarms to Work

Events and alarms are perfect for organizations that are large enough to have a person watch the events go by. For the rest of us, we need the vSphere solution to notify us automatically.

Setting up notifications

Notifications allow vCenter to communicate status to the outside world. vSphere can e-mail an address, allowing vSphere to send an alert to a smart-phone or a pager. To send an e-mail, vSphere must first have the Simple Mail Transport Protocol (SMTP) server set up. This server is typically an e-mail server in your environment that runs and accepts incoming SMTP traffic.

To configure the SMTP server:

1. **Open the vCenter client and log in.**

2. **Go to the Home page and click vCenter Server Settings.**

    The vCenter Server Settings dialog box appears. This multi-function dialog box has several headings in the left pane. The default page upon opening it is the Select License Settings page, as shown in Figure 16-5.

Figure 16-5:
The vCenter
Server
Settings
dialog box
showing
the Select
Licensing
Settings
page.

3. **Click Mail in the left pane.**

   The vCenter Server Settings dialog box changes focus to the Select Mail Sender Settings page, where you can enter the information about your organization's mail servers.

4. **Enter an SMTP server and an e-mail address to use as a sender.**

   Some e-mail systems require a valid sender; others do not. If you're going to allow alerts to be sent to business users, you need to ensure that the e-mail address is a real one because business users often reply to alerts with questions. Figure 16-6 shows the vCenter Server's Select Mail Sender Settings dialog box.

5. **Click OK.**

   You now have an SMTP server configured.

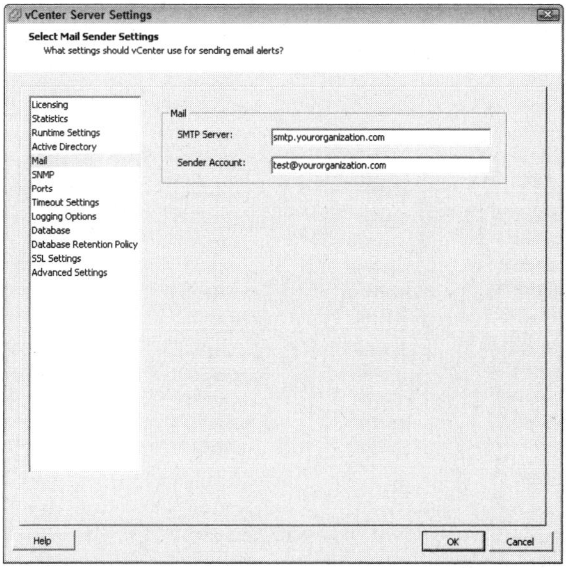

Figure 16-6:
The Select Mail Sender Settings page of the vCenter Server Settings.

Sending alerts over e-mail

Configuring your SMTP server allows vCenter to interface with the SMTP server, but it doesn't enable any alerts to go over e-mail. To send these alerts over e-mail, you must enable the alerts that you want to send:

1. **Open the vSphere Client, log in, open the Hosts and Clusters view, and navigate to the vCenter object.**

2. **Click the Alarms tab and then click Definitions to open the Alarm Definitions view.**

   The Alarm Definitions view shows all the default alarms that vCenter provides, as well as any you have created at the vCenter object.

3. **Right-click the alarm you want to modify and choose Edit Settings.**

   For this example, choose the Datastore Usage on Disk alarm. Many organizations commonly set up this alarm to send e-mail notifications.

4. **Click the Actions tab in the Alarm Settings dialog box.**

5. **Click Add.**

   An item appears in the Action list. By default, the action added is a Send a Notification Email, as shown in Figure 16-7.

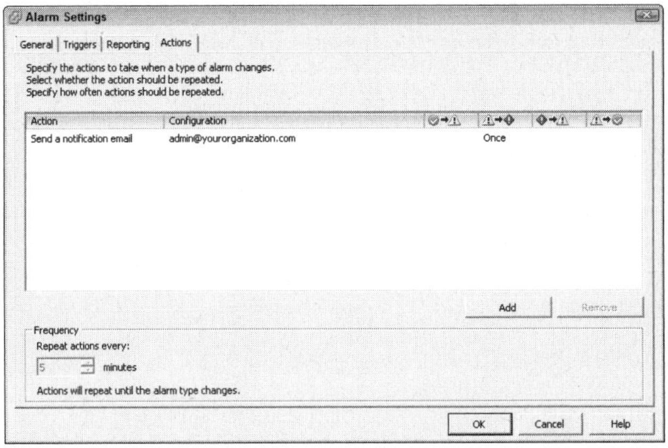

Figure 16-7:
The Actions
tab of the
Alarm
Settings.

6. **Enter the address to which you want to send the alarm in the Configuration field.**

   If you want to send to multiple e-mail addresses, you can separate them with a comma.

7. **Choose how often and when to send the e-mail.**

   Four additional attributes are to the right of the Configuration attribute. You use these attributes to control when and how often vCenter sends the e-mail. By default, the system will e-mail once when the alarm goes from Warning to Alert. You can choose to make each attribute blank, Once, or Repeat for each of the state changes, all of which are shown by icons in the attribute headings.

8. Click OK to close the Alarm Settings dialog box.

This sets the alarm to send an e-mail when it is triggered, which is handy for alerts on low space events or other important situations.

If e-mail doesn't seem to work right, check your SMTP server's security. Many servers nowadays are locked down pretty tight, to prevent spam messages.

Connecting vSphere to other monitoring systems

All this monitoring is pretty powerful, but sometimes organizations have standardized platforms. vCenter can also send a notification through a Simple Network Management Protocol (SNMP) trap to an SNMP server. *SNMP* is an industry standard protocol that allows vCenter to speak the same language as hundreds of network and server monitoring platforms. If your organization has a "single pane of glass" product, SNMP is a great way to tie the virtual infrastructure into it.

To configure the SNMP server, you need to go into vCenter Server Settings as you did for SMTP in the Setting up notifications section, and click SNMP in the navigation pane, as shown in Figure 16-8.

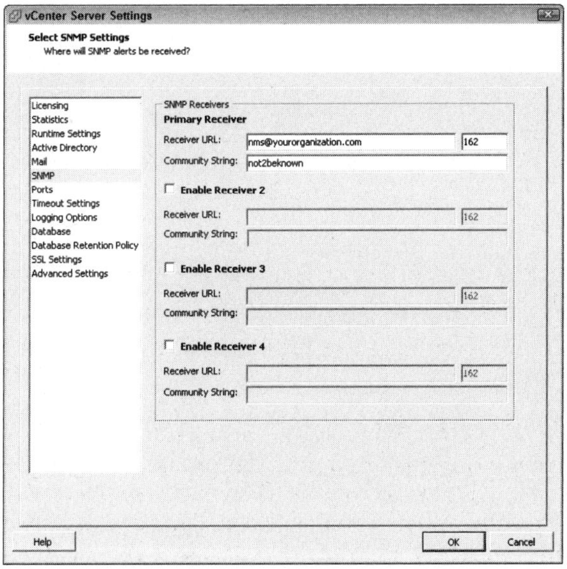

Figure 16-8:
The Select SNMP Settings page of the vCenter Server Settings dialog box.

You can have up to four receivers, and you must configure their names, ports, and community strings. After you set the SNMP settings, several default alarms will send data — for host hardware failures, for example.

You can give out too much information, and without training, someone can interpret it incorrectly. When I (Tom) first set up the vCenter to talk with an enterprise-wide SNMP server, business owners and application owners immediately had concerns because when they saw usage, they didn't under understand the differences between physical and virtual implementation. Educate your customers before providing them the details; you'll be glad you did!

Going overboard with alerting

With dozens of alarms, vSphere can overwhelm you quickly. With so many alerts, you'll begin to miss them and not react when you should. In this regard, over-alerting can be as bad as under-alerting.

Tune alarms so that they trigger only in cases where action is required. If you don't care about a particular alarm, disable it by going into the alarm settings and unchecking the Enable This Alarm check box.

Chapter 17

A Quick Tour of Your Virtual Infrastructure

*T*he vSphere client has some features designed for you, such as Scheduled Tasks, and some designed for your boss, such as Maps. Some features, such as Performance, can help moderate your discussions with end users or application owners. All these features work together so that you can fully understand and manage the virtual infrastructure, and vCenter makes that possible. This chapter looks at those features and shows you how to use them.

Diving into Datastores

In Chapter 12, we cover how to connect to shared storage and how to create a datastore. This information is pretty important, but after you've created a datastore, how do you actually get into one?

In the past, doing so was quite challenging, requiring you to navigate the ESX command line console, but now you can get in right from the vSphere Client. You simply navigate to the datastore you want to dive into from the Datastore view, right-click the datastore object, and choose Browse Datastore. The Datastore Browser window appears, as shown in Figure 17-1.

The Datastore Browser enables you to look around, upload files and download files to and from the datastore, as well as move and delete files. However, by default, the functions aren't labeled. You can easily add labels by right-clicking near the icons and choosing Show Text on Bottom. This way, you don't have to guess what the small buttons do. For environments with large datastores, you can also search a datastore by clicking the Search tab.

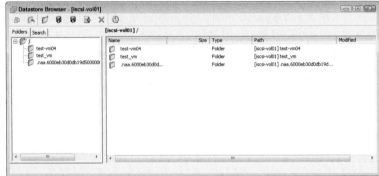

Figure 17-1:
The
Datastore
Browser
window.

Many VMs on many hosts need access to a small group of CD or DVD images, also known as ISO (.iso) files. You might create a folder for the ISO files on a shared datastore by using the Datastore Browser's New Folder button. You can then upload the ISO file to that folder by using the Upload button.

If you move a VM into the environment, you place it on a datastore, but you also need to make the move known to vCenter. To do so, you browse to the .vmx file on the datastore and add it to the Inventory. You can do so by right-clicking the .vmx file and choosing Add to Inventory or by selecting the .vmx file and clicking the Add to Inventory button in the toolbar of the Datastore Browser.

Peering into Permissions

In Chapter 15, we show you how to apply a user to an existing role and that combo to an object. vSphere includes many roles, but sometimes they don't fit. VMware even names many of the roles with (sample) right in them, begging you to modify them! You can see all the default roles on the Home page by clicking the Roles icon in the Administration panel.

Generally, we recommend that you don't modify the roles vSphere provides but that you copy them and then modify them. That way, you retain the sample role for future use. To copy a role, right-click it and choose Clone. This step makes a copy of the role, which you need to immediately rename according to your plan for it.

After you rename the role, right-click the role with the new name you have given it, and choose Edit Role. The Edit Role dialog box appears, as shown in Figure 17-2. Here, you can change the name of the role as well as the privileges the role is granted.

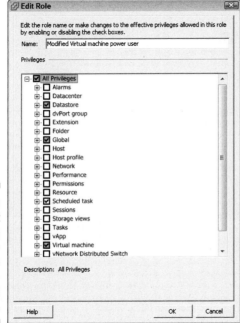

Figure 17-2:
The Edit Role dialog box, showing some of the privileges you can assign.

You can assign more than 200 specific privileges, and for the most part, they're named intuitively so that you can figure out what they do. Each privilege is a single action, so you can be very granular in defining a role's privileges. After you modify the role, you need to run a test. Create an account, map it into the role you created, and ensure that it has the rights (and restrictions) you expect.

When actually assigning the role to a user, remember that you can't do so from the Roles page of the vSphere Client. A permission is the combination of a user or group, a role, and an object. You must assign a permission to a user at the object level, as described in Chapter 15.

Perusing the Environment with Maps

Maps are handy for visualizing the vSphere environment. You can access Maps by going to the Home page of the vSphere Client and clicking the Maps icon. The Maps view appears, where inside the typical navigation pane, you can now select the objects you want to include in the map, as shown in Figure 17-3.

In large environments, the map may be too busy if you select everything, so often you just select the object you're concerned about in the navigation pane. In the upper-right corner of the pane is an Overview map that enables you to move around and zoom on the map. Below the Overview map is the Map Relationships panel, where you can further define what is shown on the map. This panel allows you to make the map show relationships among the different entities in vSphere.

One common map is the relationships between the VMs and the Hosts. To create this map, follow these steps:

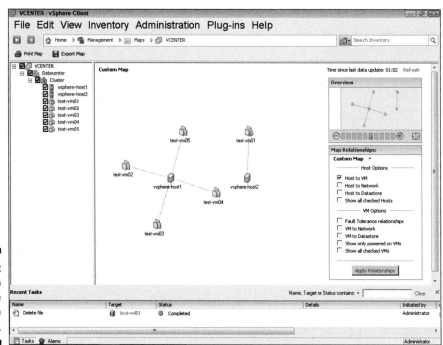

Figure 17-3: The Map view of the vSphere Client.

1. **Open the vSphere Client, log in, and go to the vSphere Client Home page.**

2. **Click the Maps icon.**

   The Maps view appears.

3. **In the navigation pane, choose your hosts and some VMs to map.**

   Don't choose any more than five VMs. As you choose VMs and Hosts, they appear in the content pane.

4. **In the Map Relationships panel, ensure that Host to VM is checked and uncheck everything else.**

5. **Click Apply Relationships.**

   The map redraws with the VMs linked to the hosts, as shown in Figure 17-3.

Because VMs can move frequently between hosts, the map may become out of date quickly. If you need to update the map, you can click the Refresh hyperlink right above the Overview map. Next to the Refresh hyperlink is a counter showing the time since the map was drawn.

Checking the Stats with Performance

Maps are good eye candy, but many administrators are more concerned with performance. Early in a virtualization project, it isn't uncommon for every performance issue to be blamed on the hypervisor. You may find yourself having to gather performance data for the hosts or virtual machines frequently. Fortunately, VMware built performance monitoring into vCenter.

To access the performance data, from the vSphere Client, navigate to the object you're interested in. Once you select the object, such as a Virtual Machine, click the Performance tab. As Figure 17-4 shows, vSphere Client draws some basic performance charts, showing you information that is frequently requested about the past day's performance.

You can modify the time range to view as well as what to look at. You set the range in the Time Range drop-down menu, located in the Performance tab. To modify what is shown, click the Advanced button at the upper-left corner of the Performance tab.

The Advanced view shows a basic chart for the object you've selected. For Hosts and VMs, the default information shown is of CPU usage, but other objects have other defaults. You can change the item being charted by selecting a different object from the Switch To drop-down menu.

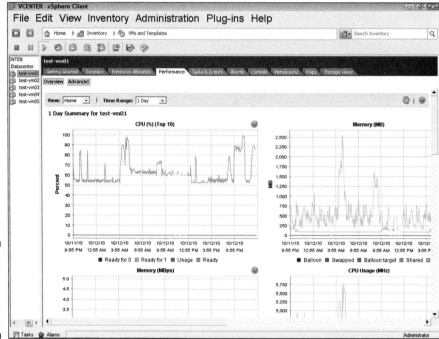

Figure 17-4:
The over-
view of a
VM's perfor-
mance.

When you require an even more specific performance chart, you can click Chart Options next to the chart name from the Advanced chart view. The Customize Performance Chart window opens, as shown in Figure 17-5, where you can choose the settings you want to chart. Like most performance charts, you can choose the range, chart type, object, and specific counter here. At the lower-right of Customize Performance Chart dialog box, you find the Counter Description panel that provides an explanation of each counter.

Some performance data shown by the vSphere Client may differ from the data available within a VM. Generally, what is in a VM can be skewed because the operating system doesn't know it's in a VM, in which case, it's not aware of limits and other restrictions. Monitoring in a VM is still helpful, though, because it represents what the VM is experiencing. So it's wise to consider both. For example, a monitor within a VM may report 100 percent CPU usage, but if you've configured it with a CPU limit of 500 Mhz, and each physical CPU is more than 500 Mhz, you may have a case where a vCPU is pinned, but the physical CPU still has ample resources available.

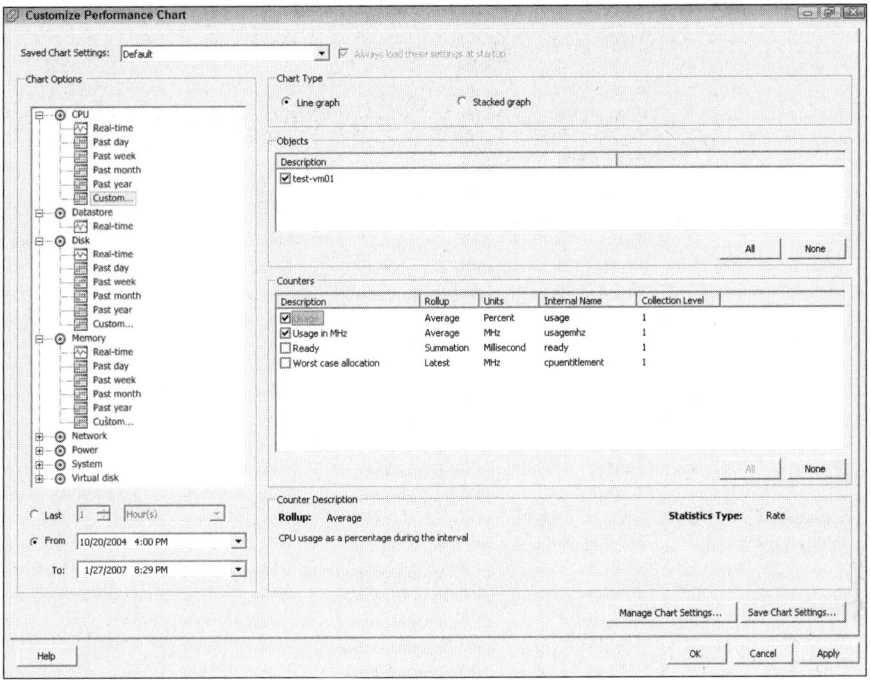

Figure 17-5:
The
Customize
Perfor-
mance
Chart dialog
box with a
CPU chart
selected.

Writing a vCenter To-Do List with Scheduled Tasks

Need to clone a VM every Tuesday? In the middle of the night? No problem! You can schedule a task to occur any time you need! You can use vCenter's internal scheduler to automate many tasks in vCenter, which lets you set up recurring tasks easily. Being able to do so is really useful — for example, if you need to create a snapshot every Monday before the Quality Assurance group begins to work.

To create a scheduled task, just follow these steps:

1. **Open the vSphere Client and click the Scheduled Tasks icon on the Home page.**

   The Scheduled Tasks view opens. Here, you can create, delete, and manage scheduled tasks.

2. **From the Scheduled Tasks view, right-click in the content pane, and choose New Scheduled Task.**

   The Schedule Task dialog box appears.

3. **Choose Create a Snapshot of a Virtual Machine in the Schedule Task dialog box and click OK.**

   The Schedule Task dialog box prompts for what type of Scheduled task, as shown in Figure 17-6. You can choose from several tasks, and each one automatically opens an appropriate wizard to assist you in setting up the task. Here, since you chose the Create a Snapshot of a Virtual Machine item in the Schedule Task dialog box, the Make a Virtual Machine Snapshot wizard opens.

Figure 17-6:
The
Schedule
Task dialog
box.

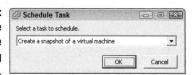

4. **In the Make a Virtual Machine Snapshot wizard, choose the VM that you want to snapshot and click Next.**

   The Describe the Snapshot page opens.

5. **Specify the name of the snapshot.**

   Use a name that describes the snapshot. Often, snapshot names reference what is about to happen, such as "Snapshot Before QA Tests Bad Code."

6. **In the description field, add information, if you need to be more verbose.**

   Snapshot Memory records the contents of the memory to the snapshot and is applicable only to running VMs. Quiesce File System pauses disk Input/Output (I/O) briefly while the snapshot is taken, allowing a better capture of the VM. Quiesce File System requires VMware Tools to be running and is often recommended if the VM and VMware Tools are running. Do not check either one.

7. **Click Next.**

   The Schedule Task page appears.

8. **Enter a task name, choose the schedule, and click Next.**

   The Notification page appears.

9. **Enter an e-mail address to notify and click Next.**

   In the Notification page, you can choose to send an e-mail when the task finishes. Doing so is helpful, because often you're scheduling the task so you do not have to be available to perform the task yourself, but you still need to ensure the task occurs. For notification to work, you must have vCenter's SMTP settings defined, which we explain in Chapter 16.

   The Summary page appears.

10. **Review your selections and click Finish.**

    You've now scheduled your task. The Scheduled Tasks view now shows the scheduled task, as shown in Figure 17-7.

The tasks that you can schedule are limited, but common and easy to set up. If you want to schedule other actions, you can, but you'll need to script them with one of the various VMware provided tools, such as vSphere CLI (Command Line Interface), vSphere PowerCLI, or the vSphere Management Assistant (vMA).

Figure 17-7:
The
Scheduled
Tasks view.

When setting up a scheduled task, it's a good idea to test it at some point before the task executes, if you can. The wizard doesn't fully validate everything about the task when you create it and can fail at runtime. We once scheduled a snapshot for the middle of the night, and it failed because one of the datastores was full. The VM was unprotected during an application upgrade; luckily, we didn't need to use the snapshot!

Chapter 18

One of These Hosts Is Not Like the Other — Host Profiles

In This Chapter

▶ Configuring a host "just right"

▶ Capturing a host's configuration

▶ Using host profiles as a management tool

*T*he Host Profiles feature was introduced in vSphere Enterprise Plus edition to address the manual, error-prone, time-consuming task of individually configuring each ESX host by hand. Prior to host profiles, an administrator would manually configure network and storage settings each time an ESX host was added to the farm. Aside from unique settings such as a host name and network addresses, most ESX hosts in a farm are configured the same. In the case of clustered ESX hosts, they have to be configured the same because it's a requirement for High Availability (HA) and Distributed Resource Scheduler (DRS) to function properly. The Host Profiles feature does just that: Captures a configuration from an ESX host and lets you apply it to other ESX hosts.

In this chapter, you find out how to prepare an ESX host to act as a reference for a new Host Profile. You attach a host profile to another ESX host and then you go through the steps to apply that host profile. You see how to modify a host profile and use it to make changes on the associated ESX hosts.

The Host Profiles feature is available only in the vSphere 4.1 Enterprise Plus edition at this time.

Preparing the Perfect Host

Imagine that you're an administrator responsible for the vSphere host farm and you're setting up your first batch of ESX hosts. After hours of tweaking and testing, you finally have your ESX host just the way you want it. You've added all the port groups to the virtual switches, tweaked all the storage paths, and even added a connection to a shared network volume containing all your company's installation media, just in case. To complete your ESX cluster, you immediately configure a second and third host the same as the first, and finally you have what you consider to be a perfect cluster.

In this situation, you may be thinking that you don't have enough ESX hosts to justify using host profiles, or maybe you have a documented process you feel is just as good as using host profiles.

But consider the following turn of events: A month goes by, and now your boss wants you to add four more ESX hosts to prepare for growth. Hastily, you click through one of your existing ESX host's configuration screens, jotting down each setting. Finally, you have your notepad of settings and proceed to configure the other four ESX hosts. When you're done, you add them to the cluster, and just in time.

Then, one of the backup power units in your server room fails during a power outage, and half the ESX hosts in the cluster go down. vSphere High Availability does its thing, and before you know it, most of the downed virtual machines are coming back up on the remaining ESX hosts. Most of them? Why not all of them? Quickly, you realize you missed adding a datastore on a couple of the ESX hosts and misspelled the datastore name on a third. For the virtual machines that did come up, only half are accessible because the network connections for one ESX host weren't configured with the right settings, and a port group is completely missing from another ESX host. Frustrated, you attempt to correct the erroneous settings and wonder how this oversight could have happened.

The good news is that if you prepare properly and use host profiles, you can prevent this scenario from happening to you.

Network considerations

Using host profiles makes it easy to capture the network configuration from an ESX host and apply the settings to other ESX hosts. However, you must meet some prerequisites outside the ESX host for this feature to work:

- ✔ **Physical network switch port settings:** The settings of the switch ports connected to the new ESX host must be identical to those of the reference ESX host. This requirement is especially true for VLAN membership of the switch port and if the port is configured for VLAN trunking.

- ✔ **Order of physical network adapters:** Isolating virtual machine network traffic from management and storage network traffic normally requires use of separate network adapters, each connected to their own physical network switch port, with each port allowed to access specific resources. When applying host profiles, it's important that the physical network switch port configuration be the same for each switch port connected to the first network adapter on each ESX host. The same goes for each of the network switch ports connected to the second network adapter of each ESX host, and so on.

✔ **Network settings:** As you apply a host profile to an ESX host, you're prompted for the network IP address values for each service console and VMKernel being configured. It's a good idea to have this information ready before applying a host profile to keep the process flowing.

Datastores all around

The Host Profiles feature configures your vSphere datastore connections for you, as long as the datastores are accessible to the ESX host. Here are a few details to ensure that everything goes smoothly:

✔ **Fibre Channel storage:** Make sure that the LUNs on your storage array are correctly presented to the ESX host's Fibre Channel Host Bus Adapter (FC HBA). Simply connecting an ESX host's FC HBAs to a Fibre Channel switch is usually not enough to get an ESX host talking with its assigned storage.

✔ **Access Control Lists (ACLs):** ACLs apply mostly to iSCSI datastores and connections to NFS storage. In order to connect to these types of storage, your ESX host's network address must be added to a list of allowed connections on each storage device. By default, these storage devices deny all connections unless they're specifically on the list.

✔ **Connection limits:** Some network storage devices allow limiting the number of connections to a given storage resource. If this is enabled for your datastores, make sure that the connection limit is set high enough to allow another ESX host to connect.

For specific information about storage and host profiles, please see the vSphere 4.1 documentation.

Connect me with Active Directory

The addition of Active Directory authentication for ESX 4.1 hosts makes it easier to give access to users with Active Directory credentials, but still requires an administrator account to add the ESX 4.1 host to Active Directory. If you want to join your ESX 4.1 hosts to Active Directory, consider the following:

- ✔ **Creating a designated AD account:** You may find it worthwhile to create a special Active Directory account with the privileges to join an ESX host to AD. Using an account set up for another purpose may put you at risk of the password being changed without notice or accidentally being locked out, both of which breaks the ability to add ESX hosts to Active Directory.

- ✔ **Domain controllers:** Servers that use Active Directory for authentication require near-constant connectivity to one of the AD domain's controllers. If the ESX host loses access to a domain controller, you won't be able to log on using AD credentials until the access is restored.

Do you know the time?

You can keep a bunch of server clocks synchronized only by setting them all from a common source. While some organizations maintain their own Network Time Protocol (NTP) servers, most rely on some external source to synchronize. If you haven't configured your ESX hosts to use an NTP server for time synchronization, now is a great time to set it up on the ESX host you use to create your host profile.

See Chapter 10 for more information on synchronizing your ESX hosts with NTP.

Capturing a Host Configuration

An ESX host being used as the source from which the host profile will be created is called a *reference host.* The reference host must be accessible from vCenter Server before you can capture a host configuration.

Follow these steps to create a host profile from a reference ESX 4.1 host:

1. **Connect to vCenter Server with the vSphere Client.**

   The Inventory panel appears.

2. **Click the Hosts tab.**

   The list of ESX hosts appears, as shown in Figure 18-1.

3. **Right-click the reference ESX host and then choose Host Profiles⇨ Create Profile from Host.**

   The Create Profile page appears, as shown in Figure 18-2.

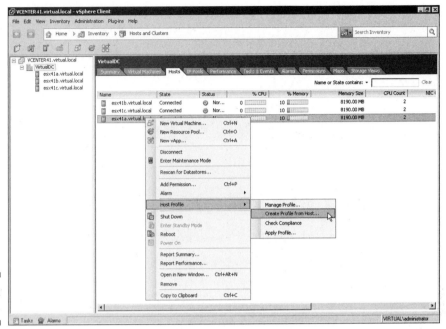

Figure 18-1:
Hosts tab.

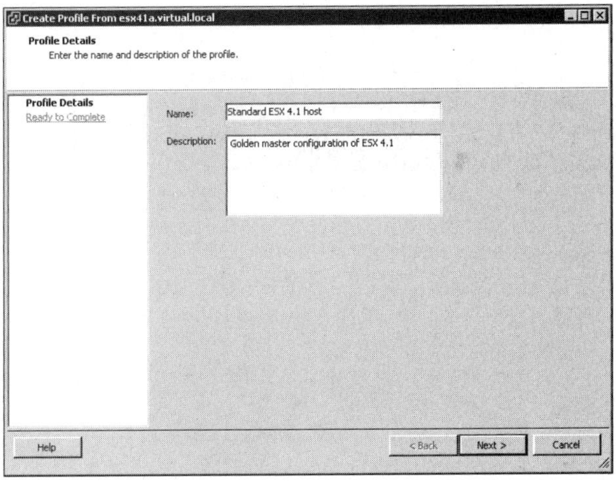

Figure 18-2:
Create
Profile page.

4. **Enter a name for the host profile in the Name field.**

5. **Enter a description of the host profile in the Description field and click Next.**

   This value should describe the configuration being captured.

A summary containing the name and description of the new host profile appears.

6. **Click Finish.**

The host profile is created.

Attaching a Host Profile

After you create a host profile, you can use it to configure other ESX hosts. The first step to configure an ESX host using a host profile is to attach the host profile to the ESX host. This process attaches a host profile to an ESX 4.1 host:

1. **Connect to vCenter Server with the vSphere Client.**

The Home Inventory window appears.

2. **Click the Hosts tab.**

The list of ESX hosts appears, as shown in Figure 18-3.

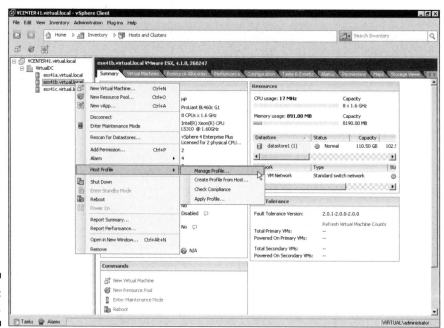

Figure 18-3:
Hosts tab.

3. **Right-click the ESX host you want to configure and then choose Host Profile⇨Manage Profile.**

   The Attach Profile window appears, as shown in Figure 18-4.

4. **Choose the host profile you want to use to configure the ESX host and click OK.**

   The selected host profile is attached to the ESX host.

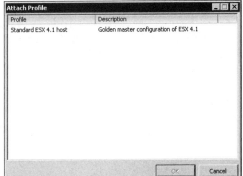

Figure 18-4:
Attach
Profile
window.

Applying a Host Profile

After a host profile is attached to an ESX host, the ESX host must be put in Maintenance mode and then the host profile applied. Follow these steps to apply the attached host profile to the ESX 4.1 host:

1. **Connect to vCenter Server with the vSphere Client.**

   The Home Inventory window appears.

2. **Click the Hosts tab.**

   The list of ESX hosts appears.

   An ESX host can be put only into maintenance mode if virtual machines are running on it. All virtual machines must be powered off or migrated to another host using vMotion.

3. **Right-click the ESX host you want to configure and then choose Enter Maintenance Mode, as shown in Figure 18-5.**

   The Confirm Maintenance Mode dialog box appears, as shown in Figure 18-6.

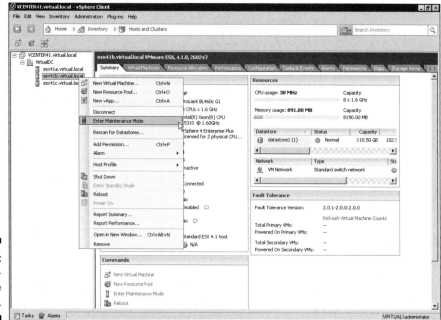

Figure 18-5:
Mainten-
ance Mode
selection.

 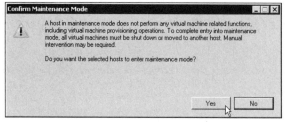

Figure 18-6:
The Confirm
Mainten-
ance Mode
dialog box.

4. Click Yes.

The ESX host is placed into maintenance mode.

5. Right-click the ESX host again and then choose Host Profiles⇨Apply.

The Apply Profile window appears, as shown in Figure 18-7. You are
prompted for an IP address and associated subnet mask for each interface, each service console, and each VMKernel interface included in the
host profile but not yet configured on the ESX host.

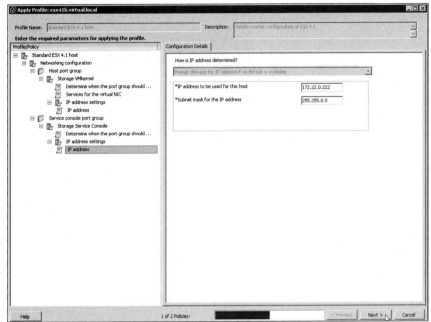

Figure 18-7:
The Apply
Profile
window.

6. **Enter the IP Address for the interface highlighted on the left side of the screen in the IP Address To Be Used For This Host field.**

   Your network administrator should provide this value.

7. **Enter the Subnet Mask for the interface highlighted on the left side of the screen in the Subnet Mask For The IP Address field and click Next.**

   In Step 6, this value is included along with the IP address.

   When all required network settings have been entered, the Configuration Tasks window appears, as shown in Figure 18-8. If you're prompted for another network address, repeat Steps 6 and 7 until you're no longer prompted.

8. **Click Finish.**

   The host profile is applied to the ESX host. Wait for the configuration to complete before proceeding to the next step.

9. **Right-click each ESX host you just configured and then choose Exit Maintenance Mode, as shown in Figure 18-9.**

   The ESX host returns to normal operation. The host profile is now applied and active.

Figure 18-8:
The Configuration Tasks window.

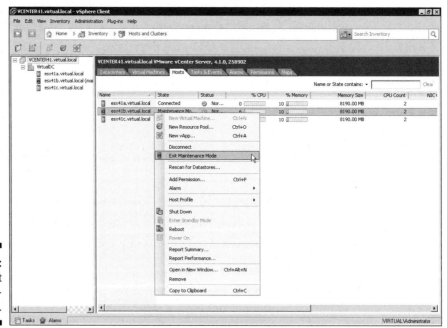

Figure 18-9:
Choose Exit Maintenance Mode.

Changing the Admin Password

Changing the administrator password on all the ESX hosts associated with a host profile is an easy task. Follow these steps to change the administrator password for a host profile:

1. **Connect to vCenter Server with the vSphere Client.**

   The Inventory pane appears.

2. **Click View on the menu bar and then select Home.**

   The Home page appears.

3. **Click the Host Profiles icon in the Management section.**

   The Host Profiles window appears, as shown in Figure 18-10.

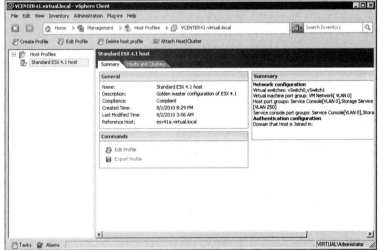

Figure 18-10:
Host
Profiles
window.

4. **Right-click the host profile to edit and then choose Edit Profile.**

   The Edit Profile window appears, as shown in Figure 18-11.

5. **Expand the menu tree in the Profile/Policy section of the screen.**

   A list of items appears.

6. **Expand the Security Configuration item.**

   Another list of items appears, as shown in Figure 18-12.

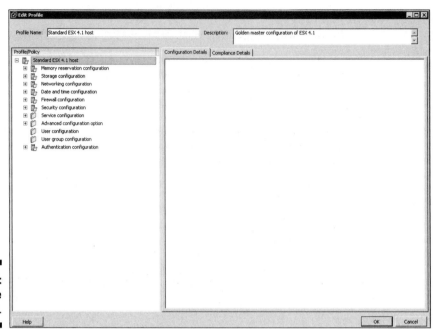

Figure 18-11:
Edit Profile
window.

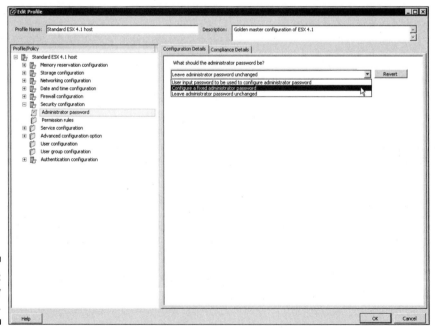

Figure 18-12:
Security
submenu.

7. **Choose Administrator Password.**

   A drop-down list appears in the Configuration Details tab.

8. **Choose Configure a Fixed Administrator Password from the drop-down list.**

   A box with two text fields appears below the drop-down list, as shown in Figure 18-13.

9. **Enter the new administrator password in the Configure Host with This Password field and then again in the Configure host with This Password field; click OK.**

   This password is the new administrator password for ESX hosts configured with this profile.

   The page closes, and the host profile is updated.

10. **Click the Hosts and Clusters tab.**

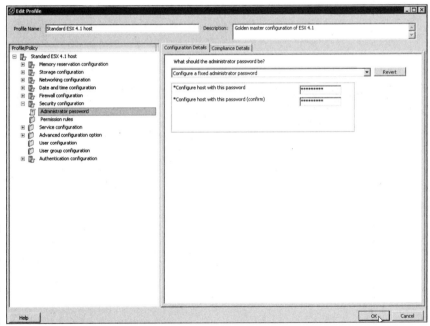

Figure 18-13:
Enter your administrator password.

A list of all ESX Hosts and Clusters attached to the host profile appears, as shown in Figure 18-14.

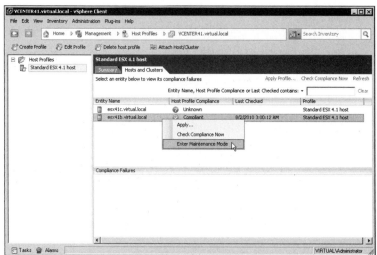

Figure 18-14:
Hosts and
Clusters tab.

11. Right-click the ESX host you want to configure and then choose Enter Maintenance Mode.

The Confirm Maintenance Mode dialog box appears, as shown in Figure 18-15.

12. Click Yes.

The ESX host is placed into Maintenance Mode.

Figure 18-15:
Confirm
Mainten-
ance Mode.

13. Right-click the ESX host again and then choose Host Profiles⇨Apply.

The Apply Profile window appears.

14. Click Finish.

The Host Profile is applied to the ESX host. Wait for the configuration to complete before proceeding to the next step.

15. **Right-click the ESX host you just configured and then choose Exit Maintenance Mode, as shown in Figure 18-16.**

    The ESX host returns to normal operation. The updated host profile is now applied and active. Repeat Steps 11 through 17 for each of the remaining ESX hosts.

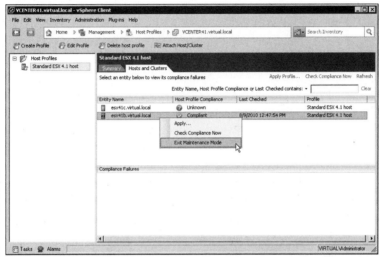

Figure 18-16:
Choose Exit
Mainten-
ance Mode.

Keeping the Host Profile Up to Date

Even after a host profile is applied, reconfiguration will be needed at some point. The easiest way to do so is to update the host profile from the reference host. Follow these steps to update the Host Profile after the reference ESX host configuration has been modified:

1. **Connect to vCenter Server with the vSphere Client.**

   The Inventory panel appears.

2. **Click View on the menu bar and then select Home.**

   The Home page appears.

3. **Click the Host Profiles icon in the Management section.**

   The Host Profiles window appears, as shown in Figure 18-17.

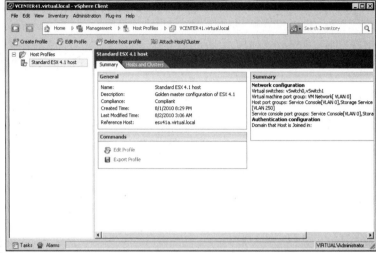

Figure 18-17:
Host
Profiles
window.

4. Right-click the host profile to update and then choose Update Profile from Reference Host, as shown in Figure 18-18.

The reference ESX host is polled, and the host profile is updated.

5. Click the Hosts and Clusters tab.

A list of all ESX hosts and clusters attached to the host profile appears, as shown in Figure 18-19.

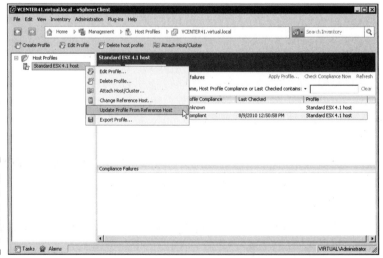

Figure 18-18:
Update
Profile from
Reference
Host option.

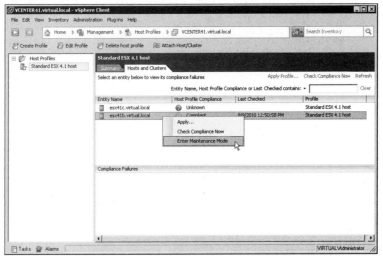

Figure 18-19:
Hosts and
Clusters tab.

6. **Right-click the ESX host you want to configure and then choose Enter Maintenance Mode.**

   The Confirm Maintenance Mode dialog box appears, as shown in Figure 18-20.

7. **Click Yes.**

   The ESX host is placed into maintenance mode.

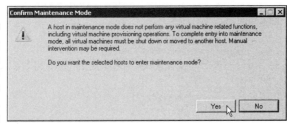

Figure 18-20:
The Confirm
Mainten-
ance Mode
dialog box.

8. **Right-click the ESX host again and then choose Host Profiles⇨Apply.**

   The Apply Profile window appears.

9. **Click Finish.**

   The Host Profile is applied to the ESX host. Wait for the configuration to complete before proceeding to the next step.

10. **Right-click the ESX host you just configured and then choose Exit Maintenance Mode, as shown in Figure 18-21.**

The ESX host returns to normal operation. The updated host profile is now applied and active. Repeat Steps 6 through 10 for each of the remaining ESX hosts.

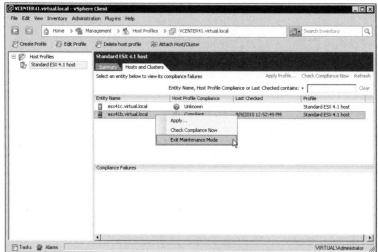

Figure 18-21:
Exit
Mainten-
ance Mode.

Part VI
Tuning and Troubleshooting vSphere

The 5th Wave   By Rich Tennant

"We're still working out the kinks in our cloud computing environment."

In this part . . .

This part covers keeping your vSphere infrastructure up and running smoothly. Chapter 19 provides guidance on making VMs play fair in the environment, making sure each VM gets an adequate share of virtual resources. Chapter 20 explains vSphere's availability features and how they contribute to VM uptime. Chapter 21 is a guide to troubleshooting vSphere, including technique, engaging VMware support, and common issues seen in vSphere environments.

Chapter 19

Making VMs Play Fair with Resource Pools

*W*hen evangelizing a virtual infrastructure, you'll find that some people may not be convinced of the benefits of a virtualization. The first issue your more skeptical customers have is about performance. When putting several VMs on a single host, it's natural to wonder how you can guarantee the performance of each one. This chapter deals with performance and how to keep any of the VMs from becoming a resource hog.

Creating a Resource Pool

Resource pools are groups that you can use to segment CPU and memory resources. You can assign an amount of resources or a limit to a resource group so that VMs are guaranteed appropriate resources. Resource groups can contain VMs or other resource groups.

A vSphere cluster always has at least one resource pool. This invisible resource pool is at the root of all the VMs and resource pools. All VMs and resource pools draw from the invisible root. Resource pools are available only from vCenter. You can create resource pools on standalone hosts, but they're available only for clusters if DRS is enabled. Performance settings can be made to a VM directly or to a resource pool. Typical performance settings for a VM are CPU, memory, and disk, but a resource pool controls only CPU and memory.

To create a resource pool, follow these steps:

1. **Open and log in to the vSphere Client.**

2. **Open the Hosts and Clusters view.**

3. **Right-click the cluster name in the navigation pane on the left and choose New Resource Pool.**

   The Create Resource Pool dialog box, shown in Figure 19-1, appears. This dialog box is split into two frames: CPU Resources and Memory Resources. Leave these settings at their defaults for now.

4. **Type a Name for the resource pool and click OK.**

   The resource pool is created.

To add a VM to the resource pool, from the Hosts and Clusters view, simply drag and drop the VM into the resource pool.

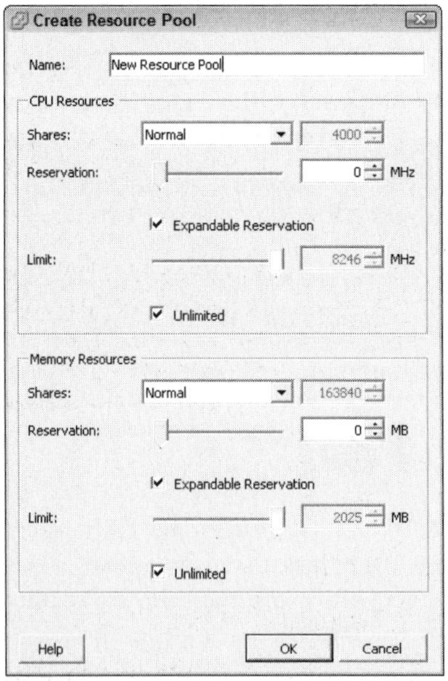

Figure 19-1:
The Create Resource Pool dialog box.

Putting Resources in Perspective

VMs share resources, which often saves money, but your kindergarten teacher probably never told you that sometimes sharing is bad! When a host becomes a bit overloaded, VMs can behave unpredictably. By default, vSphere attempts to balance between the competing VMs, but this doesn't take into account the natural differences in importance that exist among groups of VMs. For example, you may have a critical production server VM on the same host as a far less critical development server VM. Both VMs might get busy, and vSphere will do it's best to balance between the two.

Rarely are organizations without some type of resource contention. In most cases, the resource contention manifests itself without warning. Even the best-designed virtual infrastructures have occasional resource contention, so you need to plan for such occasions. Doing so upfront means less work and a better experience in the long run.

vSphere allows you to assign shares to a VM or resource pool. Within vSphere, you can use shares to control the relative priority of a resource pool or a VM. *Shares* are a basic representation of relative priority a VM has over other VMs. Shares are used by vSphere only if a resource is constrained, so an object with more shares can access the resource more than one with fewer shares. If one VM has twice as many CPU shares as another one, the first VM will be able to access the CPU twice as much as the second VM if resources are constrained. You can assign shares to CPU, memory, or disk resources.

When assigning shares in the vSphere Client, you typically use a value of high, normal, or low. These values correspond to each other with a ratio of 4:2:1. This ratio means that a VM with a high shares value will get four times the access to resources as a VM with low shares, and twice that of a VM set at normal.

A VM that's consuming resources is almost like going to a busy restaurant. If you're important in your community, you may get seated first, and the staff may be more attentive to you than to other patrons. An important VM in its community has a shares value of high, and gets seated and serviced first. If the restaurant, or host, isn't busy, you may be important (high shares), but everyone gets seated and served immediately.

To set shares on a VM, follow these steps:

1. **Open and log in to the vSphere Client.**

2. **Open the Virtual Machines & Templates view.**

3. **Right-click the VM on which you want to set the shares and choose Edit Settings.**

   The VM's Virtual Machine Properties dialog box appears. The various virtual hardware settings are on the Hardware tab.

4. **Click the Resources tab.**

   The Resources tab, shown in Figure 19-2, is where you can adjust the resources a VM is granted. When you click the Resources tab, the CPU settings appear first. You can change the Shares value in the Resource Allocation frame of the Resources tab.

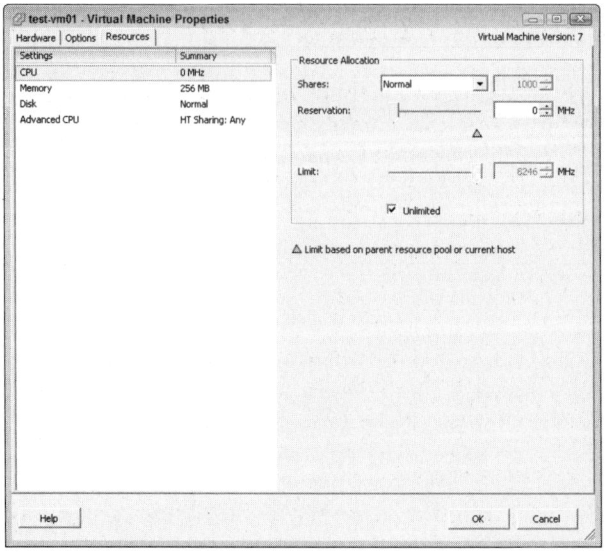

Figure 19-2:
The
Resources
tab of the
Virtual
Machine
Properties
dialog box.

5. **Using the drop-down list, set the CPU Shares value to High.**

6. **Click Memory, located under Settings on the left of the Virtual Machine Properties dialog box.**

   The Resource Allocation frame now changes to focus on Memory Allocation.

7. **Change the Memory Shares to High.**

8. **Click OK to close the Virtual Machine Properties dialog box.**

Setting Limits and Reservations for Clusters, Hosts, and Virtual Machines

Shares are helpful, but they're also relative. If you have a very overloaded cluster, shares won't help that critical VM, even if you have set it to high shares. If many more VMs are asking for resources than you have on the host, shares can't guarantee that a VM continues to perform.

Limits and reservations are more absolute, so you can be sure to keep the resources where you want. You can set limits and reservations are set on VMs and resource pools, but affect clusters, hosts, and VMs by adding or taking away resources from those objects.

Do you have a reservation?

If you want to be absolutely sure that you can eat at your favorite restaurant, even at the busiest times, you need a reservation. Similarly, a VM needs a reservation if you want to guarantee that a resource is available to it. Like a good restaurant putting a Reserved card on a table, a reservation ensures resources are available if the VM needs them.

You can set a reservation on memory and CPU resources by modifying the properties of a VM or resource pool.

Follow the steps in the "Putting Resources in Perspective" section, earlier in this chapter, to open the Virtual Machine Properties dialog box of the VM you want to modify; then continue with these steps:

1. **Click the Resources tab.**

   The Reservation value lets you drag a slider or type a number. Note that a limit may exist based on resources of the parent resource pool or other reservations drawing from the same resources.

2. **Type** 900 **in the CPU Reservation MHz field.**

   This step reserves 900 MHz for the VM's exclusive use, as shown in Figure 19-3. If the VM doesn't use the 900 MHz, it's not used elsewhere, so often reservations are used sparingly.

3. **Click OK to close the Virtual Machine Properties dialog box.**

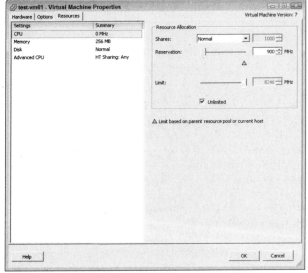

Figure 19-3: Virtual Machine Properties Resources frame with a 900 MHz CPU reservation.

Reservations are reserved when you power on a VM. So, you can easily create many reservations that prohibit many of the VMs from being turned on. Also, when setting resources, the vSphere Client shows you how much is available based on what is running at that time, not what is allocated but not running.

Enforcing hard limits

A limit prevents a VM from using more than a defined amount of resources. You set a limit by changing the Limit slider shown in Figure 19-3. Limits can keep a VM from going out of control. In general, avoiding limits is wise because if a VM needs the resources and they're available, it's best to allow the VM to consume them. However, for VMs that are prone to runaway processes or simply consume more resources than you'd like, you can set a hard limit. You can set limits in the Virtual Machine Properties window of the VM. CPU limits are in MHz, MB, and IOPS.

Avoid using limits unless you really need to. Over time, all systems tend to consume more resources, and limits can get in the way of the natural resource consumption growth. If that's the plan, then great, but limits can needlessly increase administrative burden.

Limits can be handy in some cases where you want to prevent runaway resource consumption, but they also have a nefarious, but occasionally necessary, use: Tricking your application owners. For example, many times, an application owner may not know how much memory they need for their VM. The application owner wants to be conservative, so they may guess that they need 8GB of RAM. If you think you know better, you can humor them by setting the VM to 8GB and set a limit to 4GB of RAM. Then, the guest OS will report 8GB of RAM, but the VM will be able to use only 4GB. Limits can be changed while a VM is running, so you can adjust a limit quickly if you need to. If you find you are often tricking your application owners, you may need to!

Giving preference to certain VMs

By setting shares and reservations, you can truly ensure that an important VM, such as an authentication server, gets all the resources it needs, and won't be affected by other things occurring in the virtual infrastructure. This preferential treatment can also be useful in a temporary situation. For example, your organization may have a server used for tax reports that is demanding of performance for only one month a year.

Occasionally, setting reservations on a VM can also be a good step in troubleshooting performance for an application you haven't run on VMware before.

Delegating Resources to Other VMs

You can use resource pools to lend resources to a department. If a department has a handful of VM servers, you can place them in a resource pool and grant the pool shares, reservations, and limits. Each VM in the pool can compete with the others in the pool, but they can't impact other department machines if you set up limits.

Setting up each VM to have appropriate resources is time-consuming, so with resource pools, you can quickly define the performance parameters at the resource pool. Many organizations have three resource pools at the root of the cluster, with shares set to high, normal, and low. By placing all the VMs in those three Resource pools, you can easily create some predictability in your VM performance in the case of low resources, but only if you have an equal number of VMs in each resource pool. A resource pool with high shares and many VMs may perform worse than a resource pool with Low shares and few VMs because each VM gets a relative amount of the shares available in the resource pool.

Allocating resources to a group

To allocate resources to a group, you modify the resource pool. You can do so without powering off the VMs that are in the resource pool, so be careful because you can easily create a situation where VMs don't have enough resources.

To allocate resources to a resource pool:

1. **Open and log in to the vSphere Client.**

2. **Open the properties of the resource pool by right-clicking the resource pool and choosing Edit Settings.**

   The Edit Settings dialog box appears, as shown in Figure 19-4, where you can easily set the shares, reservation, and limit of the resource pool. Keep in mind that the shares, reservation, and limit is for the entire pool, not a setting that simply propagates to VMs. So, if you set a resource pool to 5,000 MHz and you have five VMs in that pool, each one receives only 1,000 MHz if they are all equal and busy.

3. **Change the CPU Shares value to High and click OK.**

   Now, a resource pool is set to get high shares for CPU if the host is low on CPU resources.

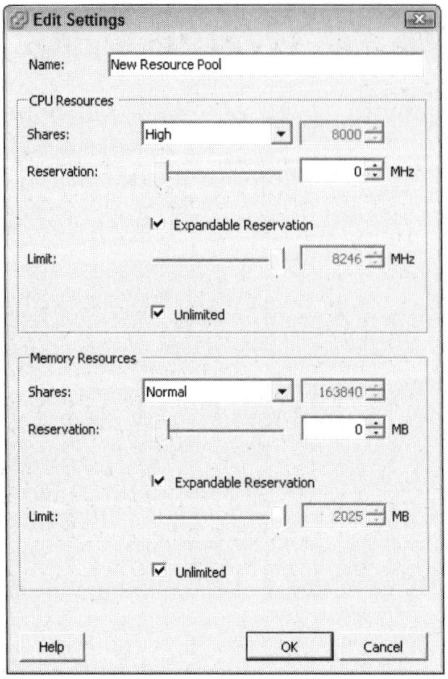

Figure 19-4:
The Edit
Settings
dialog
box of a
resource
pool.

Favoring critical machines

It's common to create a resource pool for critical VMs. Reservations for critical machines often have a high shares value and a reservation set to an appropriate amount of resources depending on how many VMs are in the pool. Generally, you allow the reservation to be expandable, which enables the reservation to expand to use resources of its parent if they're needed and available. In a critical machine resource pool, you also ensure that no limit is set because you want these VMs to get everything they may need if resources are available.

Conversely, for low-end sandbox development systems, you might set shares to low, not create a reservation, and set a limit so that the sandbox systems will never interfere with other systems.

Combining Resource Pools

You can easily modify both the settings and membership of resource pools. To move systems in an out of resource pools, just drag the VMs from the Hosts and Clusters view of the vSphere client. In some cases, such as adding a host to the cluster, you may need to choose what to do with existing resource pools.

The nesting instinct: Dividing resources with nests

Resource pools can have VMs or other resource pools as their members. Nested resource pools provide an easy way to divide resources among groups and then further divide the resources.

For example, say that you have three departments in your organization: IT, HR, and Sales. Each department has paid for a host in your cluster and expects to fully utilize the host for their production and nonproduction servers. You want to use a DRS cluster, rather than standalone servers to leverage vMotion and maximize performance. Instead of limiting all the sales VMs to one host and the HR VMs to another, you can create three top-level resource pools, each with about one host's worth of resources, and put all the VMs in that resource pool. Later, you decide that you also need to prioritize the production VMs. You might create a resource pool structure, as shown in Figure 19-5.

Don't go overboard with nesting resource pools. While resource pools can save a lot of time, too many of them can become their own source of headaches!

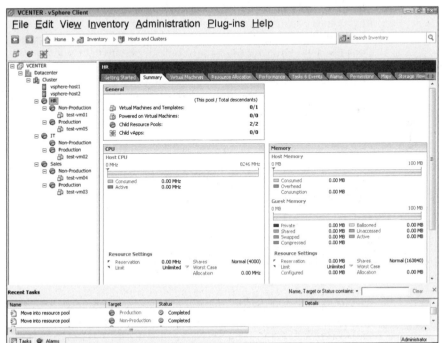

Figure 19-5:
A nested resource pool structure.

Importing VMs with their own resource settings

If a VM already has resource settings, when you add it to Inventory, the settings will persist, since they're stored in the VMX file. If the settings are set very high, you may get an error when you first boot it up because reservations are computed at the time you power on. This issue is easily resolved by editing the Virtual Machine properties as described in the earlier "Putting Resources in Perspective" section of this chapter. When you're editing the resources, simply remove any reservation and set shares to normal, and you'll be able to boot it up.

Merging resource pools when adding a host to a cluster

Because you can create resource pools in a stand-alone host or in a DRS cluster, you may have cases where you move a stand-alone host with resource pools to a cluster. When moving a stand-alone host to the cluster, the Add Host Wizard, which is covered in Chapter 13, prompts you on whether you want VMs to be moved to the cluster's invisible root resource pool or to have a new resource pool created that contains the VMs or resource pools that were on the host. Figure 19-6 shows the Add Host Wizard's Choose Destination Resource Pool page. You can usually just put the VMs in the root and move them after you've integrated the new host into the cluster.

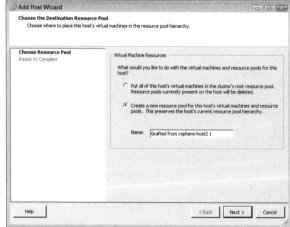

Figure 19-6:
The Choose Destination Resource Pool page of the Add Host Wizard.

Chapter 20

Using vSphere
Availability Features

*V*Mware has maintained its competitive advantage in the virtualization marketplace by discovering new ways to increase uptime of virtual machines with every major release. vSphere 4.1 represents the latest release of VMware's bare-metal hypervisor platform and respective management tools designed for supporting mission-critical workloads.

This chapter explains the different levels of availability and their associated features. You configure a cluster to use VMware High Availability (HA). You also discover how to set rules for restarting VMs during failover and how to set aside capacity to accept VMs from a failed host. You also find out about VMware Fault Tolerance (FT), its prerequisites, and when to use it.

Deciding How Much Downtime Is Too Much

The acceptable amount of downtime for a computer system varies widely across organizations and is driven by a number of factors:

- ✔ Regulatory compliance
- ✔ Service-level agreements

✔ Impact on revenue

✔ Human health and safety

✔ Emergency state

The maximum time a system can be down before impacting business defines the Recovery Time Objective (RTO). The maximum data loss that can occur during downtime defines the Recovery Point Objective (RPO). RTOs can range from absolute zero to several days depending upon the application, and RPOs can go from zero loss to several days or more.

Defining zero downtime

Even the definition of *zero downtime* can vary depending upon the sensitivity of the application. A high-volume financial trading application can be impacted by just one second of downtime, whereas a Web site may not be impacted by a couple of minutes of downtime. In the case of e-commerce, the checkout portion of that same Web site may be impacted by a few seconds of downtime during a payment. Because every organization is different, it's important to discover the availability requirements from management and business users.

Rarely will a computer operate with zero downtime — so, rarely, in fact, that even Web sites that are considered zero downtime sites achieve such a high level of availability by building an infrastructure that is redundant, eliminating single points of failure in the overall environment. In this way, devices are expected to fail, but the presented application continues to run.

Traditional server infrastructures are extremely expensive to set up in a highly available manner. They usually require specialized, proprietary hardware.

Clustering at the OS level

Many operating systems have clustering features at the OS level. These clustering solutions often use a shared disk, called the *quorum,* to keep track of resource ownership, and most are *active/passive,* meaning that only one node is busy at a time.

While many OS level clusters can work in vSphere, the only configuration supported by VMware is Microsoft Cluster Service (MSCS). In vSphere, you can create three types of MSCS clusters using VMs. While all three MSCS clusters require a shared disk, different rules apply to what you need to do:

✔ **Cluster virtual machines on one physical host:** This option provides for a two-node cluster that sits on a single physical box. Because clustering protects against physical issues, what good is this setup? Clustering on one physical host is helpful if you need a cluster set up for testing functionality, but don't want the expense of physical servers. Many organizations run this scenario for Quality Assurance and development situations.

Clustering on one physical host is usually the easiest clustering option to set up because it doesn't have as complicated a storage and network configuration as the other solutions. The disks that you create for this option can be virtual disks or non-pass-through Raw Device Mapping (RDM) disks in virtual compatibility mode.

✔ **Cluster virtual machines across physical hosts:** From an availability standpoint, this option makes more sense to many administrators. By setting up the cluster across two physical hosts, you protect against a physical host failure. Many OS level clusters allow very fast recovery, so this solution can sometimes allow for faster recovery than VMware HA. Because a disk must be available to multiple physical hosts, virtual disks aren't permitted, but both non-pass-through RDMs in virtual compatibility mode and pass-through RDMs in physical compatibility mode are usable.

✔ **Cluster a physical and a virtual machine:** The hardware for a cluster can be expensive, and often, the passive node is hardly utilized until an event occurs. The low use of the passive node prompts fiscally conservative people to ask, "What if I could have that passive node support multiple clusters? They likely won't all fail at once."

MSCS doesn't allow that option, but in vSphere, you can have a single physical host contain several passive node VMs. In this case, a VM and a physical server need to each see the shared disks, so the only option is to use a pass-through RDM in physical compatibility mode.

MSCS is complicated and has many prerequisites. Many of these prerequisites change frequently, so it is wise to check the VMware Web site for the latest information. The vSphere 4.1 guide for MSCS, named Setup for Failover Clustering and Microsoft Cluster Service is located at `www.vmware.com/pdf/vsphere4/r41/vsp_41_mscs.pdf`.

Comparing high availability and fault tolerance

High availability and fault tolerance are often interchanged incorrectly. *High availability* is a concept that measures a system against an expected duty cycle. That cycle is often 24 hours a day; in that case, you might design the system to be 99 percent available. This design sounds good, but a system that is available 99 percent of the time has about 3.65 days of downtime a year. Typical highly available systems are in four, five, or six "nines," meaning they have 99.99 percent or more availability. The key with high availability is an expectation of a short period of unscheduled downtime. In the case of "five-nines" availability, a common goal that businesses use, that 99.999 percent uptime equals 5.26 minutes of downtime a year.

Fault tolerance is different. *Fault tolerance* is often a component of high availability and refers to how well a system can handle an error, which you usually achieve by eliminating all single points of failure. Parts of most servers are fault tolerant, such as mirrored disk drives or redundant power supplies, but most servers aren't completely fault tolerant. Fully fault tolerant systems do exist and are usually used in life critical systems. A municipal emergency line (such as 911 in the United States), for example, often has two sets of call dispatch recorders that are entirely independent. If one fails, the other one can take over with no downtime whatsoever.

Most of the time, a highly available system uses many fault tolerant components. Even systems that aren't considered highly available often have fault tolerant components to allow for easier maintenance and support.

To use the VMware Fault Tolerance, you must have VMware HA enabled. However, you can have HA enabled and not use Fault Tolerance.

Using VMware High Availability

In the early days of x86 virtualization, the most common concern was, "What if you put 20 VMs on a host and the host fails?" The answer used to be, "We'll buy fault-tolerant components where we can and hope the host does not fail."

This plan clearly worked well enough because virtualization took off, but it was likely limited to nonproduction workloads. Later, VMware introduced HA in VMware ESX 3, and it has matured a lot since then. This maturity means that you can answer the question this way: "We'll buy fault tolerant components where we can, and if a host fails, vSphere will automatically restart the VMs on healthy hosts. This technology is great because vSphere protects all the VMs, not just our critical ones."

Being able to answer the question that way was a great story and really accelerated the deployment of VMware for production situations.

VMware vSphere provides HA to virtual machines by pooling ESX hosts into a cluster. The hosts are monitored, and if one of the hosts fails, the virtual machines from the failed host are restarted on other hosts in the cluster.

Prerequisites for VMware High Availability

VMware HA depends on a shared storage. HA doesn't actually move the data files around; it simply registers the failed VMs to other hosts that can see the same shared storage. Also, as with any vSphere cluster, you must have networks configured and named the same so that the VM can simply connect to the same network it always has.

Name resolution using Domain Name Services (DNS) is also important. The hosts will communicate with one another, so you want to make sure that they can find each other using the names that they are known as in vCenter.

Naturally, if you're planning on putting the VMs from a failed host on the other host, you must have space for them. Often, with server systems, having a spare system is referred to as *(N)*+1, where *(N)* is the amount of servers you need typically for production. As an example, you might have five servers that you need in production, but have a sixth in case a server fails. In general, with any *(N)*+1 plan, you must have the "1" in order for the plan to be successful. In vSphere, that "1" doesn't need to be dedicated; you just need a host-worth of capacity free in the cluster. You can also have *(N)*+2, or more in vSphere.

This idea is fine in general because it allows you to perform maintenance of a host without impacting the operations. Generally, on a cluster of five or more hosts, we recommend at least two hosts'-worth of extra capacity.

Bringing order to your VMs

Not all VMs are equal, so you can define the priority of VMs to restart following a failure in the cluster settings. If HA has to make a hard decision on what to bring on, the restart priority guides HA so that the most critical VMs are powered on first.

You set up this functionality in the Cluster settings, and you simply set a VM restart priority. The default setting is medium for the cluster, and you can either choose to disable restart or choose from a high, medium, or low priority.

After a hardware event, you might address the hardware issue and then bring the host back up. If you have DRS enabled in a fully automated mode, it will eventually rebalance the cluster. If DRS is in a manual mode, it prompts you on suggestions, and you can manually move the VMs.

Providing Your VMs High Availability

Gee, HA sounds great, but how do you set it up? Like many things in vSphere, setting up HA is easy, but you need to be sure that your cluster is configured properly. A good way to do so is to ensure that the vMotion operations work well and to go through each host to make sure there's consistency in network connections and names.

When HA is enabled on a cluster, an agent is installed on each host to communicate with the other ESX hosts in the cluster. The first five hosts added to an HA cluster are designated as *primary hosts.* Primary hosts maintain and synchronize all the information about the cluster's status. This information is used to determine when and if to initiate failover of VMs to other ESX hosts. Any hosts added beyond the first five are designated as secondary hosts. If a primary host is removed from the cluster, HA automatically promotes a secondary host to be a primary host and fill the vacancy.

When adding a ESX host to an HA cluster with at least one other ESX host, the host being added must be able to communicate with at least one primary host in the HA cluster, or the process will fail.

Responding to failure

Each member host of an HA cluster is constantly looking out for its peers. The hosts use the HA agent installed on each of them to exchange heartbeats every second with their fellow cluster members to ensure that everyone is up and running. If a host in the HA cluster fails to send a heartbeat for more than 15 seconds, and the host doesn't respond to pings on the network, HA declares that ESX host as failed. This detected failure triggers restarting the machines previously running on the failed host on alternative hosts.

Host Network Isolation varies slightly in that the host is still running, but the host is unable to communicate with other hosts in the HA cluster. If the host doesn't receive heartbeats from any other hosts in the cluster for 12 seconds, it attempts to ping other addresses, including the management network of other vSphere hosts, on the network. If that fails as well, the host declares itself isolated. The isolated host will shut down its running VMs to release the locks on its own VMs' virtual disk files, allowing other hosts to take control of the VMs. When the isolated host's network connection is unavailable for 15 seconds or more, the other hosts in the cluster treat the isolated host as failed and restart the isolated host's VMs on other cluster hosts.

The network connectivity to an ESX host should have a redundant design so that at least one network path is always available. This design nearly eliminates the likelihood of a host becoming isolated.

Enabling High Availability on a cluster

To enable HA on a cluster, first make sure that the cluster is operational and that VMotion operations work as you expect. Also ensure that DNS is working properly, as HA involves important communication between the hosts.

To enable HA on a cluster:

1. **Open and log in to the vSphere Client and navigate to the Hosts and Clusters view.**

2. **Open the Cluster settings by right-clicking the cluster object and choosing Edit Settings.**

   The Cluster Settings dialog box opens. Here, you can enable HA or DRS, as well as modify several settings that pertain to the cluster. The Cluster Settings dialog box is shown in Figure 20-1.

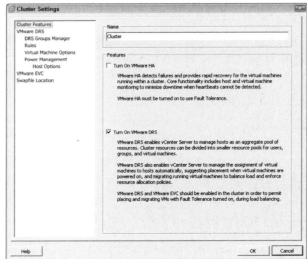

Figure 20-1:
The Cluster Settings dialog box in the vSphere Client.

3. **In the Cluster Features panel, which is shown by default, select the Turn on VMware HA option and click OK.**

The HA setup begins. The vCenter server installs the HA agent on the hosts and sets them up to support HA. Several tasks relating to installing and configuring the HA agent on the host appear in the Recent Tasks pane (see Figure 20-2).

After all the tasks are complete, HA is set up for the cluster. This set up begins protecting the cluster immediately; you don't have to opt-in the virtual machines to the service.

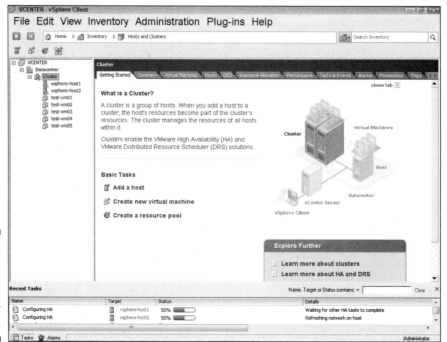

Figure 20-2:
The vSphere Client while configuring a cluster for HA.

Exploring VMware Fault Tolerance — Beyond HA

VMware High Availability enables rapid recovery of VMs in the case of hardware failure. It can also detect and recover from OS failure by moving a VM to a healthy host and rebooting the VM. Because VMs boot fast, the amount of downtime may be only a minute!

For some systems, even a minute of unplanned downtime can be catastrophic, and that's where VMware FT comes in. VMware FT takes a VM, called the *primary* VM, and creates an identical copy of it, which is called the *secondary* VM. Both VMs run in perfect synchronization, processing the same data, changing the same memory locations, writing the same data to disk. This synchronization is called *vLockstep Technology*.

VMware FT doesn't protect against application errors. If you protect a VM with FT and then the application goes into an error condition, that error will be faithfully reproduced on the secondary VM.

Prerequisites for VMware Fault Tolerance

The prerequisites for HA are pretty light, but FT is a different story altogether. It has several prerequisites, for both hosts and VMs:

✔ **Hosts:**

- vSphere Edition must be Advanced, Enterprise, or Enterprise Plus.

- Cluster must be set up and HA must operate correctly.

- CPUs must be of the same family and within 400 MHz of each other.

- CPUs must support Hardware Virtualization, and the server must have it enabled in BIOS.

- Hosts should have a dedicated 1Gbps connection to all other hosts for FT logging traffic. 10Gbps Ethernet is recommended.

✔ **Virtual machines:**

- VM must be on shared storage of NFS, FC, or iSCSI.

- VM data files must be a virtual machine disk or a non-pass-through RDM in virtual compatibility mode.

- VM data files must not be thin provisioned.

- VMs must have a single vCPU.

- VMs must not have devices attached such as (CD), serial devices, or USB devices.

- VMs must not use paravirtualized devices, SAN HBA virtualization, NIC pass-through, or vlance networking drivers.

✔ **VMs may not make use of several features:**

- **Snapshots:** Snapshots are incompatible with FT. You must remove any snapshots before enabling FT.

- **Storage vMotion:** You can use Storage vMotion to migrate a fault-tolerant VM by turning FT off and moving the VM. After it's moved, you can turn FT back on. While FT is off, the VM isn't protected in a continuous way, but it's still eligible for VMware HA protection.

- **Linked Clones:** Linked Clones use a sophisticated pointer map and are incompatible with FT.

- **VMware Consolidated Backup:** VMware Consolidated Backups make use of snapshots, and thus are incompatible with FT.

These requirements are so strict that when writing this chapter, we didn't have appropriate hardware in our labs. We had to reach out to other organizations to secure hardware on which to test FT. The requirements for FT are strict, but compared to providing continuous fault tolerance in physical hardware, VMware Fault Tolerance is much easier and less expensive!

Calculating the cost of VMware Fault Tolerance

Many editions of vSphere include VMware FT, but it's not free. Using VMware FT requires a more complicated infrastructure, due to the high bandwidth logging interface, as well as additional CPU and memory requirements for the secondary VM. On both the primary and secondary VM, vSphere sets up the VM to have a memory reservation equal to the memory assigned to the VM so that FT-enabled VMs can't take advantage of oversubscription technologies. Because FT uses the shared storage, it doesn't require duplicate disk space, but you must use a Thick disk, and FT scrubs the disk on first conversion so that it's zeroed out.

Enabling VMware Fault Tolerance

If your infrastructure meets the requirements of VMware FT and you want to enable it, you can do so easily. Depending on the setup of the VM and the host, you may be able to do so while the VM is running. However, we always shut down the VM that VMware FT will be enabled on. Shutting down the VM ensures the best results and enables vSphere to quickly configure the VM for FT.

To enable VMware Fault Tolerance on a VM:

1. **Log in to the vSphere Client and go to the VMs and Templates view.**

2. **Right-click the VM and choose Fault Tolerance⇨Turn on Fault Tolerance.**

   The Turn on Fault Tolerance dialog box appears noting the changes that vSphere must make to the VM in order to enable it. Common changes are that the DRS automation level for this VM will change to disabled and that a Memory reservation equal to the memory assigned to the VM will be set up. If the VM is currently thin or thick provisioned, but not fully zeroed out, the dialog box will also note that vCenter will convert the disk file and take some time. Figure 20-3 shows an "intimidating" dialog box noting all three concerns.

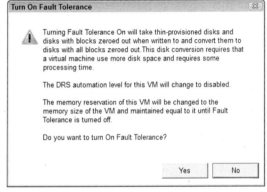

Figure 20-3: Scary "Warning" dialog box about Fault Tolerance.

3. **Click Yes.**

   In the Recent Tasks pane, note that several tasks are performed by the system to enable FT on the VM. When the tasks are finished, the vSphere Client changes the VM's icon to a darker VM icon, as shown in Figure 20-4.

One task that occurs when you turn on FT is that a secondary VM is created, named the same as the first, and appended with (secondary). To prevent confusion, this secondary VM isn't shown by the vSphere Client in the navigation pane, but you can see it by clicking the Datacenter object and then the Virtual Machines tab, as shown in Figure 20-4.

Fault Tolerance is now enabled for the VM, but you still need to boot up the VM. Do so in the normal way, and you now have a fully fault-tolerant solution!

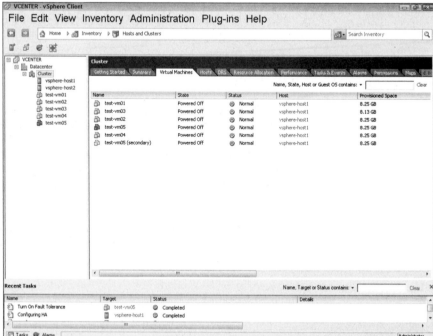

Figure 20-4:
The vSphere
Client
showing
VMs with
FT enabled.

You can open the console of both the primary and secondary VMs, but the secondary console is always read-only. You can see that the secondary VM processes the same instructions, draws the same graphics, and follows the primary VM exactly.

Protecting multi-VM applications

Protecting a single VM may be easy with VMware FT, but many applications span several VMs. If you want to protect the application, you must ensure that all the servers are protected in one way or another. All servers that are VMs must meet the prerequisites. If a physical server provides any services, that server must also be set up with another product to be fault tolerant. So, to truly be fault tolerant, all components involved in the solution must be fault tolerant. If you build a fault tolerant application using several VMware FT enabled VMs and connect them all to the same nonredundant network switch, you probably haven't really achieved the goal of fault tolerance.

Making the Rules (and Breaking Them)

Automated systems such as DRS are quite helpful, but what if they put two VMs that are redundant to one another on the same host? If the host fails, it might take out all of VMs.

By default, VMware HA takes its job seriously. So seriously, in fact, that when you enable it, it ensures that if a host fails in the cluster, there are enough resources to relocate the affected machines to other hosts. This feature is called *admission control,* and you can leave it enabled, or you can disable it. Figure 20-5 shows the default VMware HA properties, and you can define the rules around how a VM can boot up.

Generally, you want to keep admission control enabled so that you don't oversubscribe the cluster to the point that a host failure will hurt the overall performance of the VMs. Sometimes, you need to disable admission control so that you can perform maintenance, or it may simply be overkill in a cluster full of nonproduction VMs. Admission control ensures that if a host does fail, HA has space to move a VM to, ensuring that no VM gets left behind.

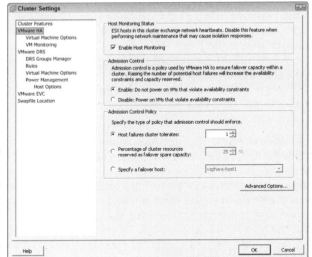

Figure 20-5: VMware HA properties surrounding admission control.

Managing acceptable failure settings

The Admission Control Policy setting's default of "1" for Host Failures Cluster Tolerates is great if you have a few hosts in the cluster, but in a cluster with many hosts, you may want to allow for more than one simultaneous host failure.

You can set how much capacity to reserve in case of a failure by changing the options in the Admission Control Policy pane. You have three options:

- ✔ **Host Failures Cluster Tolerates:** This default setting is configured to one host failure, which means that the HA system will reserve one host's worth of resources across all the other hosts. You can configure up to four hosts. When vSphere computes how many resources to reserve in place of a host, it assumes that the most powerful host is the one that might fail and determines how many VM slots are needed based on the largest VMs in the cluster. These slots are logical groups of resources that the HA engine uses to simplify the computation. Because HA is so conservative, it maximizes protection, but this conservative approach can result in admission control preventing VMs from powering up even if the cluster still has resources available. In general, Host Failures Cluster Tolerates admission control is often used when hosts and VMs are somewhat uniform.

- ✔ **Percentage of Cluster Resources Reserved as Failover Spare Capacity:** This setting lets you be more granular than the Host Failures Cluster Tolerates setting. You can choose any amount up to 50 percent. This solution is flexible because it simply reserves a percentage of overall capacity. It's especially appropriate when each host has a different amount of available resources. However, in practice, this setting has the negative effect of not ensuring that the excess capacity is contiguous. So, if you need to reserve 16GB for a host failure and you have 16 hosts, you could have 16GB on one host that is reserved, or you could have 1GB on each of the 16 hosts. If VMs that need to be relocated each need 2GB, having only 1GB on each host means that HA won't have a place to put the failed VMs! HA integrates with DRS to move stuff around, so it may be able to sort things out, but the recovery will take a lot longer.

- ✔ **Specify a Failover Host:** This option specifies a single host to take the VMs in the event that one fails. When you enable this option, the host that you specify is removed from automatic VM placement and DRS operations. This option allows for only a single host failure and works best when the hosts have the same amount of resources.

Configuring behaviors for critical situations

VMware HA can protect against more than a host failure. You can enable VM monitoring in the Cluster HA settings, as shown in Figure 20-6. VM Monitoring makes the host monitor the VM for a heartbeat provided by the VMware Tools installed in the VM. If a heartbeat isn't received in a set period of time, the HA agent monitors that VM's I/O usage to determine whether the VM is indeed down. If no activity shows, HA begins the process to reboot the VM.

This capability is powerful, and it extends HA's capabilities from the hardware to the VM itself. It also protects against operating system and application hangs. In vSphere, application developers can also make use of the Software Development Kit (SDK) to take this heartbeat functionality to the application layer. Application monitoring is relatively new, but VMware expects future applications to be able to integrate with the HA service.

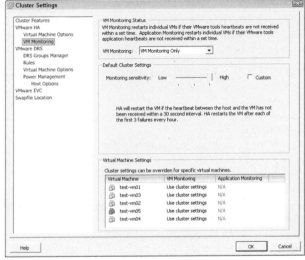

Figure 20-6: VM Monitoring settings in Cluster Settings.

Saving space for visitors during maintenance

One of the best things about vSphere is the ability to do many operations while the VMs are active elsewhere in the cluster. To do so, you put a host in maintenance mode, and the VMs on the host move to other hosts in the cluster.

Usually, a set of servers can tolerate one failure, but not always two. So, while performing maintenance, be sure that you have enough capacity so that everything is running as it should be, plus strive to get the host back into service as quickly as possible.

Chapter 21

Troubleshooting vSphere

- -

- -

*I*n any vSphere environment, given enough time, things will go wrong. It's not necessarily a reflection of poor administration, or even karma coming back to get you. Inherently, vSphere environments grow and get complex over time, meaning increased possibility of problems.

This chapter provides you with some basic troubleshooting techniques for your vSphere environment. You discover some of the more common issues that pop up in vSphere and how to quickly identify them. You also find some tips to prevent future trouble.

Conducting General Troubleshooting

When you first have an issue, take a step back and capture the bigger picture. Look for something that's common among the affected systems and see whether there's a correlation with another environmental issue, such as storage or network. If you come up empty for answers externally, you'll need to do some troubleshooting.

In any troubleshooting process, you need to take each step one by one. The key to good troubleshooting is to ensure that you can isolate the root cause. To do so, you need to make sure that you track your actions.

When an issue arises, you first need to look at what may have changed recently in the environment. Often, recent changes, such as patches or updates, may be the issue. Some patches that apply successfully cause issues by increasing host security, so systems that connect to the host also occasionally need updates.

Looking at what changed is often the best way to start. When an issue arises, removing or backing out a recent change is often the first step to take.

After backing out a recent change, continue troubleshooting by evaluating the environment, making one change at a time. Sometimes, the change is based on best practices, and other times, the change is a result of a gut feeling. Make one change and test the result. Remember that the Internet (especially community forums and sites) can provide a lot of tips. In all cases, if you work on a team, remember to brainstorm and approach the situation as a team, as multiple troubleshooters working independently can cause more harm than good.

Not all issues are the result of recent changes. Sometimes, issues can crop out of nowhere, but the troubleshooting steps you take are similar.

ESXi: Easier or harder to troubleshoot?

VMware has two versions of the bare metal hypervisor, ESX and ESXi. ESXi doesn't have a service console, so it requires a different approach when troubleshooting. So, is ESXi easier or harder to troubleshoot?

Most engineers might say that ESXi is harder to troubleshoot, but because it's smaller, fewer things can go wrong. Without a service console, ESXi has fewer security patches, so there are fewer upgrades that might disrupt the host.

You can accomplish most tasks in ESXi from the vSphere Client, just as you can with ESX. For automation, use the VMware vCLI, PowerCLI, or the vMware SDK.

Super-secret Tech Support Mode

When troubleshooting ESXi, you may need to enter *Tech Support Mode* (TSM). TSM is a feature that provides a basic Linux-based console, but it is limited. Not all ESX commands work in Tech Support Mode, but it was greatly enhanced in ESX 4.1.

TSM works for local or remote connections. You can enable them individually or both at the same time. It's usually best to enable only what you need.

VMware recommends using TSM only when VMware Support instructs you to. When using TSM, set the timeout so that it automatically disconnects any active sessions and exits Tech Support Mode.

To enable TSM on an ESXi 4.1 host:

1. **Open and log on to the vSphere Client.**

2. **Navigate to the Hosts and Clusters view and choose the host in the navigation pane.**

3. **Click the Configuration tab, click Security Profile, and then click the Properties hyperlink.**

   The Services Properties window appears, as shown in Figure 21-1.

4. **Choose the Local Tech Support or the Remote Tech Support (SSH) items and click Options.**

   The Options dialog box appears.

5. **Click Start.**

   The Tech Support Mode starts.

6. **Click OK.**

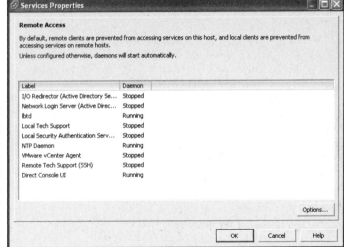

Figure 21-1: The Services Properties window, where you can enable TSM.

PSOD

You probably know what a Blue Screen of Death (BSOD) is, but what about a Purple Screen of Death (PSOD)? A PSOD has other common names, but it's commonly referred to at VMware as a purple diagnostic screen, as shown in Figure 21-2.

A PSOD can be caused by several issues, such as

- Hardware errors
- Storage errors

- ✔ Driver issues
- ✔ Virtual Machine Monitor (VMM) faults

```
VMware ESXi [Releasebuild-244038 X86_64]
#PF Exception(14) in world 4106:idleI0 ip 0x418031e9c3d1 addr 0x18
cr2=0x18 cr3=0x40187000 cr4=0x16c
frame=0x4100c0057928 ip=0x418031e9c3d1 err=0 rflags=0x10246
rax=0x0 rbx=0x41000e4cba60 rcx=0x417ff1c63720
rdx=0x0 rbp=0x4100c0057a18 rsi=0x80
rdi=0x41000e4cba60 r8=0x58 r9=0x0
r10=0x0 r11=0x64 r12=0x0
r13=0x80 r14=0x41000e4cba60 r15=0x41000e4cbaa8
0:5174171/vmm0:CLNF 1:5303/hostd 2:4532641/vmm0:ATAS 3:5180725/vmm1:FPFS
4:1858435/hostd 5:4101/idle5 6:5174172/vmm1:CLNF 7:5135/hostd
8:4104/idle8 9:4600276/vmm0:HRAS *10:4106/idle10 11:5170531/vmm1:HVAS
12:4908408/vmm0:CXAS 13:4600277/vmm1:HRAS 14:5170530/vmm0:HVAS 15:4111/idle15
Code starts at  0x418031a00000
0x4100c0057a18:[0x418031e9c3d1]bnx2x_poll+0xa0 stack: 0x4100c0057a98
0x4100c0057a98:[0x418031da2f26]napi_poll+0xed stack: 0x4100c0057ad8
0x4100c0057b58:[0x418031a31a1f]WorldletBHHandler+0x426 stack: 0x417ff1c1e590
0x4100c0057bc8:[0x418031a28767]BHCallHandlersInt+0x106 stack: 0x4100c0057c18
0x4100c0057c18:[0x418031a28c31]BH_Check+0x144 stack: 0x4100c0057d00
0x4100c0057c48:[0x418031a35298]IDT_HandleInterrupt+0x12b stack: 0x418040000000
0x4100c0057c68:[0x418031a35762]IDT_IntrHandler+0x91 stack: 0x4018
0x4100c0057d48:[0x418031aaf1e6]gate_entry+0x25 stack: 0x0
0x4100c0057e58:[0x418031b95f8e]CpuSchedIdleLoopInt+0x8f9 stack: 0x4100c0057e88
0x4100c0057e68:[0x418031b97e07]CpuSched_IdleLoop+0x16 stack: 0x2
0x4100c0057e88:[0x418031a38c07]Init_SlaveIdle+0x9e stack: 0x0
0x4100c0057fe8:[0x418031c4356b]SMPSlaveIdle+0x3d1 stack: 0x0
VMK uptime: 19:21:44:38.955 TSC: 504515770193937?
FSbase (0x0) GSbase (0x0) kernelGSbase (0x0)
Starting coredump to disk
using slot 1 of 1... 987666666665432110 DiskDump Successful.
#PF Exception(14) in world 4106:idle10 ip 0x418031c16040 addr 0x40
Debugger is listening on serial port ...
Press Escape to enter local debugger
```

Figure 21-2:
The Purple
Screen
of Death
(PSOD).

Like a Microsoft product BSOD, a PSOD has a wealth of information. Information about the product version, and the actual error text, and also the CPU register information is displayed. You can usually ascertain the cause of the issue, but if you get a PSOD, it's usually a good idea to contact VMware Support.

VMware has several articles on how to troubleshoot a PSOD at its Web site. Check out `http://kb.vmware.com/selfservice/microsites/search.do?language=en_US&cmd=displayKC&externalId=1004250` for a comprehensive article about purple screen errors.

Taking Advantage of Log Files

When bad things happen, you may not be there to catch them in the act. Fortunately, ESX has dozens of logs that can shed light on issues. Despite having so many logs, experienced vSphere administrators frequently encounter several common issues:

- ✔ **Service Console log:** The Service Console log, located at `/var/log/messages` provides details on the Linux-based operating system used in the service console. This log is useful for diagnosing issues related to management connectivity and the Linux console.

- ✔ **VMKernel log:** The VMKernel log, located at `/var/log/vmkernel`, provides information on the virtual machines on the vSphere host. This log can grow quite large.

- ✔ **VMkernel Warnings log:** Since the VMkernel log, located at `/var/log/vmkwarning`, can grow so large, VMware takes the warning and errors from the VMKernel log and writes them to the VMkernel warnings log as well. This log is the first place many admins go when diagnosing vSphere host issues.

- ✔ **VMkernel Summary:** This summary, located at `/var/log/vmksummary`, provides data regarding availability and uptime. It is helpful for determining how a host is running.

- ✔ **vCenter Agent log:** This log file, located at `/var/log/vmware/vpx`, focuses on the communication between the host and the vCenter Server. It's helpful for troubleshooting connectivity issues between the vSCenter server and the ESX host.

- ✔ **Virtual Machines:** When a VM has an issue, it has a log named `vmware.log` in the same directory as the VM configuration file.

When working with VMware tech support, you may be asked to send the logs to VMware for analysis. With so many logs, how do you decide which ones to send, and what format do you use?

As you may have guessed, VMware considered that issue already and made it quite easy to grab the relevant logs right from the vSphere Client. To create a support bundle of logs, simply choose Administration➪Export System Logs.

This step opens the Export System Logs dialog box, as shown in Figure 21-3. Here, you can choose the devices from which to export the logs. Usually, it's best to include only what you may suspect is part of the problem because creating the system log bundle can take quite a long time, and the logs can also be sizable. VMware Support often gives you a location that you can upload to using File Transfer Protocol (FTP).

The vSphere Client makes sure that you can easily grab the vSphere log bundle, but what if your problems are related to the network? You can also create a bundle on the host by typing vm-support at the command line. If you're using ESXi, you need to activate Local Tech Support Mode to run the `vm-support` command. However, consider how to get the logs off the vSphere host without networking! If you have functional shared storage and another machine connected to the shared disk that has networking, you can copy the log bundle to the shared storage datastore and then grab it from the datastore using the Datastore Browser in the vSphere Client.

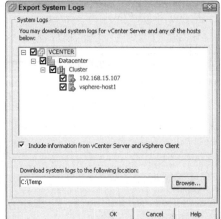

Figure 21-3:
The Export
System Logs
dialog box.

Troubleshooting a SAN

Storage Area Networks (SANs) are very flexible and powerful, but also very complex. Troubleshooting a SAN primarily occurs on the fabric and at the array, but some aspects of SAN troubleshooting focus on the vSphere host.

Refresh and rescan

After presenting a volume to a vSphere host, you may not see it immediately. Often, you'll want to see the volume immediately so that you can rescan the host to discover new volumes.

You can also rescan when removing a volume, which, in fact, is a good way to ensure that the volume is indeed no longer available to the host.

SCSI locks

Certain operations on a Virtual Machine File System (VMFS) datatstore require temporary locks. These locks are called SCSI reservations, and they give a host exclusive access to the datastore for a short period of time.

SCSI reservations occur more often on datastores with many VMs. Limiting the size of a VMFS volume reduces the amount of VMs that are impacted when a SCSI reservation occurs.

Certain features of vSphere can result in more frequent SCSI reservations. A VM set to use thin provisioning requires a SCSI reservation each time it has to expand a disk file. On rapidly growing or busy VMs, this condition can result in many SCSI reservations.

SCSI reservations aren't normally a big deal, but too many reservations can result in hosts losing access to datastores. If everything seems fine in your cluster and then one day you notice that some VMs go offline while others are still running, you may have a SCSI reservation conflict. If a conflict happens and it's constrained to a single host, you may be able to evacuate the host and reboot it. Otherwise, you may need to contact VMware Support or your Storage Array vendor.

Solving High Availability Errors

HA can be a savior in a crisis, but it's often one of the most error-prone areas of vSphere. No large vSphere environment is without occasional HA troubleshooting. The following sections describe a few items to watch out for.

Reconfigure for VMware HA over and over

Even after HA is running, you may need to reconfigure it frequently. When adding a host to a cluster, the host won't fully participate in HA until you choose the Reconfigure for VMware HA process. Whenever you have a problem with HA on a host, the first step is usually to reconfigure for VMware HA. This process attempts to reinstall and set up the HA agent on the host.

Admittance errors

By default, when you enable HA, admission control is enabled. Many administrators new to vSphere don't know or care what admission control does, until suddenly, one day out of the blue, they get slapped in the face with an error telling them they don't have enough resources to power on a VM! This problem can often follow modification of a VM's reservation, and many administrators searching for the error and seeing that it's admission control, shut off admission control.

Don't be that administrator! Admission control is there to ensure that when you tell your constituents their VMs are protected with HA, you are not a liar!

Instead, take a look at your HA settings, which we explain in Chapter 20. If you have one VM with a huge reservation that may be skewing the default settings, then it may make sense to move to a different admission control policy.

My whole blade chassis failed, and HA did nothing!

When building your environment, you bought two blade chassis and filled them halfway with blades. You were concerned about a whole chassis going down, so you ensured that your cluster of 16 blades had 8 in each chassis. Then disaster struck, and one whole chassis failed! You think about how great HA is and then you hear that it didn't do anything! This problem is a rude awakening when you configure your shiny new blades, and such a failure isn't something that is well understood.

When HA is set up on a cluster, each host active in the cluster has a role (see Chapter 20). Some are primary HA nodes, and others are secondary nodes. The first five hosts in a cluster are the primary nodes, and they stay that way until a host fails and enters maintenance mode or when an administrator does a Reconfigure for VMware HA from the vSphere Client. In order for HA to work, a primary node must coordinate the VM failover, so in the preceding scenario, if all five primary nodes were in the chassis, HA would be rendered useless in a failure.

VMware is working on making specifying primary and secondary nodes more configurable, and several unsupported ways are available for modifying which hosts are primary nodes. In the future, these unsupported ways may become fully supported. For now, if you use blades, it's best to include eight hosts per cluster, split evenly between two chassis. This way, a primary node will always be alive in the event of a whole chassis failure.

Isolation island

When a host loses network connectivity, the VMs running on it may still run fine. HA can detect the network issue and begin to fail the VMs over. To do so, the HA agent periodically pings the isolation address, which is, by default, the default gateway of the service console. If the default gateway is unavailable, the HA agent can evacuate the host, which can be a good thing if the host is indeed no longer on the network.

In a complicated network, having multiple isolation addresses may be better, and you can have up to ten. You can create ten by setting the `das.isolationaddress1` through `das.isolationaddress10` parameters in the advanced options of the cluster HA settings. If you do use multiple isolation addresses, it's usually a good idea to allow more time to detect the failure. This setting is the `das.failuredetectiontime` — it's noted in milliseconds and should be set to at least 20 seconds (`20000`).

Troubleshooting Oversubscribed Hosts

When you first set up a virtual infrastructure, performance of the guest virtual machines will likely be stellar. With minimal competition, every VM gets the resources that it demands. However, as you put more VMs on the infrastructure, things may begin to slow down a bit. The following sections cover some troubleshooting tips on how to keep the VMs performing optimally.

Disabling unneeded devices

Each VM has a set of virtual hardware that it uses. Each device in a virtual hardware profile uses some resources, so you should disable or remove any devices that aren't needed. Doing so can also improve security because the device isn't available to an attacker.

Install/update VMware Tools

Whenever you upgrade vSphere versions, you'll want to update the VMware Tools. In this way, you ensure that the latest drivers are installed, and you also add VMware-specific drivers, such as the balloon driver that helps to manage memory consumption. The VMware Tools kit also sets several registry settings to optimize the performance of the VM.

Tools updated on every reboot

You may be wondering how to ensure that your VMware Tools stay updated. Each VM has a setting in the VM properties to do exactly that, and many administrators don't even know it! To enable VMware Tools automatic update, go to the properties on the VM, click the Options tab and choose the VMware Tools item. In the corresponding settings, choose Check and Upgrade Tools During Power Cycling.

Automatic updates of VMware tools provides an easy way to keep things in sync, but it can result in automatic driver installations and changes. Before enabling the automatic update, be sure that you feel comfortable with the system taking these actions without user or administrator intervention.

If you choose to enable Check and Upgrade Tools During Power Cycling, when systems first boot after a host upgrade, the VMs immediately reboot. As part of the upgrade to the host, plan for the VM double-boot. This reboot doesn't immediately occur if you vMotion a guest over to the upgraded host, but the double-boot will occur on the next reboot.

Don't overuse reservations

When troubleshooting a performance problem, one common issue is over-use of reservations. Remember that resources committed with a reservation aren't available to other VMs, so you can quickly get into some trouble.

In situations where you must set reservations, consider that the ideal reservation is not too big and not too small. To determine the size of the reservation, you can use the performance monitoring tools to see historical trends. With that information, you can set a reservation that ensures the VM has the resources it needs to function. VMs can request more resources if they require them, but VMs never use less than their reservation. (See Chapter 19 for more on reservations.)

CPU ready and why it matters

CPU instructions in ESX are scheduled on physical CPUs. On a physical server, the operating system doesn't have to wait for a CPU to be available each time it wants to schedule an instruction. VMs are different, so they wait for a CPU. This wait is called *CPU ready,* and it refers to the time spent while a VM has work to do, but must wait for a CPU to be available for an instruction. Lower numbers are better, but the mere presence of the hypervisor means CPU ready will never really be zero.

This metric matters because if your CPU ready times are high, your system may be performing badly. Each VM may have a different CPU ready time, and you'll notice that multi-processor VMs have a generally higher CPU ready time. This situation is sometimes best understood by thinking of a rollercoaster.

The rollercoaster has eight seats. If you get in line, like a vCPU waiting to be scheduled, you'll wait until your turn. Once it's your turn, you'll take any available seat, and away you go!

What if you're with a friend? You likely want to ride together, just as a VM with two vCPUs needs to schedule them together. To do so, you may need to allow a person or two to pass in front of you to fill in all the empty spaces, depending on who is in front of you and which spaces are open. Here, because you want to ride, but can't, your CPU ready time increases!

What if you're part of a group of four friends? As a four vCPU system, you may need to wait even longer for the right circumstances to be available. Meanwhile, that single rider gets to keep getting back on to fill in empty spaces!

As you can see, it's usually a good idea to start every VM at one vCPU, unless you have evidence that more than one vCPU will be needed. This way, you can reduce the amount of time a VM waits to run.

Handling vCenter Troubles

Once in a while, vCenter Server will throw you a curveball. As sturdy as vCenter is, its ability to clearly tell you why it won't do something is severely lacking. Most errors are unique enough that you can easily search for them in the VMware Knowledgebase, but you need to know about a few common ones, which we describe in the following sections.

Cannot convert template to a VM

VMware vSphere administrators like to reuse resources whenever possible, including VM templates from other versions of VMware. An example is adding VM templates from VMware ESX 3.5 by directly registering the template into vCenter. Attaching a component that is no longer accessible or valid (such as a virtual CD-ROM drive) to a VM template can prevent the template from being converted to a virtual machine. This problem is due to incompatible entries in the VM template's `.vmtx` (vm template config) file.

Fixing the issue requires direct editing of the configuration file on the ESX host. You must remove the VM template from the inventory in vCenter, from the config file edited, and from the VM template reregistered in vCenter. You can find this process outlined in VMware Knowledgebase article 1021563.

Guest customization errors

Guest customization errors can be quite annoying because you can't see the error until the end of the template deployment. Generally, these issues are hard to troubleshoot because you have limited access to the guest until it's successfully customized.

If the customization of a Windows system fails, you can check the log at `%SYSTEMROOT%\Temp\guestcust.log`. This log file often has information about why a VM may not have been customized correctly or at all.

vCenter Server stopped and won't start

VMware vCenter Server is a central command station for vSphere. What happens when vCenter stops and won't start again? For the most part, nothing happens to the VMs under vCenter's management, but having vCenter Server in a nonfunctional state is definitely a critical issue.

Occasionally (and sometime more often), passwords for Windows "service" accounts get changed by other administrators without warning. Check the Services management console on the vCenter Server's host to see whether you can manually start the vCenter Server service. See whether the vCenter Server service is configured to run as a Windows Active Directory account. If so, try starting the service. Windows will immediately tell you if there's a problem with the configured credentials.

When vCenter was installed, did you use the default Microsoft SQL Express database? If your vCenter Server has been running for a while, it may have reached the 4GB database size limit that exists in the Express versions of Microsoft SQL Server. In this case, you can upgrade the database version in-place, replace the Express version with a full version of SQL Server, or you can move the database to another SQL Server. All these options are well-documented processes.

Another condition that can kill vCenter Server is a full disk volume containing the vCenter Server logs, the database, or both. Clearing off some space on the volume will give vCenter Server space to write to its log files. If vCenter seems to be consuming disk space at a higher rate than normal, check the logging level. Logging is increased for troubleshooting, and that logging may have been left at the more verbose setting unintentionally.

Dealing with VM Crashes

Physical machines can crash for many reasons, and the same is true for virtual machines. Common causes of many of the crashes include application issues, operating system misconfiguration, or driver issues.

With VMs, you usually don't have to worry about persistent hardware issues because a VM is actually software. However, you do have the same troubleshooting steps you'd otherwise have. VMs also have some occasional issues that aren't normally a concern in a physical environment.

Low VMFS space

The VMFS datastore contains multiple VM disk files (VMDK) that contain data. If you use vSphere's powerful thin-provisioning features, these VMDKs will each grow as needed. Some VMs may grow slowly, and others may grow fast. With different rates of growth, you may find that a VMFS fills up. With a full VMFS datastore, many VMs, especially those that are thin provisioned, can fail. In this event, the operating system will crash or simply hang.

Fixing a full VMFS can be tricky. Generally, the first thing you do is check to see whether any files can be deleted. On each datastore in a large environment, you often find one or more orphaned VMs. Deleting these orphaned files can free up some space quickly and get you back in business, but remember that a VMFS datastore doesn't have "Trash Can" functionality.

If there are no VMs to delete, you can move a VM to another datastore. Because you have no disk space on the datastore, you won't be able to use Storage vMotion, so you'll need to shut down the VM to migrate it.

After you free up disk space, any VM that did experience a failure needs to be rebooted.

Missing or ghost hardware

Many VMs are moved on to a virtual platform from a physical system. This common procedure, called *Physical To Virtual* (P2V), often leaves devices in the hardware specifications of the guest VM. After the VM is operational, it's a good idea to remove any of the old devices and items that are no longer needed.

Incorrect HAL in Windows

Windows has a Hardware Abstraction Layer (HAL) that provides a barrier between the running software and the hardware. A HAL in Windows often denotes whether the Windows system is a multiprocessor or uniprocessor system. You won't often have to pay attention to HAL mismatches because growing on demand in the physical server world is not easy, but in vSphere, it's quite common.

Adding or removing a processor to a VM is a trivial task requiring no more downtime than a reboot. After doing so, however, it's important to check the HAL to ensure that you have the right one loaded. Running a uniprocessor HAL on a system with more than one vCPU decreases performance and stability. Running a multiprocessor HAL on a system with only one vCPU can lead to crashes and extremely degraded performance. Sometimes, Windows Plug and Play can detect and upgrade the HAL automatically, but it usually doesn't automatically downgrade the HAL.

Handling Networking Issues

In all vSphere implementations, Networking is key for the success of the management and availability of the VMs. Many of the networking issues are unique to vSphere because of the different ways a vSphere host is usually set up. Several networking symptoms are quite common:

✔ **Some VMs can talk, others cannot!** Probably nothing is more frustrating than a situation where some VMs on a host can communicate fine, but others can't. This problem can often be due to a VLAN having an issue. Because a host can run VMs from multiple VLANs, it may seem to be just a single host when a whole VLAN is having an issue.

VLAN issues are easy to test by moving a VM available for testing to the affected VLAN. Sometimes, however, you'll find that it isn't at the VLAN level and that some VMs work and some don't even within a VLAN!

✔ **Even Media Access Control addresses work, while others don't.** In this case, you should look at the Media Access Control (MAC) addresses of the VMs. Each MAC address is a number, denoted in hexadecimals. Many port aggregation methods rely on sending even numbers over one physical connection and odd numbers over the other connection. The system should detect a failure and move all communication to the surviving link, but sometimes a link doesn't fail hard. This situation is especially common with fiber connections, where the glass may not be letting all the data through.

✔ **Routing vMotion, or worse!** vMotion failures can be tough to troubleshoot. One common issue is not getting a nonrouted VLAN assigned to vMotion. In this case, while you can do a vMotion through a router, the results can be unpredictable. vMotion expects there to be a very high-speed connection as it copies memory contents over the wire. Ensure that you have a fast connection and that all the systems using vMotion can do so over a Layer-2 connection.

Part VII
The Part of Tens

The 5th Wave   By Rich Tennant

"Oh, I'll get us in — I used to run tech support at an
internet access company."

In this part . . .

The Part of Tens directs you to indispensible resources *For Dummies* readers have come to know and love, and we tell you about them ten at a time. Chapter 22 provides details on ten tools to automate management of your vSphere environment. Chapter 23 covers ten places to further your vSphere knowledge online. Chapter 24 gives you ten powerful pro tips for a successful vSphere deployment.

Chapter 22

Ten Tools to Make vSphere Management Easier

In This Chapter

▶ Automating repetitive tasks in vSphere

▶ Simplifying everyday vSphere administration

*V*Mware vSphere is a somewhat complex solution, and VMware has done a great job at building out the vSphere architecture. As a vSphere administrator, you'll begin to notice yourself doing the same task the same way over and over again. These repetitive tasks are time-consuming and cut into your infrastructure administration duties. This chapter gives you ten tools to help automate your vSphere infrastructure.

VMware PowerCLI

    communities.vmware.com/community/vmtn/vsphere/automationtools/powercli

VMware vSphere PowerCLI (see Figure 22-1) is a Microsoft PowerShell–based Snap-in designed to make even the most complex vSphere task easy to script in PowerShell. PowerCLI covers all aspects of vSphere management, including storage, network, hosts, virtual machines, and guest operating systems. PowerCLI is free, has more than 200 PowerShell commands (cmdlets), and includes both documentation and samples.

Figure 22-1:
VMware
PowerCLI.

VMware Project Onyx

`labs.vmware.com/flings/onyx`

Onyx (see Figure 22-2) is a stand-alone application that sits between the vSphere Client and the vCenter Server. Onyx listens to the network communication between them and generates executable PowerShell code that mimics the commands being passed. You can modify this code for your own purposes and place it in a reusable PowerShell script. Onyx is a huge time-saver, particularly if you know how to work via vSphere Client, but don't have the time or patience to figure out how to do the same thing in PowerCLI.

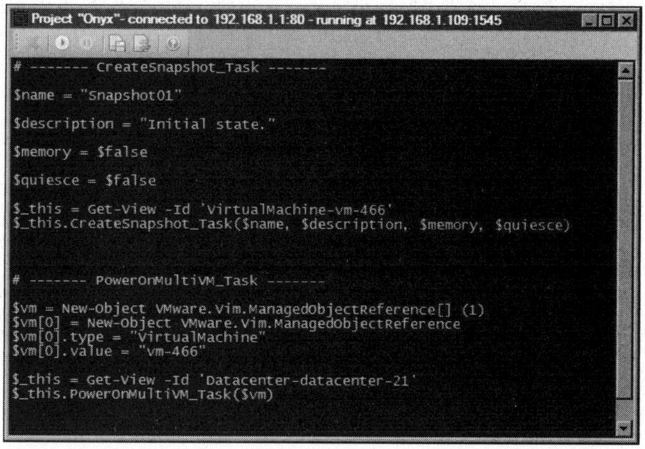

```
Project "Onyx"- connected to  192.168.1.1:80 - running at  192.168.1.109:1545

# ------- CreateSnapshot_Task -------

$name = "Snapshot01"

$description = "Initial state."

$memory = $false

$quiesce = $false

$_this = Get-View -Id 'VirtualMachine-vm-466'
$_this.CreateSnapshot_Task($name, $description, $memory, $quiesce)


# ------- PowerOnMultiVM_Task -------

$vm = New-Object VMware.Vim.ManagedObjectReference[] (1)
$vm[0] = New-Object VMware.Vim.ManagedObjectReference
$vm[0].type = "VirtualMachine"
$vm[0].value = "vm-466"

$_this = Get-View -Id 'Datacenter-datacenter-21'
$_this.PowerOnMultiVM_Task($vm)
```

Figure 22-2:
VMware
Labs' Onyx
tool.

DynamicOps Cloud Automation Center

www.dynamicops.com

The IT personnel at Credit Suisse developed DynamicOps management software in 2004 to address the challenges of deploying virtualization across several distinct business groups with unique requirements. In 2008, with thousands of virtual machines under management and having identified a business opportunity, the bank spun off DynamicOps as a company.

DynamicOps Cloud Automation Center (DCAC) lets you rapidly create and deploy on-demand IT services within the boundaries of your corporate IT policy. DCAC (see Figure 22-3) manages deployment of virtual and physical machines, using shared resources, in private and/or public clouds. Other investment banks and leaders in financial services, consumer products, manufacturing, healthcare, education, and government use the software to manage tens of thousands of VMs worldwide.

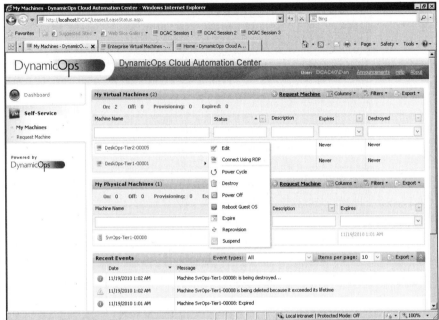

Figure 22-3:
DynamicOps
Cloud
Automation
Center.

vSphere Mini Monitor

www.nickapedia.com

vSphere Mini Monitor (VMM) is a simple tool created to keep an eye on activity in your vSphere environment. VMM (see Figure 22-4) notifies you of all kinds of activities, such as creation, deletion, or reconfiguration of VMs. It even lets you know about new sessions connecting to your vCenter Server.

Veeam FastSCP

www.veeam.com

FastSCP (see Figure 22-5) is not just another Secure Shell (SSH)–based secure copy tool. FastSCP is able to copy files up to six times faster than other Secure Copy (SCP) tools due to its compression and empty block removal features built right into the FastSCP engine. It's easy to use, vSphere-ready, and free from Veeam.

Figure 22-4:
vSphere
Mini
Monitor.

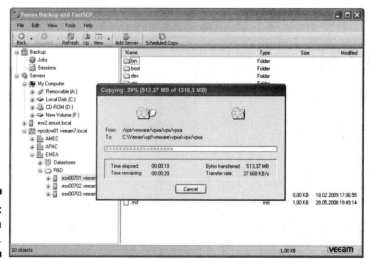

Figure 22-5:
Veeam
FastSCP.

Ultimate Deployment Appliance (UDA)

www.rtfm-ed.co.uk/vmware-content/ultimate-da

The Ultimate Deployment Appliance v2.0 (UDA 2.0) is a popular PXE Boot appliance that you can use to deploy VMware ESX 4 and other operating systems automatically. As long as your new server is capable of PXE-booting from network, the UDA will take control of the new server and load on ESX 4, ready for configuration. UDA (see Figure 22-6) is available as a virtual appliance and can be imported directly to your vSphere environment using vSphere Client and vCenter Server.

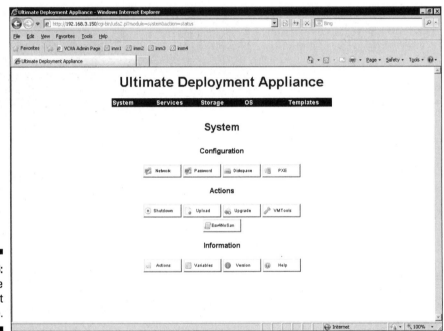

Figure 22-6: Ultimate Deployment Appliance.

Virtual Guest Console

```
labs.vmware.com/flings/vgc
```

With VMware Virtual Guest Console (VGC) you can perform actions such as creation of snapshots or deployment and execution of files inside the guest OS, across multiple virtual machines, using a single command in the user interface. VGC (see Figure 22-7) can also facilitate file transfers between VMs, hosts, or any combination of the two. This tool is particularly handy when you need to perform mass operations, such as shutting down all the VMs on a farm, requiring only that each VM is running VM Tools.

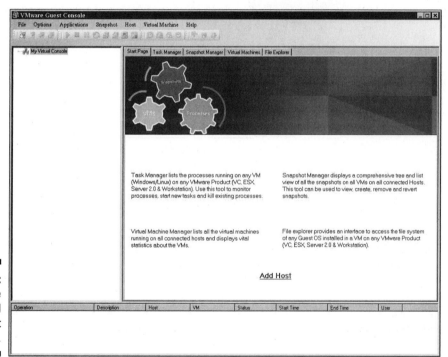

Figure 22-7:
VMware
Labs' Virtual
Guest
Console.

xtravirt vSphere Client RDP Plug-In

www.xtravirt.com

The xtravirt vSphere RDP Plug-In (see Figure 22-8) integrates the Microsoft Windows Remote Desktop Client with the VMware vSphere Client. Using Remote Desktop to connect virtual machines offers a better user experience compared to the built-in VMware console, especially in higher-latency situations, such as slow or low-bandwidth network connections.

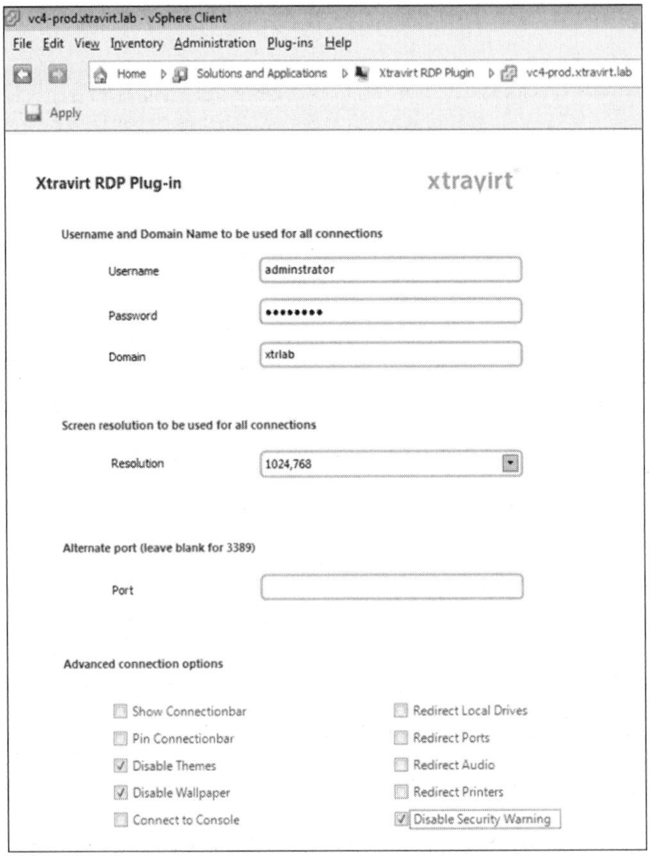

Figure 22-8: xtravirt vSphere Client Plug-In.

Openfiler

www.openfiler.com

Openfiler is an open-source storage appliance with a built-in, easy-to-use management interface. It supports iSCSI, NFS, and CIFS, making it perfect for use with vSphere. Openfiler (see Figure 22-9) runs on your vSphere infrastructure and looks like any other network-based storage array, when in fact, it's completely software-based and can utilize even local storage on your ESX hosts. Use Openfiler when you need shared storage for your lab, but can't justify buying expensive storage hardware, or when you want to make the most of your host's local disk space.

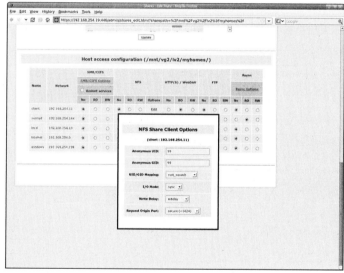

Figure 22-9: Openfiler open-source storage appliance.

Stratusphere UX

www.liquidwarelabs.com

Liquidware Labs Stratusphere UX is the ultimate tool to help you prepare for a Virtual Desktop initiative. Stratusphere (see Figure 22-10) unobtrusively gathers data from your users' existing physical desktops. The data gathered includes the usage of applications, network stats, intensity of disk usage, hardware and software inventory, and other detailed information. Stratusphere then processes the data and generates reports to tell you which users' desktops are the best candidates to transition to virtual desktops, and it profiles desktop use to help with figuring out your standard virtual desktop configurations.

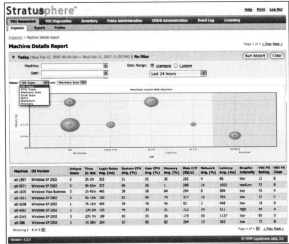

Figure 22-10:
Liquidware
Labs'
Stratus-
phere UX.

Chapter 23

Ten Places to Improve Your vSphere Know-How

In This Chapter

▶ Finding out more about vSphere

▶ Benefitting from ten free repositories of expert knowledge

*V*Mware vSphere is a complex product and solution. Thanks to the generosity of VMware experts and enthusiasts, Web sites have popped up across the Internet with information about VMware virtualization. Here is a list of ten places online we've found quite helpful. We hope you'll find them useful for improving your vSphere know-how.

DABCC.com

`www.dabcc.com`

Founded by Doug A. Brown (the DAB in DABCC.com), this site has grown exponentially over the past few years. DABCC.com is packed with insightful and educational articles by contributing writers throughout the virtualization industry. DABCC also acts as a massive aggregator of virtualization news and publications and is an excellent starting point for searches.

Mike Laverick's RTFM Education

www.rtfm-ed.co.uk

RTFM (which stands for "Read the Flippin' Manual") is the brainchild of Mike Laverick, well-known virtualization expert. RTFM is media-rich with videos, podcasts, downloadable guides, and applications. RTFM is home to Ultimate P2V, a comprehensive, community-created physical-to-virtual conversion tool for creating VMware VMs from physical machines.

NTPRO.NL

www.ntpro.nl

Established by Eric Sloof of the Netherlands back in July 2004, NTPRO.NL is loaded with online training, videos, tools, and more. NTPRO.NL is also home to the vmClient, a simple tool for direct console access and power control of virtual machines.

Petri IT Knowledgebase

www.petri.co.il/virtualization.htm

Petri IT Knowledgebase is full of useful posts, guides, and utilities for all types of technologies, but has an especially good virtualization section. Founded by Daniel Petri, the Petri IT Knowledgebase is a top resource when looking for how-to information not found in the VMware manuals.

virtualization.info

www.virtualization.info

Since 2003, virtualization.info has had its finger on the pulse of the virtualization industry. Alessandro Perilli gives you the inside scoop on all things virtualization, including product reviews, predictions, white papers, Webcasts, and interviews. If you want to know what's new, check out this site.

VMware Knowledgebase

http://kb.vmware.com

When vSphere gives you trouble, the official VMware Knowledgebase (KB) is the place to go. The VMware KB is the definitive source for known issues and fixes. If you have an error message from vSphere, search here first.

VMware Communities

http://communities.vmware.com

VMware Communities are where VMware administrators, experts, and engineers connect to discuss everything VMware. There's even a points system to acknowledge users who provide useful correct answers. Search the VMware Communities site with your next vSphere question, and you'll likely find that someone else has already asked it and been answered by one of the many experts patrolling the forums.

vSphere Land

http://vSphere-land.com

Founded by Eric Seibert, top VMTN community member and VMware guru, vSphere Land has grown into a massive repository of VMware-related information. The site contains numerous tips, tricks, and other great ideas for new and experienced vSphere admins alike.

xtravirt

http://xtravirt.com

xtravirt.com is packed with white papers, news, blogs, and downloads related to virtualization and VMware vSphere. Referred to as the "Virtualization Knowledge Portal," it provides extensive content and even some tools to help you with your everyday administration.

Yellow Bricks

`www.yellow-bricks.com`

Yellow Bricks was founded by Duncan Epping, a consulting architect for VMware. The site contains excellent deep-dive information on VMware HA and DRS, as well as a number of comprehensive VMware and vSphere-related posts. In case you're wondering, the site's name is derived from an Arctic Monkeys song, "Old Yellow Bricks."

Chapter 24

Ten Pro Tips for a Successful vSphere Deployment

In This Chapter

▶ Getting the configuration right the first time

▶ Avoiding common pitfalls during vSphere setup

*V*Mware vSphere is the most robust virtualization platform on the market. Its popularity and presence in the enterprise yields a realm of knowledge and expertise surrounding the best practices for deploying vSphere, much of it through hands-on experience. Here are ten tips used by virtualization experts and veterans alike to ensure a smooth and successful vSphere deployment.

Plan to Make the Most of vSphere Memory Optimization

One of the best features of vSphere virtualization is its ability to optimize memory use through *transparent page sharing* (TPS). TPS optimizes memory consumption by eliminating redundant blocks of data that is common across VMs and replacing them with pointers to a common set of memory blocks.

Take full advantage of TPS by placing similar virtual machines together, especially those with the same applications installed, and TPS will take care of the rest.

Monitor Utilization on Datastores with Thin-Provisioned VMs

Thin provisioning allows you to fit more virtual machines per datastore, because the space consumed by thin-provisioned virtual disks is equal to the actual data inside the VM. While most virtual machines don't stick around long enough to consume the entire virtual disk, the keepers creep up in size. As the permanent VMs grow, they expect space to be available for that growth. Eventually, the datastore reaches capacity, and VMs looking for space to grow will be impacted and fail.

Fortunately, vCenter does a great job of tracking allocated versus actual datastore capacity and can even alert you when certain thresholds are met. Consider using virtual machines pre-allocated (thick-provisioned) virtual disks for production applications to eliminate the risk altogether.

VM Snapshots Are Quiet Space Consumers

Snapshots are something like a safety net: You're able to make changes, knowing that you can roll back the machine to the point in time when the snapshot was created. If the changes are unsuccessful, you simply revert to the snapshot. The problem occurs when the changes are successful and you keep the snapshot around "just in case," and then forget it. A snapshot can eventually grow to the size of the base virtual disk, but the additional space consumption isn't reflected by a VM's virtual disk capacity shown in a VM's settings. A virtual machine with a forgotten snapshot not only consumes disks in an inconspicuous way, but it also exposes the VM to risk of failure if the datastore containing the VM reaches capacity.

As snapshots grow in size, they take much longer to remove. Removing a large snapshot can take hours, even days to complete. After you start removing a snapshot, you can't do anything else to the VM until the process has finished.

Clean Templates Make for Happy VMs

A virtual machine template in vSphere is a virtual machine configured to act as a source image from which new virtual machines are cloned. Building a set of virtual machine templates for your environment is a time-consuming task, but a worthwhile investment in VM integrity.

If you take shortcuts or rush the creation of VM templates to save time, you will pay for it in the end. Check to confirm that all virtual media (such as CD/ DVD and floppy disk images) are detached and not just disconnected, that the installed version of VM Tools is up-to-date, and that the VM's guest OS has all the current updates before converting a machine into a VM template. These simple checks will save time, minimize problems, and make troubleshooting much easier later on.

The Summary tab for a virtual machine in vCenter Server shows you the state of VM Tools and will even tell you whether the existing version of VM Tools running in a virtual machine is out of date.

Automate the Startup/Shutdown of VMs

Every day, unforeseeable events occur in the datacenter. Even with redundant power feeds connected to redundant power sources and everything in-between, sometimes unexpected downtime is unavoidable for less-than-mission-critical machines.

Unlike traditional servers running individual operating systems, VMs won't come back up unless they have specifically been set for automatic power-on in vCenter. If you run vCenter, domain controllers, DNS servers, or any other system critical to vSphere in virtual machines, these VMs need to be powered on in a specific order to bring the infrastructure back online. The same is true in the rare case these infrastructure VMs need to be shut down for host maintenance.

Take the time to configure automatic startup/shutdown of VMs to improve recovery time in the event of failure and make your job easier during maintenance.

Not Everyone Needs vCenter Access

A common misconception is that everyone who interacts with a virtual machine requires access to vCenter Server. This belief couldn't be further from the truth. There is actually a limit to the number of simultaneous connections to a vCenter Server, which you can easily exceed in large environments.

Find out what operations need to be executed by the virtual machine user and offer alternatives capable of providing the same functionality. Many times, this functionality can be provided by Remote Desktop access on the Windows side and SSH access on the Linux side. VMware also provides utilities to allow users to carry out simple operations, such as power controls and snapshots from a Web-based GUI.

vSphere Clusters of a Feather

vSphere clustering is the optimal deployment configuration for leveraging high availability and workload optimization through vCenter. A key component to this functionality is vSphere's capability to move and run a VM on a different ESX host, whether by vMotion or just simple HA and shared storage.

One thing that can really put a damper on the excitement is when a VM can't move between hosts because of processor incompatibility. Some of these challenges are overcome in vSphere 4.1, but the best way to prevent them from happening is to build out clusters with identical server hardware. Ideally, deploying identical servers in a vSphere cluster is the best way to go.

The next best option is using servers with processors sharing common instruction sets. See the VMware Hardware Compatibility Guide on the VMware Web site for specific makes and models of CPUs.

Don't Get vMotion Sickness

A prominent feature of vSphere is the Distributed Resource Scheduler (DRS), which constantly looks for opportunities to improve workload distribution by shuffling VMs across ESX hosts within a cluster. DRS ranks the effectiveness of each recommendation, from one to five stars, with five stars being the most effective. vSphere environments with vMotion capability allow DRS to move the virtual machines while still running.

Some administrators go for the "set it and forget it" approach — that is, set DRS to fully automated mode and tell it to act on any recommendation it comes up with, even those with a single star. In response, DRS begins moving virtual machines all around the cluster to optimally balance workloads.

Occasionally, the impact of moving a VM onto a host in the cluster will trigger DRS to move another VM off the same host onto another, causing a domino effect. This phenomenon is known as *vMotion sickness*. To minimize the likelihood of this happening, don't set DRS below a three-star minimum when DRS is configured in fully automated mode.

Working through Hostname Resolution

Certain virtual environments, especially those in highly regulated industries, present challenges in adding new host names to their Domain Name Service (DNS) servers. When ESX hosts are deployed, they require the administrator to give the machine a host name and to provide the IP addresses of one or more DNS servers. The ESX host expects to be able to look up its peers by name via DNS, for the purposes of cluster communication and management. The same expectation holds true for the vCenter Server.

A common workaround is to manually place host name entries in the vCenter Server's host lookup file so that the vCenter Server can resolve the ESX hosts by name. If the ESX hosts aren't registered in DNS, but are added to vCenter Server using their host names, the ESX hosts won't know how to reach each other using their names. This situation, in turn, triggers a nondescript HA configuration error in vCenter Server.

To avoid this situation altogether, either add the ESX and vCenter Server host names to DNS or add all the ESX hosts to vCenter Server using their IP address instead of their name.

Putting VM Tools — Everywhere

VMware created VM Tools as a way to bridge the management communication gap between the guest operating system inside a VM and the ESX host it runs on, while maintaining secure separation between the two. VM Tools also includes guest OS-specific optimized drivers for network, disk, and other virtualized components presented to the guest OS. Certain features are enhanced by VM Tools, such as adding the capability to quiesce the virtual disk of a running VM to take a point-in-time snapshot or to initiate the shutdown of a guest OS in a VM instead of just powering it off. Installing VM Tools is critical to monitoring the health of a virtual machine, and it should be a standard component in every VM (and VM template) created in your virtual infrastructure.

Index

• S •

• *W* •

• X •

• Y •

• Z •